SMP 16–19

Pure 2

Coordinate geometry, trigonometry
and further calculus

CAMBRIDGE
UNIVERSITY PRESS

Much of this book is based, with adaptation by Alexandra Round, on earlier SMP books to which the following people contributed.

Simon Baxter
Chris Belsom
Stan Dolan
Doug French
Andy Hall
Barrie Hunt
Lorna Lyons
Paul Roder
Jeff Searle
David Tall

PUBLISHED BY THE PRESS SYNDICATE OF THE UNIVERSITY OF CAMBRIDGE
The Pitt Building, Trumpington Street, Cambridge, United Kingdom

CAMBRIDGE UNIVERSITY PRESS
The Edinburgh Building, Cambridge, CB2 2RU, UK
40 West 20th Street, New York, NY 10011–4211, USA
477 Williamstown Road, Port Melbourne, VIC 3207, Australia
Ruiz de Alarcón 13, 28014 Madrid, Spain
Dock House, The Waterfront, Cape Town 8001, South Africa

http://www.cambridge.org

First published 2002

Printed in the United Kingdom at the University Press, Cambridge

Typeface Minion and Officina   *System* QuarkXpress®

A catalogue record for this book is available from the British Library

ISBN 0 521 78798 X paperback

Acknowledgements

The authors and publishers would like to thank the following for supplying photographs:

page 53 National Aeronautics and Space Administration, USA (earth); © Bettmann/CORBIS (Everest)

Cover photograph: Peter Menzel/Science Photo Library
Cover design: Angela Ashton

Contents

Using this book

Most sections within a chapter consist of work developing new ideas followed by an exercise for practice in using those ideas.

Within the development sections, some questions and activities are labelled with a **D**, for example **2D**, and are enclosed in a box. These involve issues that are worth exploring through discussion – either teacher-led discussion in the whole class or discussion by students in small groups, who may then feed back their conclusions to the whole class.

Questions labelled **E** are more demanding.

1 Iterative processes

Sequences can be used to describe many patterns and processes. They can be powerful when a set of data can be written as a sequence in which each term depends only on the terms that have come before.

If you have already studied the inductive definition of sequences in *Pure 1*, you may omit Sections A and B below, or use them for revision.

A Inductive definition (answers p. 123)

When describing a sequence, certain notations are used. If U is the sequence 3, 7, 11, 15, 19, ... then

$$u_1 = 3 \text{ is the first term,}$$
$$u_2 = 7 \text{ is the second term,}$$
$$u_5 = 19 \text{ is the fifth term, and so on.}$$

The subscript indicates the term of the sequence U. So the ith term of sequence U is written as u_i.

1 U is the sequence 1, 7, 13, 19, ...
   (a) What are the values of u_1 and u_4?
   (b) What value would you expect for u_5?
       Give an equation connecting u_5 and u_4.
   (c) Give an equation connecting u_{i+1} and u_i.

2 T is the sequence defined by $t_1 = 5$ and $t_{i+1} = t_i + 9$.
   (a) What are the values of t_2, t_3, t_4, t_5?
   (b) What is the value of t_{20}?

> A sequence U may be given by an **inductive definition**. Such a definition requires
>
> (i) a starting value or values, for example u_1, the first term;
> (ii) a **recurrence relation**, i.e. a formula which will generate any term from the previous term or terms, for example
> $$u_{i+1} = u_i + 6.$$

3 For each sequence write out the first five terms and the value of the 20th term.

(a) $u_1 = -5$ and $u_{i+1} = u_i - 2$ (b) $u_1 = 2$ and $u_{i+1} = 3u_i$

(c) $u_1 = 2$ and $u_{i+1} = -2u_i$ (d) $u_1 = 5$ and $u_{i+1} = \dfrac{1}{u_i}$

4E For different starting values, obtain a sufficient number of terms to enable you to describe the patterns of the sequence $u_{i+2} = u_i + u_{i+1}$. (You will need starting values for u_1 and u_2.)

A sequence can use the subscript value in the recurrence relation. For example if $u_1 = 1$ and $u_{i+1} = u_i + (i+1)$ then $u_2 = 1 + (2) = 3$, $u_3 = 3 + (3) = 6$. The familiar triangle number sequence is the result: 1, 3, 6, 10, 15, ...

Example 1

Find an inductive definition for the sequence 1, 2, 6, 24, 120, ...

Solution

$u_1 = 1$ and the pattern is then
$u_2 = 2 \times u_1$, $u_3 = 3 \times u_2$, $u_4 = 4 \times u_3$, and so on.
So $u_1 = 1$, $u_{i+1} = (i+1)u_i$.

5 Write out the first six terms of the sequence U where $u_i = 0$ and $u_{i+1} = u_i + 2i$.

$u_1 = 0$

6 Find an inductive definition for the sequence 2, 4, 12, 48, 240, ...

Exercise A (answers p. 123)

1 Write down the first five terms of the sequence U where $u_{i+1} = 2u_i$ and $u_1 = 4$.

2 Investigate the following sequences.

(a) $u_{i+1} = \dfrac{2}{3}u_i$, $u_1 = -3$ (b) $u_{i+1} = \dfrac{1}{u_i^2}$, $u_1 = 2$ (c) $u_{i+1} = \dfrac{-5}{u_i}$, $u_1 = 1$

3 Investigate and describe the sequence T where

$$t_{i+1} = \dfrac{t_{i-1}}{t_i} \qquad \text{and} \qquad t_1 = 1, t_2 = 2.$$

4 Find inductive definitions for these sequences.

(a) $1, \frac{1}{3}, \frac{1}{9}, \frac{1}{27}, \frac{1}{81}, \ldots$ (b) $1, -\frac{1}{3}, \frac{1}{9}, -\frac{1}{27}, \frac{1}{81}, \ldots$

B The general term (answers p. 123)

1 A sequence S has a zero starting value and a term-to-term rule (recurrence relation) $s_{t+1} = s_t + 6$.

(a) What is s_{50}?

(b) Why is it inappropriate to use an inductive method to calculate s_{50}?

Clearly, there are drawbacks if only inductive definitions are used to generate the terms of a sequence. It can be very useful to have a formula for the general term.

2 Why is $2 \times 1.1^{n-1}$ the general term of the sequence T where

$$t_{i+1} = 1.1 t_i \quad \text{and} \quad t_1 = 2?$$

3 What are the terms of the sequence U where

$$u_i = (-1)^i \frac{1}{i^2}?$$

4 Using an inductive method investigate the sequence U where u_i is the number of ways to connect pairs of dots among a set of i dots.

Find a recurrence relation for this sequence.

5 Using an inductive method investigate the sequence T where t_i is the number of ways to arrange i flower pots in a row.

Find a recurrence relation for this sequence.

> A sequence of alternating signs can be achieved by using a factor of $(-1)^i$ or $(-1)^{i+1}$ in the general term.

Example 2

Find an expression for the ith term of the sequence $-1, 3, -5, 7, \ldots$

Solution

It is helpful to think of the terms as

$$-1 \times 1, +1 \times 3, -1 \times 5, +1 \times 7, \ldots$$

The $-1, +1, -1, +1, \ldots$ sequence is generated by $(-1)^i$.
The $1, 3, 5, 7, \ldots$ sequence is generated by $2i - 1$.
So $u_i = (-1)^i (2i - 1)$.

Exercise B (answers p. 123)

1   Write out the first five terms of the sequences with these ith terms.
(a) $u_i = 3i + 2$ (b) $u_i = 5 \times 2^i$ (c) $u_i = 3i^2$
(d) $u_i = 10 - i$ (e) $u_i = 10 - (\frac{1}{2})^i$ (f) $u_i = 10 + (\frac{1}{2})^i$

2   (a) Write out the first five terms of the sequences with these ith terms.
(i) $u_i = (-1)^i$
(ii) $u_i = (-1)^{i+1}$
(iii) $u_i = (-1)^{i+2}$
(iv) $u_i = (-1)^i 2^{i-1}$

(b) Write down the general term of each of these sequences.
(i) $4, -4, 4, -4, 4, \ldots$
(ii) $-4, 4, -4, 4, -4, \ldots$

3   For each of the following sequences copy and complete the table.

Term	1	2	3	4	5	6	9	100	i
A	2	5	8	11					
B	2	4	8	16					
C	$\frac{1}{2}$	$\frac{1}{3}$	$\frac{1}{4}$	$\frac{1}{5}$					
D	-1	2	-3	4					
E	1	-2	3	-4					
F	2	-4	6	-8					
G	1	-4	9	-16					

4   A company is excavating in order to build a new warehouse. As the excavated area increases more soil can be removed. The amount of soil (in cubic metres) removed on each sucessive day is modelled by the sequence T where

$$t_{i+1} = 1.2 t_i \quad \text{and} \quad t_i = 100.$$

A building control surveyor visits the site and observes almost 900 m^3 of soil being excavated that day. How many days can she conclude the digging has been under way?

5   House prices in a town are rising at a constant rate of 15 per cent each year. In how many years will house prices double?

C Mortgages, loans and depreciation (answers p. 124)

A mortgage is a way of borrowing money in order to purchase a house, which is then used as security for the loan. A mortgage is usually taken out with a building society or bank, although it is also possible to take out a mortgage with other institutions such as a county council.

In order to understand how the simplest kind of mortgage works, you can see what happens in the case of a mortgage of £40 000 borrowed at an interest rate of 10 per cent (the current mortgage rate may be different from this). The repayments are commonly made for 20 or 25 years, although this can be varied. Suppose you make monthly repayments of £395. How many years will it take to repay the loan?

1   Copy and complete the following:

£

| YEAR ONE: | Initial loan | 40 000 | (Interest for the year is added at the beginning of the year.) |

Interest   ——

Total debt

Repayments 12 @ £395   4 740
Outstanding balance   ——

YEAR TWO: Loan outstanding
                Interest   ——

Total debt

Repayments 12 @ £395   ——
Outstanding balance   ——

This continues until the loan is completely repaid.

2   Let $£L_n$ be the loan outstanding at the beginning of year n.
    (a) Write down L_1.
    (b) Express L_{n+1} in terms of L_n.

3D   Use a program or spreadsheet to find how long it will take to repay the mortgage.

Software you produce for this question will be useful with a little adaptation for questions throughout this chapter.

4   How many years will it take to repay a £100 000 mortgage at 8 per cent interest with monthly repayments of £800?

5   It is possible to set up an algebraic calculation for the repetitive routine
    you used to solve the mortgage problem above.

   YEAR ONE: Final debt $= 40\,000 \times 1.1 - 4740$

   YEAR TWO: Final debt $= (40\,000 \times 1.1 - 4740) \times 1.1 - 4740$

   $= 40\,000 \times 1.1^2 - 4740 \times 1.1 - 4740$

   Obtain similar expressions for the final debts at the end of year three
   and year four.

6   After n years, the outstanding debt is

$$40\,000 \times 1.1^n - 4740 \times 1.1^{n-1} - 4740 \times 1.1^{n-2} - \ldots$$

$$- 4740 \times 1.1^2 - 4740 \times 1.1 - 4740$$

$$= 40\,000 \times 1.1^n - 4740(1.1^{n-1} + 1.1^{n-2} + \ldots + 1.1^2 + 1.1 + 1)$$

$$= 40\,000 \times 1.1^n - 4740 \sum_{i=1}^{n} 1.1^{i-1} \qquad (1)$$

   (a) Explain why

$$\sum_{i=1}^{n} 1.1^{i-1} = \frac{1.1^n - 1}{0.1}$$

   (b) Hence simplify expression (1) for the outstanding debt after
        n years.

7E Find the monthly repayment required so that a mortgage of £50 000 at
    11 per cent per annum is repaid at the end of 25 years.

Exercise C (answers p. 125)

1   A car is purchased new for £9995. Its falling value or **depreciation** is
    modelled using the recurrence relation

$$v_{n+1} = 0.85v_n + 200, \qquad v_0 = 9995$$

   where v_n is the value in pounds after n years.
   (a) What is the value of the car after one year?
   (b) What is the value of the car after ten years?
   (c) Obtain a formula for v_n in terms of n.
   (d) The value tends towards a limit. What is this limit?

2   A woman takes out a loan of £4000 to buy a car. The interest rate is
    0.75 per cent per month, and she repays the loan at £150 per month.
   (a) Write a recurrence relation.
   (b) How long will it take the woman to repay the loan?
   (c) How much does she pay altogether?

3 Suppose the woman in question 2 wants to repay the loan over a period of five years. Calculate her monthly repayments.

D Convergent sequences (answers p. 125)

Consider the sequence defined by $u_1 = 2$, $u_{i+1} = \dfrac{1}{u_i} + 1$.

1 Use a calculator to find u_2, u_3, u_4, u_5 and u_6.

2 Use a spreadsheet or other program to continue the sequence as far as u_{12}.

The last three terms you should have obtained are 1.617 977 528, 1.618 055 556 and 1.618 025 751.

The terms of the sequence seem to be changing less as you proceed and settling down at a value. This is called the **limit** of the sequence; it is about 1.618. Such a sequence is said to be **convergent**.

What is special about the limit? If the sequence settles down to some fixed number x, so that u_{i+1} and u_i are both equal to x, then it must be a solution of the equation

$$x = \frac{1}{x} + 1$$

3 Show that $x = \dfrac{1}{x} + 1$ can be written as $x^2 - x - 1 = 0$ and that the solutions of this equation are $\frac{1}{2}(1 \pm \sqrt{5})$.

4 Write $\frac{1}{2}(1 + \sqrt{5})$ as a decimal.

Exercise D (answers p. 125)

1 (a) Find u_9 and u_{10} for the sequence $u_1 = 1$, $u_{i+1} = \frac{1}{3}(u_i^3 + 1)$.
　　(b) Suggest a limit of the sequence. Explain why it is a solution of $x^3 - 3x + 1 = 0$ and check that it is.

2 Explain why the limit of the sequence $u_1 = 3$, $u_{i+1} = \sqrt{\dfrac{20}{u_i}}$ is $\sqrt[3]{20}$.
　Find u_9 and u_{10}, and compare them with $\sqrt[3]{20}$.

3 Find u_4 and u_5 for the sequence $u_1 = 3$, $u_{i+1} = \frac{1}{2}\left(u_i + \dfrac{7}{u_i}\right)$. What is special about the limit of the sequence?

4 Find u_2, u_3, u_4 and u_5 for the sequence $u_1 = 4$, $u_{i+1} = \dfrac{100}{u_i^2}$. Does the sequence have a limit?

E Iterative formulas for solving equations (answers p. 125)

Suppose you have an iteration giving a convergent sequence. You can now write down an equation for which the limit is a solution.

The reverse process is more important. You may wish to solve a particular equation. Can you write it in a form that leads to a suitable iteration?

Example 3

Find the positive root of the equation $x^3 - 8x - 7 = 0$ correct to 3 decimal places.

Solution

Step 1: Rewrite the equation.

$$x^3 - 8x - 7 = 0$$
$$\Rightarrow \quad x^3 = 8x + 7$$
$$\Rightarrow \quad x = \sqrt[3]{8x + 7}$$

This suggests the iterative formula

$$x_{i+1} = \sqrt[3]{8x_i + 7}$$

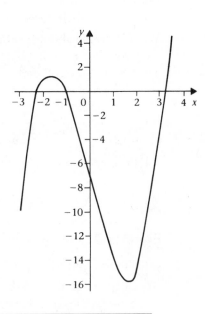

Step 2: Sketch the graph to locate the roots.

Step 3: From the graph, choose a suitable value for x_1.

$x_1 = 3$ is near the required solution.

Step 4: Use the formula to generate the iterative sequence.

$$x_2 = \sqrt[3]{8 \times 3 + 7}$$
$$= 3.141\ 380\ 652$$
$$x_3 = 3.179\ 129\ 979$$

1D

(a) Find x_4.

(b) Continue to find x_5, x_6, x_7, etc. until you are confident that you know the solution to 3 decimal places. How can you decide when to stop?

(c) In writing out your solutions, how many decimal places is it sensible to give for your intermediate results?

Exercise E (answers p. 125)

1 For the equation
$$2x^2 - 5x + 1 = 0$$
find which of the following are possible iterative formulas and show how they can be obtained.

(a) $x_{i+1} = \sqrt{\dfrac{5x_i - 1}{2}}$

(b) $x_{i+1} = \dfrac{1 + 2x_i^2}{5}$

(c) $x_{i+1} = \dfrac{1}{2}\left(5 - \dfrac{1}{x_i}\right)$

(d) $x_{i+1} = \dfrac{1}{5 - 2x_i}$

(e) $x_{i+1} = \frac{1}{2}\sqrt{1 - 5x_i}$

(f) $x_{i+1} = 2x_i^2 - 4x_i + 1$

2 Consider the equation $x^3 = 10$.
  (a) (i) Show that the equation can be arranged into the form
  $$x = \sqrt{\dfrac{10}{x}}.$$

  (ii) By letting $x_1 = 2$, and using an iterative formula, obtain the positive solution for $x^3 = 10$, to 5 decimal places.
  (b) (i) Show that the equation can be rearranged to $x = \sqrt{\sqrt{10x}}$.
  (ii) By letting $x_1 = 2$ and using an iterative formula, obtain the positive solution for $x^3 = 10$, to 5 decimal places.

3 Using an initial value of $x_1 = 3$ and an iterative formula, find a positive solution of $2^x = 3x$ to 4 decimal places.

4 (a) By sketching appropriate graphs, find an interval that contains the root of
  $$x^2 - 1 = 6\sqrt{x}$$

  (b) Show that $x = \sqrt{6\sqrt{x} + 1}$ is a rearrangement of this equation.
  (c) By choosing an appropriate starting value, solve the equation, giving your answer correct to 6 decimal places.

5 (a) Show that the equation $x^3 + 2x = 1$ has a root that lies between 0 and 1.

(b) Show that $x = \dfrac{1 - x^3}{2}$ is a rearrangement of the equation.

(c) Find the root between 0 and 1 correct to 5 decimal places using a starting value of   (i) 0,   (ii) 1.

(d) What happens if you take a starting value of 2?

6 This question concerns the equation $2x^2 - 5x + 1 = 0$ and three possible rearrangements given in question 1. All answers should be given to 6 decimal places.

(a) Show that the equation $2x^2 - 5x + 1 = 0$ has one root in the interval $[0, 1]$ and another in the interval $[2, 3]$.

(b) Consider the iterative formula $x_{i+1} = \sqrt{\dfrac{5x_i - 1}{2}}$.

   (i) Explain why the starting value $x_i = 0$ cannot be used.

   (ii) Solve the equation using starting values of 1, 2 and 10. Record the number of iterations used for each starting value.

(c) Solve the equation using the iterative formula

$$x_{i+1} = \frac{1}{2}\left(5 - \frac{1}{x_i}\right)$$

and starting values 1, 2 and 10.

Record the number of iterations used for each starting value.

(d) Solve the equation using the iterative formula

$$x_{i+1} = \frac{1 + 2x_i^2}{5}$$

and starting values 1, 2 and 3.

(e) Comment on the suitability of each formula.

F Convergence (answers p. 126)

In exercise E you solved the equation $2x^2 - 5x + 1 = 0$ using a variety of formulas and starting points, of which some converged rapidly, some converged more slowly, some converged to a root in a different interval, and some did not converge at all.

It is plain that the choice of iterative formula is critical if you are to obtain a sequence which converges quickly.

1 (a) Give a rough estimate for $\sqrt[3]{10}$.

(b) Explain how the rearrangement $x = \dfrac{10}{x^2}$ is obtained from $x^3 = 10$.

Use the iterative formula $x_{i+1} = \dfrac{10}{x_i^2}$, together with the starting value that you gave in part (a), to evaluate $x_2, x_3, ..., x_{10}$. What do you find?

It is helpful to know when a sequence is likely to converge *before* working out all the values. These questions show how a graphical approach can help to predict convergence.

2 Consider the rearranged equation $x = \dfrac{10}{x^2}$.

This is equivalent to the two simultaneous equations

$$y = x \qquad \text{and} \qquad y = \frac{10}{x^2} = g(x), \text{ say}$$

and its solution lies at the intersection of the two graphs.

(a) For $0 \leqslant x \leqslant 3$, plot $y = x$ and $y = \dfrac{10}{x^2}$ on the same graph. You can now illustrate the solution procedure for a particular starting value, say $x_1 = 2$.

$$x_1 = 2 \implies g(x_1) = \frac{10}{2^2} = 2.5$$

Therefore $x_2 = 2.5$.

(b) On your graph, plot and join the points (x_1, x_1), (x_1, x_2) and (x_2, x_2). How could you have used your graph to locate the points (x_1, x_2) and (x_2, x_2) *without* doing any calculations?

(c) *Without* further calculation, plot and successively join up the points (x_2, x_3), (x_3, x_3), (x_3, x_4), (x_4, x_4). The diagram you have obtained is called a **cobweb diagram.**

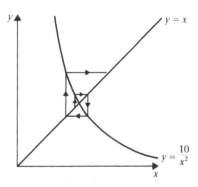

3 What does the cobweb diagram of question 2 illustrate about the iteration attempted in question 1?

4 (a) Draw a cobweb diagram for the function g(x) illustrated. (It is not necessary to give g(x) an equation – simply use the construction described in question 2.)

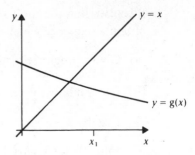

(b) What would happen in this case to the sequence defined by $x_{i+1} = g(x_i)$?

Not all graphs give rise to a cobweb diagram.

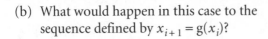

This is called a **staircase diagram**.

5 (a) What happens if x_1 is on the other side of the root in the graph for question 4?

(b) Draw a similar diagram for the function on the right, choosing values for x_1 above and below the root.

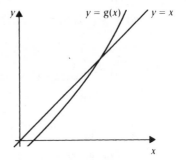

6 What property of g(x) determines whether you get a staircase or a cobweb diagram?

7 By considering the staircase and cobweb diagrams above, explain how the gradient of g(x) determines whether an iteration based upon $x_{i+1} = g(x_i)$ will converge or diverge.

8 Consider the equation $x^3 = 10$.

(a) Show how to obtain the iterative formula

$$x_{i+1} = \frac{1}{3}\left(2x_i + \frac{10}{x_i^2}\right)$$

(b) Using appropriate staircase or cobweb diagrams, investigate the convergence of the iterative sequence obtained for different initial values.

Example 4

Illustrate the convergence of the iterative formula

$$x_{i+1} = \sqrt{\frac{10}{x_i}}$$

with starting value $x_1 = 2$ using a cobweb diagram.

Solution

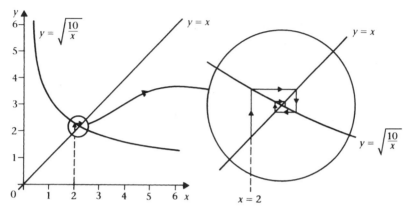

Convergence occurs here because, near the root, the graph is sufficiently flat.

The convergence of iterative sequences is of interest in various areas of mathematics. For example, the iterative process based upon the sequence $x_{i+1} = \lambda x_i(1 - x_i)$ is at the heart of the recently developed mathematical theory of **chaos**.

Exercise F (answers p. 127)

1   Illustrate the convergence of the iterative formula $x_{i+1} = \frac{1}{3}(2^{x_i})$ on a cobweb or staircase diagram using a starting value of 3. (See exercise E, question 3.)

2   In exercise E you found a root of the equation $x^3 + 2x = 1$ between 0 and 1 using the iterative formula $x_{i+1} = \dfrac{(1 - x_i^3)}{2}$.

   (a) Show on a cobweb diagram that a starting value of 0 converges, showing five iterations.

   (b) Illustrate the divergence when a starting value of 2 is used.

3 (a) Given $f(x) = \dfrac{1}{2}\left(5 - \dfrac{1}{x}\right)$ and $g(x) = \dfrac{1 + 2x^2}{5}$, find $f'(2.28)$ and $g'(0.219)$. What light is thrown on exercise E question 6 (c) and (d)?

   (b) If $h(x) = \sqrt{\dfrac{5x - 1}{2}}$, then $h'(2.28) \approx 0.55$. Explain why the sequence of exercise E question 6(b) converges slowly.

4 (a) Show that the equation $x = \frac{1}{4}e^x$ can be written alternatively as $x = \ln(4x)$.

   (b) Find the limits of sequences based on each of the forms in (a), with starting value 1 in each case.

   (c) Illustrate (b) by staircase diagrams.

5 One scout troop heated soup in a well-insulated electric stewpot. The temperature θ °C after t minutes was given by $\theta = 8t$.

   Another troop heated the same amount of soup in a saucepan on an open fire. There was heat loss to the air and the temperature was given by $\theta = 120(1 - e^{-0.1t})$.

   (a) What was the temperature in each case after 8 minutes?

   (b) After T minutes, the temperature was the same by both methods. Find T to 2 decimal places.

6 The line AB in the diagram divides the area of the circle in the ratio $1 : 7$.

   O is the centre and angle AOB $= \theta$ radians. Show that $\theta = \sin \theta + \frac{1}{4}\pi$. Solve this equation, giving your answer to 3 decimal places.

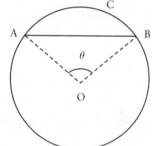

After working through this chapter you should

1 know how to recognise, define and describe a sequence in terms of a recurrence relation

2 understand the principles of mortgages

3 be able to use the iterative formula $x_{i+1} = g(x_i)$ to obtain a root of an equation to a given degree of accuracy

4 be able to rearrange equations into the form $x = g(x)$

5 appreciate that the iterative method based upon $x = g(x)$ may or may not converge

6 be able to illustrate convergence or divergence on a cobweb or staircase diagram.

2 Circles, tangents and normals

A The equation of a circle (answers p. 128)

Pythagoras' theorem can be used to find the equation of a circle. The necessary ideas are developed in the following questions.

1 (a) Use Pythagoras' theorem to find the distance of the point $(3, 3)$ from the origin.

   (b) Use Pythagoras' theorem to find the distance of the point $(4, 6)$ from the point $(1, 2)$.

A circle is made up of all the points that are a fixed distance from its centre. The distance from the centre is the radius r of the circle.

2 (a) Use Pythagoras' theorem to decide which of the following points lie on a circle with centre $(0, 0)$, radius 5.

$$(4, 3), (2.5, 2.5), (-3, 4), (-5, 0), (1, -4.5)$$

   (b) Write down an equation connecting x and y which is satisfied by all points (x, y) which lie on this circle.

   (c) Use a graph plotter to draw the graph of this equation. (For some graph plotters, you may need to rearrange the equation to give y in terms of x. This form of the equation will involve a square root, so the graph will be drawn in two sections, one part using the positive square root, and one using the negative square root.)

3 (a) Use Pythagoras' theorem to decide which of the following points lie on a circle with centre $(2, 5)$, radius 25.

$$(27, 5), (17, 25), (-5, 29), (-22, -2), (-18, -10)$$

   (b) Write down an equation connecting x and y which is satisfied by all points (x, y) that lie on this circle.

   (c) Use a graph plotter to draw the graph of this equation.

4 (a) Use Pythagoras' theorem to prove that the equation of a circle centre $(0, 0)$ and radius r is $x^2 + y^2 = r^2$.

   (b) Prove that the equation of a circle centre (a, b) and radius r is $(x - a)^2 + (y - b)^2 = r^2$.

The equation of a circle of radius r about the point (a, b) is
$$(x - a)^2 + (y - b)^2 = r^2$$
When the circle has its centre at the origin, $a = b = 0$, so the equation becomes
$$x^2 + y^2 = r^2$$
This can be rewritten as
$$y = \pm \sqrt{r^2 - x^2}$$

Example 1

Find the equation of the circle radius 4, centre $(2, 3)$. Does the point $(5, 5)$ lie inside or outside the circle?

Solution

The equation of the circle is $(x - 2)^2 + (y - 3)^2 = 16$.

The distance between the points $(2, 3)$ and $(5, 5)$ is $\sqrt{3^2 + 2^2} = \sqrt{13}$.

Since $\sqrt{13}$ is less than the radius of the circle, $(5, 5)$ must lie inside the circle.

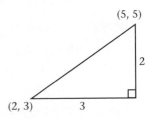

Example 2

Find the radius and coordinates of the centre of the circle having equation $x^2 - 2x + y^2 + 4y + 1 = 0$.

Solution

You need to write the equation in the form $(x - a)^2 + (y - b)^2 = r^2$. The method of completing the square is used to do this.

$$(x - 1)^2 - 1 + y^2 + 4y + 1 = 0 \qquad \text{Complete the square on the } x \text{ terms ...}$$

$$(x - 1)^2 + (y + 2)^2 - 4 = 0 \qquad \text{... and on the } y \text{ terms}$$
$$(x - 1)^2 + (y + 2)^2 = 4$$

The circle has radius 2 and centre $(1, -2)$.

Exercise A (answers p. 128)

1   Find the equations of the following circles with centre the origin.

(a) radius 15 units

(b) diameter 8 units

(c) circumference 10 units

(d) passing through the point $(12, 16)$

2 Find the equations of the following circles.

(a) radius 3 units, centre $(1, 1)$

(b) diameter 16 units, centre $(-4, 6)$

3 A lighthouse has a grid reference $(20, 85)$ on a map, where each unit represents one nautical mile. The light is powerful enough to be seen from up to 18 nautical miles away. Write an equation involving E, the easterly map reference, and N, the northerly map reference, to show the boundary beyond which ships cannot see the lighthouse.

4 Do the following points lie inside or outside the circles given by the equations?

(a) $(3, 2)$; $(x-1)^2 + (y-4)^2 = 9$

(b) $(4, -1)$; $(x+1)^2 + (y-2)^2 = 30$

5 Find the radius and the coordinates of the centre of the circle given by each of the following equations.

(a) $x^2 - 4x + y^2 - 2y + 1 = 0$

(b) $x^2 - 2x + y^2 - 8 = 0$

(c) $4x^2 - 4x + 4y^2 + 2y + 1 = 0$

6E Find the centre, radius and equation of the circle passing through the points $(6, 9)$, $(13, -8)$ and $(-4, -15)$.

(Hint: You could let the equation be $(x-a)^2 + (y-b)^2 = r^2$, or plot the points and consider a geometric approach.)

7E Find the possible equations of circles, radius 10 units, which pass through the points $(10, 9)$ and $(8, -5)$. Which of these equations describes a circle which also passes through the point $(-6, -3)$?

B Intersections of lines and circles

Example 3

Where does the line $y = -2x + 10$ intersect the circle $x^2 + y^2 = 25$?

Solution

Substitution shows that the graphs meet where

$$x^2 + (-2x + 10)^2 = 25$$
$$x^2 + 4x^2 - 40x + 100 = 25$$
$$5x^2 - 40x + 75 = 0$$
$$x^2 - 8x + 15 = 0$$
$$(x - 3)(x - 5) = 0$$
$$x = 3 \text{ or } 5$$

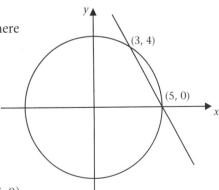

From the equation of the line, $y = 4$ or 0.

The points of intersection are $(3, 4)$ and $(5, 0)$.

Exercise B (answers p. 129)

1   Find in each case where the line meets the circle. Find the centre and radius of the circle and draw a sketch showing the line, circle and intersection points.

(a) line $y = 2x$,   circle $x^2 + y^2 - 10x = 15$

(b) line $y = -x + 4$,   circle $x^2 + y^2 = 10$

(c) line $2x + y = 11$,   circle $x^2 + y^2 - 6x = 1$

(d) line $y = 3x + 6$,   circle $x^2 + y^2 - 2x + 2y = 8$

(e) line $x + 2y = 14$,   circle $x^2 + y^2 - 4x - 2y = 15$

2   Show that the line $x + y = 5$ does not intersect the circle $x^2 + y^2 = 8$.

3   Where does the circle $x^2 + y^2 = 6$ meet the circle $x^2 + y^2 - 8y + 10 = 0$? Show the two circles on a sketch.

C Tangents and normals to curves (answers p. 129)

You know that the gradient of a curve at a point is defined as the gradient of the tangent to the curve at that point. Sometimes it is necessary to find the equation of the tangent at a point. You can find the gradient of the curve, and hence of the tangent, by differentiating. The tangent is a straight line, so its equation is of the form $y = mx + c$.

Example 4

(a) Find the gradient of the graph $y = 2x^3 - 3x + 5$ at the point $(-1, 6)$.

(b) Hence find the equation of the tangent at $(-1, 6)$.

Solution

(a) $\dfrac{dy}{dx} = 6x^2 - 3$. At the point $(-1, 6)$, the gradient is $6 \times (-1)^2 - 3 = 3$.

(b) The tangent has gradient 3 and passes through the point $(-1, 6)$. If (x, y) is another point on the tangent, then

$$\frac{y - 6}{x - (-1)} = 3$$

$$\Rightarrow y - 6 = 3(x + 1)$$

$$\Rightarrow y = 3x + 9$$

The equation of the tangent is $y = 3x + 9$.

A line with gradient $-\frac{1}{2}$ makes a right angle with a line with gradient 2.

Each line is said to be **normal** to the other.

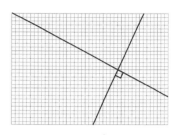

1D If a line is drawn with a gradient g, what can you say about the gradient of a line which is normal to it?

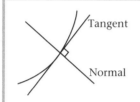

A line is said to be a **normal** to a curve at a given point if it is normal to the tangent at that point.

Exercise C (answers p. 129)

1 Find the equations of the tangents to each of the following graphs at $(2, 3)$.
   (a) $y = 3 + 2x - x^2$
   (b) $y = x^3 - 5$
   (c) $y = 7 + x^2 - x^3$

2 Find the equation of the tangent to $y = x + 2x^2$ at the point whose x-coordinate is 3.

3 Find the equations of the tangents to each of the following graphs at $(0, 5)$.
   (a) $y = 5 + x - x^3$
   (b) $y = 5 - 3x + 2x^3$
   (c) $y = 5 + 4x^2 + 3x^3$

4 The graph of $y = \frac{1}{3}x^3$ has tangents drawn at $x = 1$ and at $x = -1$. These two tangents and the normals to the tangents form a rectangle.
   (a) Sketch the graph with the tangents and normals shown.
   (b) Find the equations of the two tangents.
   (c) Find the equations of the two normals.
   (d) Use your answers to (b) and (c) to find the coordinates of all four corners of the rectangle.
   (e) What is the area of the rectangle?

5   Tangents and normals drawn on the graph of
    $y = x^2$ form a square as shown.

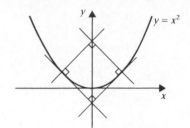

(a) Find the coordinates of the four corners
     of the square.

(b) Show that the area of the square is $\frac{1}{2}$.

6   The normal to the graph of $y = x^2$ at $(1, 1)$ cuts
    the graph at A as shown.

    Find A.

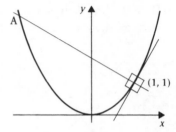

7   Find where the normal to $y = x^2 + x + 3$ at $(2, 9)$ meets the curve again.
    Show the curve and normal on the same sketch.

8   Find the equations of the tangents and normals to the curves at the
    given points. Use a graph plotter to check your answers.

    (a) $y = \dfrac{1}{x}$ at $(2, \frac{1}{2})$ (b) $y = \sqrt{x}$ at $(9, 3)$

    (c) $y = x + \dfrac{9}{x}$ at $(3, 6)$ (d) $y = x - \sqrt{x}$ at $(1, 0)$

    (e) $y = x^3$ at $(2, 8)$ (f) $y = x^{1/3}$ at $(8, 2)$

9E Find where the tangent to $y = x^3 + x^2 - 7$ at $(2, 5)$ meets the curve
    again.

D Tangents and normals to circles (answers p. 130)

It is possible to find the gradient of a tangent or normal to a circle
without using differentiation.

The diagram shows the circle with centre C $(2, 3)$ which passes
through P $(5, 7)$; the tangent at P has also been
drawn.

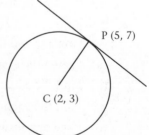

1   How are the radius and tangent at a point related?

2   What is the gradient of PC?

3   What is the gradient of the tangent?

4   Show that the equation of the tangent is
    $4y = -3x + 43$.

Example 5

A circle has centre $(-1, 2)$ and radius 13. Find the equations of the tangent and the normal to the circle at the point $(11, 7)$.

Solution

The gradient of the radius through $(11, 7)$ is $\frac{5}{12}$.
So the gradient of the tangent is $-\frac{12}{5}$.
If (x, y) is a point on the tangent, then

$$\frac{y-7}{x-11} = -\frac{12}{5}$$

$$\Rightarrow \quad 5(y-7) = -12(x-11)$$
$$\Rightarrow \quad 5y - 35 = -12x + 132$$
$$\Rightarrow \quad 5y + 12x = 167$$

If (x, y) is a point on the normal, then

$$\frac{y-7}{x-11} = \frac{5}{12}$$

$$\Rightarrow \quad 12(y-7) = 5(x-11)$$
$$\Rightarrow \quad 12y - 84 = 5x - 55$$
$$\Rightarrow \quad 12y - 5x = 29$$

Exercise D (answers p. 130)

1. The point $(8, 9)$ lies on the circle with centre $(2, 1)$.
   (a) What is the radius of the circle?
   (b) Find the equations of the tangent and the normal to the circle at $(8, 9)$.

2. The point $(-4, 5)$ lies on the circle with centre $(-1, 4)$. Find the equations of the tangent and the normal to the circle at this point.

3. A circle has equation $x^2 - 6x + y^2 - 2y - 7 = 0$.
   (a) Find the centre of the circle.
   (b) Find the equations of the tangent and the normal to the circle at the point $(1, 2)$.

4. The tangents at A $(-5, 1)$ and B $(7, 5)$ on the circle $x^2 + y^2 - 4x = 46$ meet at P. Find the coordinates of P and the distances AP and BP.

5   (a)   Show that A $(4, 8)$ lies on both the circles

$$x^2 + y^2 + 4x = 96 \qquad \text{and} \qquad x^2 + y^2 - 16x - 10y + 64 = 0$$

     (b)   Show that the tangent at A to the first circle passes through the centre of the second circle.

     (c)   Does the tangent at A to the second circle pass through the centre of the first circle?

     (d)   Find the other point of intersection of the two circles.

After working through this chapter you should

1   be able to find the equation of a circle, given its centre and radius

2   be able to find the centre and radius of a circle, given its equation

3   be able to find the equation of a tangent or normal to a graph at a given point

4   be able to find the equation of a tangent or normal to a circle at a given point.

3 Trigonometric functions

A Inverse functions and equations (answers p. 130)

You have used the functions sin, cos and tan to find lengths and angles, and also as periodic functions to model periodic motion.

Angles may be measured in degrees or in radians, and all ideas concerning the degree sine function, for example, have their counterparts for the radian function. In this chapter, you will revise and extend earlier work, keeping to degrees and the degree functions. Radians will re-appear in the next chapter.

1 (a) Sketch the graph of $y = \sin x°$.

   (b) Use your calculator (in degree mode) to find $\sin^{-1}(-0.46)$.
   (You may find the $\sin^{-1}$ function called arcsin or asin.)
   Show your answer on your graph.

   (c) Find the two solutions in the interval $0 \leqslant x \leqslant 360$ of the equation $\sin x° = -0.46$.

2 Sketch the graph of $y = \sin^{-1} x$. Describe its relation to the graph of $y = \sin x°$.

3 (a) Use your calculator to find $\cos^{-1}(0.88)$ and $\cos^{-1}(-0.88)$.
   (You may find $\cos^{-1}$ called arccos or acos.)

   (b) Sketch the graph of $y = \cos^{-1} x$.

4 Find all the solutions of the equation $\cos x° = 0.29$ in the interval $0 \leqslant x \leqslant 360$.

5 Find all the solutions of $\sin \frac{1}{2}x° = 0.75$ in the interval $0 \leqslant x \leqslant 720$.

The graphs of the inverse functions $y = \sin^{-1} x$ and $y = \cos^{-1} x$ are reflections in $y = x$ of parts of the graphs of $y = \sin x°$ and $y = \cos x°$.

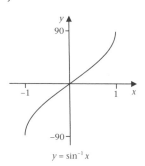

$y = \sin^{-1} x$

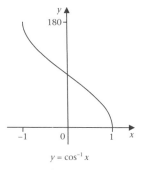

$y = \cos^{-1} x$

In each case the domain is $-1 \leqslant x \leqslant 1$. The ranges are given by $-90 \leqslant \sin^{-1} x \leqslant 90$ and $0 \leqslant \cos^{-1} x \leqslant 180$.

When solving an equation like sin $x° = a$ or cos $x° = b$, the inverse function will only give you one solution. By sketching a graph it is possible to find other required solutions.

Example 1

Solve the equation cos $(2t + 50)° = 0.8$ for $0 \leqslant t \leqslant 360$.

Solution

You first need to solve cos $x° = 0.8$ where $x = 2t + 50$. A calculator gives $x = 36.9$.

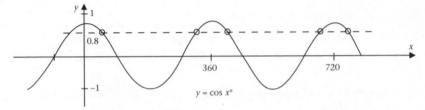

From the graph, $x = 36.9, 360 \pm 36.9, 720 \pm 36.9, \ldots$

So $2t + 50 = 36.9, 360 - 36.9, 360 + 36.9, 720 - 36.9, 720 + 36.9$

   $2t = -13.1, 273.1, 346.9, 633.1, 706.9$

   $t = (-6.6), 136.6, 173.5, 316.6, 353.5$

There are four solutions in the required interval. Note that values of x were needed from 50 to 770.

6   You have already met the definition $\tan x° = \dfrac{\sin x°}{\cos x°}$.

(a)   What is the greatest possible domain for the function tan?

(b)   Sketch the graph of $y = \tan^{-1} x$. ($\tan^{-1} x$ may also be called arctan x or atan x.)

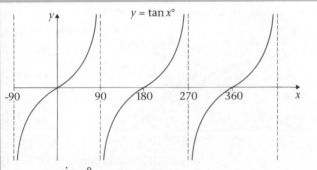

$\tan x° = \dfrac{\sin x°}{\cos x°}$ $\{\cos x° \neq 0\}$

$\tan x°$ is an odd function: $\tan (-x)° = -\tan x°$.

$\tan^{-1} x$ has domain all real numbers, range $-90 < \tan^{-1} x < 90$.

Exercise A (answers p. 131)

1   For each of these equations find all the solutions in the interval
    $-360 \leqslant x \leqslant 360$.

   (a) $\sin x° = 0.2$ (b) $\cos x° = -0.3$

   (c) $3 \sin x° = 2$ (d) $\cos 2x° = 0.4$

2   Find the solutions in the interval $0 \leqslant t \leqslant 360$ of these equations.

   (a) $\sin(t - 23)° = -0.14$ (b) $\sin(2t + 68)° = 0.21$

   (c) $\cos(\tfrac{1}{2}t + 11)° = 0.53$ (d) $\tan(3t - 30)° = 1.28$

   (e) $5 \sin t° = 2 \cos t°$

3   Sketch the graphs of $y = \sin(t - 23)°$ and $y = \cos(\tfrac{1}{2}t + 11)°$, marking the
    intersections with the t-axis. Show your answers to question 2(a) and
    (c) on your graphs.

4   Consider the equation $\sin x° = 0.91$.

   (a) Find the four solutions in the interval $0 \leqslant x \leqslant 720$.

   (b) Write down the two solutions in the interval $3600 \leqslant x \leqslant 3960$.

   (c) Write down the two solutions in the interval $360n \leqslant x \leqslant 360(n + 1)$.
    Does your formula apply if n is negative?

5   Sketch the graphs of

   (a) $y = \tan 2x°$ (b) $y = \tan(x + 45)°$

B   **$r \sin (\theta + a)°$** (answers p. 131)

You have seen how to solve equations of the form $a \sin \theta° = b \cos \theta°$.
This section looks at equations of the form $a \sin \theta° + b \cos \theta° = c$.

Two men are trying to carry a wardrobe through a doorway which is
too low to allow them to carry it upright. The wardrobe is 2.5 metres
high and 1.5 metres wide and the doorway is 2 metres high. If the men
tip the wardrobe, as shown in the diagram, they will be able to carry it
through the doorway.

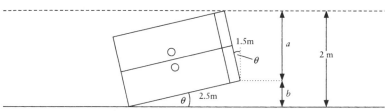

| **1D** | Explain why $2.5 \sin \theta° + 1.5 \cos \theta° \leqslant 2$ if the wardrobe is to go through the doorway. |

You do not yet know how to solve the equation
2.5 sin $\theta°$ + 1.5 cos $\theta°$ = 2 using analytic methods. In the questions
which follow you will look at alternative ways of writing this equation
in order to solve it.

The graphs of 1.5 cos $\theta°$ and 2.5 sin $\theta°$ are illustrated. The function
1.5 cos $\theta°$ + 2.5 sin $\theta°$ is the sum of the two separate functions.

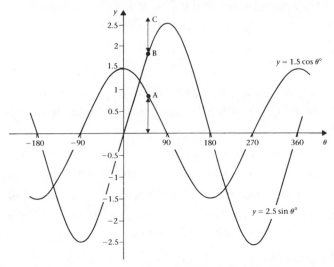

2 (a) In order to find the sum of two graphs, you may use the method
of 'pointwise addition'. The value of the graph at A is added to the
value at B in order to give the value at C. By adding pointwise the
two graphs shown above, obtain a sketch of the graph of

$$y = 2.5 \sin \theta° + 1.5 \cos \theta° \qquad \text{for } -180 \leqslant \theta \leqslant 360$$

(b) Check your sketch using a graph plotter, and write down an
approximate solution to the equation

$$2.5 \sin \theta° + 1.5 \cos \theta° = 2 \qquad \text{between 0 and 90}$$

(c) The wardrobe can be rotated through any angle between 0° and 90°.

   (i) What is the greatest height of the top corner above the
ground, and for what value of θ is this height achieved?

   (ii) Through what range of angles can the wardrobe be tipped so
that it fits through the door?

3 (a) Use a graph plotter to examine the graph of
$y = 3 \sin \theta° + 4 \cos \theta°$.

(b) The resulting graph should be of the form $y = r \sin(\theta + \alpha)°$. Find
the values of r and α from your graph.

(c) Repeat parts (a) and (b) for one or two more graphs of the form
$y = a \sin \theta° + b \cos \theta°$.

4   Questions 2 and 3 suggest that the graph of $y = a \sin \theta° + b \cos \theta°$ is identical to a graph of the form $y = r \sin(\theta + \alpha)°$. The diagram shows how the two expressions are connected.

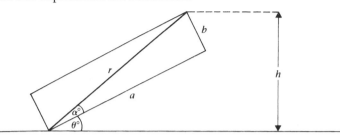

(a) Explain why

(i) $h = a \sin \theta° + b \cos \theta°$

(ii) $h = r \sin(\theta + \alpha)°$

(b) Express r and α in terms of a and b.

5   (a) Use the result in question 4 to express $4 \sin \theta° + 7 \cos \theta°$ in the form $r \sin(\theta + \alpha)°$.

(b) Verify your answer using a graph plotter.

The expression $a \sin \theta° + b \cos \theta°$ is equivalent to the expression $r \sin(\theta + \alpha)°$, where r and α can be found from the triangle

$$r = \sqrt{a^2 + b^2} \text{ and } \alpha° = \tan^{-1} \frac{b}{a}$$

$r \sin(\theta + \alpha)°$ is a sine wave, amplitude r, phase-shifted by $\alpha°$ in the negative x-direction.

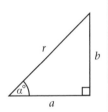

Example 2

Solve the equation $6 \sin \theta° + 9 \cos \theta° = 7$ for values of θ in the range $0 \leqslant \theta \leqslant 360$.

Solution

$6 \sin \theta° + 9 \cos \theta°$ is equivalent to the expression $r \sin(\theta + \alpha)°$, where r and α are found from the triangle shown below.

$$r = \sqrt{6^2 + 9^2} = 10.82 \quad \text{and} \quad \alpha = \tan^{-1} \tfrac{9}{6} = 56.31$$

So $6 \sin \theta° + 9 \cos \theta° = 10.82 \sin(\theta + 56.31)°$

$\implies$ $10.82 \sin(\theta + 56.31)° = 7$

$\implies$ $\sin(\theta + 56.31)° = 0.6472$

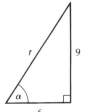

For the equation $\sin x° = 0.6472$, where
$x = \theta + 56.31$, a calculator gives $x = 40.33$.

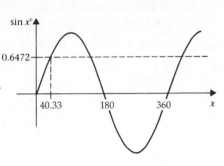

From the sketch graph, you can see that
the solutions are

$x = 40.33, 139.67, 400.33, 499.67$, and so on.

Since $x = \theta + 56.31$,

$\theta = -16.0, 83.4, 344.0, 443.4$, and so on.

The solutions in the range $0 \leqslant \theta \leqslant 360$ are

$\theta = 83.4, 344.0$ correct to 1 decimal place.

Exercise B (answers p. 132)

1 (a) Express $3 \sin \theta° + 2 \cos \theta°$ in the form $r \sin(\theta + \alpha)°$.

(b) Solve the equation $3 \sin \theta° + 2 \cos \theta° = 3$ for $0 \leqslant \theta \leqslant 90$.

2 (a) Explain why the maximum value of $5 \sin \theta° + 12 \cos \theta°$ is 13.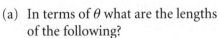

(b) Solve the equation $5 \sin \theta° + 12 \cos \theta° = 9$ for $0 \leqslant \theta \leqslant 360$.

3E Any point on the ellipse has coordinates
of the form $(4 \cos \theta°, 3 \sin \theta°)$.

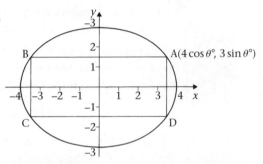

(a) In terms of θ what are the lengths
of the following?

(i) AD

(ii) AB

(iii) the perimeter of the rectangle
ABCD?

(b) If the rectangle ABCD has a perimeter of 14 units, explain why
$3 \sin \theta° + 4 \cos \theta° = 3.5$.

(c) Solve the equation $3 \sin \theta° + 4 \cos \theta° = 3.5$, and hence find the
lengths of sides of the rectangle whose perimeter is 14.

(d) What is the largest possible perimeter, and for what value of θ
does it occur?

4E The octopus ride is a common feature of fun-fairs. There are various
designs: the one illustrated moves in a combination of horizontal
circles.

The diagram below shows the position after an arm of the octopus ride
has moved through an angle of $\theta°$.

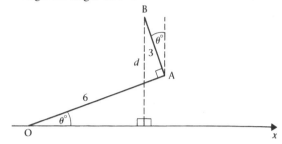

To simplify matters, assume that the arm rotates about O, but that the
chairs (at B, etc.) do not rotate about A.

(a) Explain why the chair at B will move in a circle, and find the
     centre and radius of this circle.

(b) Calculate, in terms of θ, the distance, d, of B from the x-axis.

(c) Write the expression for d in the form $r\sin(\theta + a)°$.

(d) For what values of θ is the chair at B farthest from the x-axis?

C Addition formulas (answers p. 132)

In section B you considered the use of the expression $r\sin(\theta + \alpha)°$.
Here we are concerned with general formulas for the sine and cosine
of the sums of angles. Consider a rotated rectangle with a diagonal of
length 1 unit.

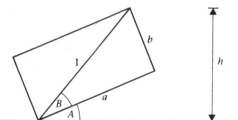

1D

(a) Use the diagram to explain why
$$\sin(A + B) = a\sin A + b\cos A$$
Hence obtain the expansion
$$\sin(A + B) = \sin A\cos B + \cos A\sin B$$

(b) Similarly, explain why
$$\cos(A + B) = a\cos A - b\sin A$$
Hence show that
$$\cos(A + B) = \cos A\cos B - \sin A\sin B$$

(c) Check the identities you obtain by substituting various values
for A and B.

Other formulas for $\sin(A - B)$ and $\cos(A - B)$ can be obtained from the formulas for $\sin(A + B)$ and $\cos(A + B)$ simply by replacing B by $-B$. You should familiarise yourself with the following identities, which are known as the **addition formulas**, together with the **double angle formulas** for $\sin 2A$ and $\cos 2A$ which are derived from them.

Addition formulas

$\sin(A + B) = \sin A \cos B + \cos A \sin B$

$\sin(A - B) = \sin A \cos B - \cos A \sin B$

$\cos(A + B) = \cos A \cos B - \sin A \sin B$

$\cos(A - B) = \cos A \cos B + \sin A \sin B$

2D

Put $B = A$ in each of the four addition formulas. What do you find?

Show that $\quad \cos 2A = 2 \cos^2 A - 1$

and $\quad \cos 2A = 1 - 2 \sin^2 A$.

Double angle formulas

$\sin 2A = 2 \sin A \cos A$

$\cos 2A = \cos^2 A - \sin^2 A$

$\qquad = 2 \cos^2 A - 1$

$\qquad = 1 - 2 \sin^2 A$

Trigonometric form of Pythagoras' formula

$1 = \cos^2 A + \sin^2 A$

The addition formulas, and hence the double angle formulas, were developed assuming that all the angles were acute. In fact they all apply for angles of any size, positive or negative.

We can use $\equiv$ to write each of the above identities, to indicate 'identically equals', because it holds true for all values of A. The $\equiv$ notation can be used for all mathematical identities, where an equality is true for all values of the variables.

Example 3

Use an addition formula to show that $\cos(x + 90)° = -\sin x°$.

Solution

$$\cos(x + 90)° = \cos x° \cos 90° - \sin x° \sin 90°$$
$$= \cos x° \times 0 - \sin x° \times 1$$
$$= -\sin x°$$

Note that the graph of $y = \cos(x + 90)°$ is the standard cosine graph translated 90° to the left. This gives a reflection of the graph of $y = \sin x°$ in the x-axis.

Exercise C (answers p. 133)

1 (a) Use the formula for $\sin(A + B)$ to show that

$$\sin(x + 60)° = \frac{1}{2} \sin x° + \frac{\sqrt{3}}{2} \cos x°$$

(b) Check this result using a graph plotter.

2 (a) Use an addition formula to simplify $\sin(x + 180)°$.

(b) Explain your result graphically.

3 (a) Show that $\cos(A + B) + \cos(A - B) = 2 \cos A \cos B$.

(b) Simplify $\cos(A - B) - \cos(A + B)$.

4 (a) By writing $\sin 75°$ as $\sin(45° + 30°)$, show that $\sin 75° = \dfrac{\sqrt{3} + 1}{2\sqrt{2}}$.

(b) Use the method of part (a) to express $\sin 15°$ in surd form (i.e. square roots).

5 If A and B are acute angles with $\sin A = \frac{4}{5}$ and $\cos B = \frac{12}{13}$, find $\sin(A + B)$ and $\cos(A + B)$ without using a calculator. (The Pythagorean triangles with sides 3, 4, 5 and 5, 12, 13 may be useful in finding $\cos A$ and $\sin B$.)

6 Simplify the following expressions.

(a) $\cos 2A \cos A - \sin 2A \sin A$

(b) $\sin 3B \cos 2B + \cos 3B \sin 2B$

(c) $2 \sin 3C \cos 3C$

(d) $\cos(A + B) \cos A + \sin(A + B) \sin A$

(e) $\sin(A + B) \cos(A - B) + \cos(A + B) \sin(A - B)$

7 Show the following.

(a) $(\cos A + \sin A)(\cos B + \sin B) = \sin(A + B) + \cos(A - B)$

(b) $(\sin A + \cos A)^2 = 1 + \sin 2A$

(c) $(\sin A + \cos B)^2 + (\cos A - \sin B)^2 = 2[1 + \sin(A - B)]$

(d) $\dfrac{\sin 3A}{\sin A} + \dfrac{\cos 3A}{\cos A} = 4 \cos 2A$

8   Verify the double angle formulas with angles of your own choice.

9   (a)   Given $\cos A = \frac{1}{8}$, find $\cos 2A$ and $\cos \frac{1}{2}A$.

(b)   Given $\sin A = \frac{3}{5}$, find $\sin 2A$, $\cos 2A$ and $\sin 4A$.

(c)   Given $\cos A = \frac{1}{2}$, find $\cos 2A$ and $\cos 4A$.

10   Solve these equations for $0 \leqslant x \leqslant 360$.

(a) $\sin 2x° = \cos x°$

(b) $\sin x° + \cos 2x° = 0$

(c) $\cos 2x° = 7 \cos x° + 3$

(d) $\cos 2x° = 1 + \sin x°$

(e) $\sin 2x° = \tan x°$

11   (a)   By writing $\sin 3x° = \sin(x + 2x)°$, show that
$\sin 3x° = 3 \sin x° - 4 \sin^3 x°$.

(b)   Express $\cos 3x°$ in terms of $\cos x°$. Verify your answer using a graph plotter.

D   Extending the method for $r \sin (\theta + \alpha)°$ (answers p. 134)

The method of section B, although useful, has only been developed for the expression $a \sin \theta° + b \cos \theta°$ on the assumption that a and b are positive. Other possibilities are now considered.

1   (a)   Use the diagram to find an expression for x

(i)   in terms of r, θ and α,

(ii)   in terms of a, b and θ.

(b)   Use your result from (a) to obtain an
alternative expression for
$a \cos \theta° - b \sin \theta°$.

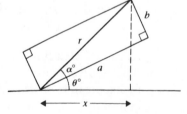

2   By expressing y in two different ways, explain
why $a \sin \theta° - b \cos \theta° = r \sin(\theta - \alpha)°$.

3   Using the same diagram, explain why
$a \cos \theta° + b \sin \theta° = r \cos(\theta - \alpha)°$.

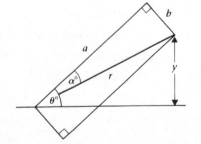

The expression you have just found is an alternative to the expression used in section B where you wrote $a \sin \theta° + b \cos \theta° = r \sin(\theta + \alpha)°$.

4   (a)   Express $7 \sin \theta° + 4 \cos \theta°$ in the form $r_1 \sin(\theta + \alpha_1)°$.

(b)   Express $4 \cos \theta° + 7 \sin \theta°$ in the form $r_2 \cos(\theta - \alpha_2)°$.

(c)   By plotting the two graphs show that these give the same result.

(d)   What is the relationship between α_1 and α_2?

$$a \sin \theta° + b \cos \theta° = r \sin(\theta + \alpha)°$$
$$a \sin \theta° - b \cos \theta° = r \sin(\theta - \alpha)°$$
$$a \cos \theta° + b \sin \theta° = r \cos(\theta - \alpha)°$$
$$a \cos \theta° - b \sin \theta° = r \cos(\theta + \alpha)°$$

where $r = \sqrt{a^2 + b^2}$ and $\alpha = \tan^{-1} \dfrac{b}{a}$

It is not necessary for α to be acute, although practically it is easier to work with if it is.

Exercise D (answers p. 134)

1 This graph may be regarded either as a sine graph or as a cosine graph, phase-shifted either to the right or to the left.

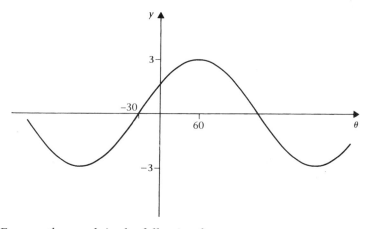

Express the graph in the following forms.
(a) $r \sin(\theta + \alpha)°$ (b) $r \cos(\theta - \alpha)°$
(c) $r \sin(\theta - \alpha)°$ (d) $r \cos(\theta + \alpha)°$

2 Express each of the following as a phase-shifted sine or cosine wave.
(a) $7 \cos \theta° + 24 \sin \theta°$ (b) $12 \sin \theta° + 5 \cos \theta°$
(c) $9 \sin \theta° - 40 \cos \theta°$ (d) $4 \sin \theta° + 2 \cos \theta°$

3 Solve these equations for $0 \leqslant \theta \leqslant 360$.
(a) $3 \sin \theta° - 4 \cos \theta° = 2$
(b) $9 \cos \theta° - 5 \sin \theta° = 4$
(c) $10 \cos \theta° + 7 \sin \theta° = 8$

E   Formulas for tan (answers p. 134)

This section develops and uses addition and double angle formulas for the tangent function.

1D   (a) By using addition formulas for $\sin(A + B)$ and $\cos(A + B)$, show that

$$\tan(A + B) = \frac{\tan A + \tan B}{1 - \tan A \tan B}$$

(b) Deduce formulas for $\tan(A - B)$ and $\tan 2A$.

Example 4

Find a formula for $\tan 3A$ in terms of $\tan A$.

Solution

Using the addition formula,

$$\tan 3A = \tan(A + 2A) = \frac{\tan A + \tan 2A}{1 - \tan A \tan 2A}$$

Now the double angle formula gives

$$\tan 3A = \frac{t + \dfrac{2t}{1 - t^2}}{1 - t\dfrac{2t}{1 - t^2}} \qquad \text{where } t = \tan A$$

$$= \frac{t(1 - t^2) + 2t}{1 - t^2 - t \times 2t}$$

$$= \frac{3t - t^3}{1 - 3t^2} = \frac{3 \tan A - \tan^3 A}{1 - 3 \tan^2 A}$$

$$\tan(A + B) = \frac{\tan A + \tan B}{1 - \tan A \tan B}$$

$$\tan(A - B) = \frac{\tan A - \tan B}{1 + \tan A \tan B}$$

$$\tan 2A = \frac{2 \tan A}{1 - \tan^2 A}$$

Exercise E (answers p. 134)

1 (a) If $\tan A = \frac{1}{2}$ and $\tan B = \frac{1}{3}$, find $\tan(A + B)$. Check by using a calculator to find A and B, assuming that they are acute angles.

  (b) Given $\tan C = 2$ and $\tan D = 3$, find $\tan(C + D)$. How could you have predicted your answer from (a)?

2 Let $A = \tan^{-1} \frac{1}{8}$, $B = \tan^{-1} \frac{1}{2}$, $C = \tan^{-1} \frac{1}{5}$. Without using a calculator, find $\tan(A + B)$ and $\tan(A + B + C)$. Deduce the value of $A + B + C$.

3 Given $A = \tan^{-1} \frac{1}{5}$, find $\tan 2A$ and $\tan 4A$. Deduce that $4A \approx 45°$.

4 (a) Show that, if the angle between the graph of $y = mx$ and the x-axis is A, then $\tan A = m$.

  (b) Show that the angle between the lines $y = 2x$ and $y = \frac{1}{3}x$ is 45°.

5 Given $\tan 2A = \frac{3}{4}$, find the two possible values of $\tan A$.

After working through this chapter you should

1 be able to sketch graphs of various trigonometric functions and solve simple trigonometric equations

2 be able to write an expression of the form $a \sin \theta \pm b \cos \theta$ in the form $r \sin(\theta \pm \alpha)$ or $r \cos(\theta \pm \alpha)$ and vice versa

3 be familiar with the addition formulas and double angle formulas for the sine and cosine functions (p. 30)

4 be familiar with the graph and inverse function of $\tan x$

5 be familiar with the addition formulas and the double angle formula for the tangent function (p. 30).

4 Differentiating trigonometric functions

A Radians

You have already seen evidence that, when x is measured in radians,

$$y = \sin x \implies \frac{dy}{dx} = \cos x \qquad \text{and} \qquad y = \cos x \implies \frac{dy}{dx} = -\sin x$$

These results are important in many unexpected contexts so we shall use the radian functions on all occasions when differentiation or integration may be involved.

The addition formulas and all the other concepts from the last chapter apply just as well with the radian functions. Exercise A below underlines this while also including some revision.

Remember that π radians $= 180°$.

For graphs and equations, the degree symbol is included when you are required to work 'in degree mode' – as in $y = \sin x°$ and $\cos x° = 0.8$. When there is no degree symbol, you should think 'in radian mode' unless told otherwise.

Look back at exercises C and E of the last chapter. Many of the questions apply equally to the radian functions and to the degree functions. Notice that no degree symbol was written in these cases.

Exercise A (answers p. 135)

1 Sketch the graphs of $y = \sin x$ and $y = \cos x$ for $-2\pi \leqslant x \leqslant 4\pi$.

2 Sketch the graphs of the following.
   (a) $\sin^{-1} x$ (b) $\cos^{-1} x$ (c) $\tan^{-1} x$
   State the domain and range of each of these inverse functions.

3 Copy and complete this table, giving exact values (including surds where appropriate).

x	0	$\frac{1}{6}\pi$	$\frac{1}{4}\pi$	$\frac{1}{3}\pi$	$\frac{1}{2}\pi$	$\frac{2}{3}\pi$	$\frac{3}{4}\pi$	$\frac{5}{6}\pi$	π	$\frac{5}{4}\pi$	$\frac{3}{2}\pi$	$\frac{7}{4}\pi$	2π
$\sin x$			$\frac{1}{2}\sqrt{3}$										
$\cos x$			$\frac{1}{2}$										

4 Simplify each of these, using the addition formulas or otherwise.
   (a) $\sin(x + \pi)$ (b) $\cos(\frac{1}{2}\pi - x)$
   (c) $\cos(\frac{1}{2}\pi + x)$ (d) $\sin(2\pi - x)$

5 (a) Write $10 \sin(x + 1.2)$ in the form $a \sin x + b \cos x$, giving a and b to 2 significant figures.
   (b) Write $8 \sin x + 5 \cos x$ in the form $r \sin(x + \alpha)$.

6 Confirm the addition formula $\cos(A - B) = \cos A \cos B + \sin A \sin B$ by substituting the following values and using a calculator (in radian mode).

    (a) $A = 2, B = 1.7$ (b) $A = 3.8, B = 0.9$

    (c) two values of your own choice

7 Solve the equation $3 \sin(x + 0.4) = 2.7$ for $0 \leqslant x \leqslant 4\pi$.

8 Sketch the graphs of (a) $y = 2 \sin x$, (b) $y = \sin 2x$, (c) $y = \sin(x - 2)$.

B Differentiation (answers p. 136)

In the diagram, AB is an arc of the circle of radius 1 with centre O.
Angle AOB = θ radians.

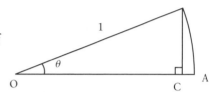

1D (a) Obtain expressions for the lengths of BC and the arc AB.

       Explain why $\dfrac{\sin \theta}{\theta} \approx 1$ for small positive θ. What does this tell you about the graph of $y = \sin x$?

    (b) Use a calculator to find $\sin 0.1$.

    (c) Use $\cos x = 1 - 2 \sin^2 \tfrac{1}{2}x$ to provide a quadratic approximation for $\cos x$ when x is small. What is the error in this approximation when $x = 0.3$?

    (d) Show that the gradient of $y = \sin x$ at $x = a$ is approximately $\dfrac{\sin(a + h) - \sin a}{h}$ if h is small. Show that this is approximately $\cos a - \tfrac{1}{2} h \sin a$.

    (e) Explain why $y = \sin x \Rightarrow \dfrac{dy}{dx} = \cos x$.

2 Use the derivative of $\sin x$ to show that

$$y = \cos x \Rightarrow \frac{dy}{dx} = -\sin x,$$

either by using graphs or by the method of question 1.

$$y = \sin x \Rightarrow \frac{dy}{dx} = \cos x$$

$$y = \cos x \Rightarrow \frac{dy}{dx} = -\sin x$$

We can use these results to find derivatives of functions such as $\sin 2x$, $5 \cos x$ and $10 \sin 0.1\pi x$. The graphs of such functions are related to those of $\sin x$ and $\cos x$ by means of stretches in the x- and y-directions. You have seen that a stretch of factor $\frac{1}{b}$ in the x-direction and a stretch of a in the y-direction maps $y = \sin x$ onto $y = a \sin bx$.

Exercise B (answers p. 136)

1. On the same axes sketch the graphs of $y = \sin x$ and $y = 5 \sin x$ for $0 \leqslant x \leqslant 2\pi$.

   (a) Describe the stretch which maps $y = \sin x$ onto $y = 5 \sin x$.

   (b) What is the effect of this stretch on the gradient of the graph of $y = \sin x$?

   (c) Suggest what the derivative of $y = 5 \sin x$ might be.

2. On the same axes, sketch the graphs of $y = \sin x$ and $y = \sin 3x$ for $0 \leqslant x \leqslant 2\pi$.

   (a) Describe the stretch which maps $y = \sin x$ onto $y = \sin 3x$.

   (b) What is the effect of this stretch on the gradient of the graph of $y = \sin x$?

   (c) Suggest what the derivative of $y = \sin 3x$ might be.

3. Investigate the derivative of $y = 5 \sin 3x$ in a similar way.

4. Using the ideas of the previous questions, find the derivatives of these.

   (a) $y = \cos 2x$ (b) $y = 10 \sin 2x$ (c) $y = \sin 0.5x$

5. (a) Sketch graphs of $y = 3 \cos 2x$, $y = 3 \cos 2x + 4$ and $y = 3 \cos 2x - 1$.

   (b) What is the derivative of each of these functions?

6. (a) What are the derivatives of these functions?

      (i) $y = a \sin x$ (ii) $y = \sin bx$ (iii) $y = a \sin bx$

   (b) Write down the corresponding result for cosine functions for part (a) (iii).

7. Find $\dfrac{dy}{dx}$ for each of these.

   (a) $y = \frac{1}{2} \sin x$ (b) $y = 5 \cos x$ (c) $y = 0.1 \sin x + 0.5$

   (d) $y = \sin 4x$ (e) $y = \cos 2\pi x$ (f) $y = \sin 0.2x$

   (g) $y = 3 \cos 2x$ (h) $y = 6 \sin \frac{1}{2}\pi x$ (i) $y = 4 + 3 \sin \frac{1}{3}x$

8. Copy and complete this table.

y	$\sin x$	$4 \sin 5x$		$\cos x$	$10 \cos \frac{1}{2}x$
$\dfrac{dy}{dx}$	$\cos x$		$6 \cos 3x$	$-\sin x$	$3 \sin \frac{1}{3}x$

9 Write down the indefinite integral of each of these.

   (a) $8 \cos x$ (b) $3 \sin 7x$ (c) $4 \cos 0.1x + 3 \sin 0.1x$

10 Find the shaded areas in the following graphs.

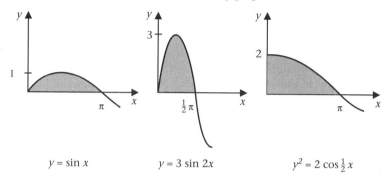

$y = \sin x$ $y = 3 \sin 2x$ $y^2 = 2 \cos \frac{1}{2} x$

$$y = a \sin bx \implies \frac{dy}{dx} = ab \cos bx$$

$$y = a \cos bx \implies \frac{dy}{dx} = -ab \sin bx$$

$$\int a \sin bx \, dx = -\frac{a}{b} \cos bx + k$$

$$\int a \cos bx \, dx = \frac{a}{b} \sin bx + k$$

C Applications (answers p. 137)

You can formulate many problems in terms of radians so that it is easier to answer questions about rates of change. For example, suppose the height of the tide in a harbour at time t is as shown.

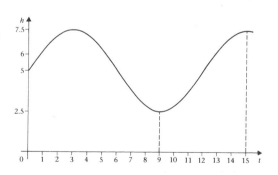

1D (a) What is the period of the function which describes the height of the tide?

   (b) If the height of the tide is h metres at time t hours, then explain why

$$h = 2.5 \sin \tfrac{1}{6} \pi t + 5$$

Differentiating to find the rate at which the tide is changing at any time,

$$\frac{dh}{dt} = \tfrac{5}{12}\pi \cos \tfrac{1}{6}\pi t$$

2   Why $\tfrac{5}{12}\pi$?

When $t = 0$, $\dfrac{dh}{dt} = \tfrac{5}{12}\pi = 1.3$ (to 2 s.f.)

The tide is rising most rapidly when $t = 0$ (and also when $t = 12$, 24, ...), and the rate of rise is 1.3 metres per hour. You can use the formula for $\dfrac{dh}{dt}$ to find the rate of change at any time.

3   (a) When $t = 4$, what is the value of $\dfrac{dh}{dt}$ to 2 significant figures?

   (b) State what this means.

   (c) At what other times will $\dfrac{dh}{dt}$ have this value?

Example 1

A pendulum is pulled to one side and then released from rest, after which its displacement x cm from the central position after t seconds is given by $x = 1.5 \cos \pi t$. Write down the period and amplitude of the motion, and calculate the first two times when $x = 1$, and its velocity at these times.

Solution

By inspection of the function, period $= \dfrac{2\pi}{\pi} = 2$ seconds and amplitude $= 1.5$ cm.

$$x = 1 \text{ when } \cos \pi t = \frac{1}{1.5} = 0.666 \ldots,$$

$$\pi t = 0.8410, \quad 2\pi - 0.8410 \ldots$$

So $t = 0.268$ and $t = 1.732$ are the first two times, to 3 decimal places.

The velocity $v = \dfrac{dx}{dt} = -1.5\pi \sin \pi t$.

Substituting,

when $t = 0.268 \ldots,$ $v = -3.52$ cm s^{-1}

when $t = 1.732 \ldots,$ $v = 3.52$ cm s^{-1}

The negative sign in the first velocity indicates that the pendulum is then moving in the opposite direction to that in which x is increasing.

Exercise C (answers p. 137)

1   A mass oscillates up and down at the end of a spring. The length of the
    spring in centimetres after time t seconds is given by the equation

$$L = 12 + 2.5 \cos 2\pi t$$

(a) Find the derivative, $\dfrac{dL}{dt}$. Sketch the graphs of L and $\dfrac{dL}{dt}$ against t.

(b) Calculate the following when $t = 0, 0.1, 0.25, 0.4$ and 0.5.

    (i)   the length of the spring   (ii)   the velocity of the mass

Comment on the results.

2   The height in metres of the tide at a harbour entrance is given by

$$h = 0.8 \cos \tfrac{1}{6}\pi t + 6.5$$

where t is the time in hours measured from high tide.

(a) Find the derivative, $\dfrac{dh}{dt}$. Sketch graphs of h and $\dfrac{dh}{dt}$ against t for a
     24-hour interval.

(b) Calculate the two times during the first 12 hours when the height
     of the tide is 6 metres. Find the rate of change of height at both
     these times and comment on the results.

(c) When is the tide falling most rapidly during the first 12 hours?
     Find the rate at which it is then falling.

(d) When is the speed of the tidal current least and when is it greatest?
     What factors are important in deciding when it is safe to enter or
     leave the harbour?

3   The height in metres above ground level of a chair on a big wheel is
    given by

$$h = 5.6 - 4.8 \cos \tfrac{1}{30}\pi t$$

where t is the time measured in seconds.

(a) Find the derivative, $\dfrac{dh}{dt}$, and sketch graphs of h and $\dfrac{dh}{dt}$ against t

for a two-minute interval.

(b) Between what times is the chair descending at a rate greater than
     0.4 metre per second? When is the chair descending most rapidly
     and at what speed?

4   (a) The heights of the tide at Sheerness on a certain September day
         were 4.6 m at high water and 1.7 m at low water.

    (i)   Assuming a period of 12 hours and measuring the time in
       hours from high tide, sketch a graph of the height from
       6 hours before to 6 hours after high water.

    (ii)   Suggest a suitable formula for h, the height in metres, in
       terms of t, the time in hours.

(b) The currents in the Thames estuary near to Sheerness are given in the following table.

Hours before high water	5	4	3	2	1
Current in knots	0.7	1.0	1.1	1.0	0.7

(i) Assuming that the currents after high water are the same, but in the opposite direction, sketch the graph of current against time from 6 hours before to 6 hours after high water.

(ii) Suggest a suitable formula for the current in knots in terms of the time in hours.

(iii) How is this related to the height equation found in part (a)?

(c) (i) Find the rate of change of h and sketch a graph of $\dfrac{dh}{dt}$ against t for the same values as those in the previous graphs.

(ii) Comment on the relationship between this and the graph of the current.

D More trigonometric functions (answers p. 138)

There are three other trigonometric functions that are sometimes useful. They are secant (usually abbreviated to sec), cosecant (cosec) and cotangent (cot). They are defined by

$$\sec \theta = \frac{1}{\cos \theta}, \qquad \operatorname{cosec} \theta = \frac{1}{\sin \theta}, \qquad \cot \theta = \frac{1}{\tan \theta}$$

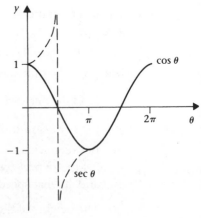

1 The diagram shows the graph of $\cos \theta$ for

$0 \leqslant \theta \leqslant 2\pi$ and part of the graph of $\sec \theta = \dfrac{1}{\cos \theta}$.

Copy the diagram and complete the graph of $\sec \theta$.

2 (a) Sketch on one diagram the graphs of $\sin \theta$ and $\operatorname{cosec} \theta$.

(b) Sketch on one diagram the graphs of $\tan \theta$ and $\cot \theta$.

3 You know that, for any value of θ,

$$\sin^2 \theta + \cos^2 \theta = 1 \quad (1)$$

(a) By dividing each term of equation (1) by $\cos^2 \theta$, show that
$$\tan^2 \theta + 1 = \sec^2 \theta$$

(b) By dividing each term of equation (1) by $\sin^2 \theta$, show that
$$1 + \cot^2 \theta = \operatorname{cosec}^2 \theta$$

$$\sec \theta = \frac{1}{\cos \theta}, \qquad \operatorname{cosec} \theta = \frac{1}{\sin \theta}, \qquad \cot \theta = \frac{1}{\tan \theta}$$

For any value of θ,

$$\cos^2 \theta + \sin^2 \theta = 1$$
$$1 + \tan^2 \theta = \sec^2 \theta$$
$$\cot^2 \theta + 1 = \operatorname{cosec}^2 \theta$$

You have already seen how to use identities such as $\cos^2 \theta + \sin^2 \theta = 1$ to simplify equations. You can use the two new identities in the same way.

Example 2

Solve the equation

$$\tan^2 \theta + 2 \sec \theta = 2 \qquad \text{for } 0 \leqslant \theta \leqslant 2\pi$$

Solution

$$\sec^2 \theta - 1 + 2 \sec \theta = 2 \qquad (\text{using } \tan^2 \theta = \sec^2 \theta - 1)$$
$$\Rightarrow \qquad \sec^2 \theta + 2 \sec \theta - 3 = 0$$

Using $x = \sec \theta$, this becomes the quadratic equation

$$x^2 + 2x - 3 = 0$$
$$\Rightarrow \qquad (x + 3)(x - 1) = 0$$
$$\Rightarrow \qquad x = -3 \quad \text{or} \quad x = 1$$

So
$$\sec \theta = -3 \text{ or } \sec \theta = 1$$
$$\Rightarrow \qquad \cos \theta = -\tfrac{1}{3} \text{ or } 1$$
$$\Rightarrow \qquad \theta = 1.91, 4.37, 0, 6.28$$

Exercise D (answers p. 139)

1 (a) By replacing $\sec^2 \theta$ by $1 + \tan^2 \theta$ show that the equation
$$\sec^2 \theta + \tan \theta = 3$$
is equivalent to the equation
$$\tan^2 \theta + \tan \theta - 2 = 0$$

(b) Factorise the left-hand side of this equation.

(c) Solve the equation to find all values of θ between $-\pi$ and π.

2 Solve $2 \cot^2 \theta + \operatorname{cosec} \theta + 1 = 0$ for $-\pi \leqslant \theta \leqslant \pi$.

3 Solve the following equations for $0 \leqslant \theta \leqslant 2\pi$.

(a) $2 \sec^2 \theta = 9 \tan \theta + 7$ (b) $\operatorname{cosec}^2 \theta = 3 \cot \theta + 5$

4　Prove the following identities:

(a) $\tan\theta + \cot\theta = \sec\theta\,\mathrm{cosec}\,\theta$

(b) $\sec^2 x + \mathrm{cosec}^2\,x = \dfrac{4}{\sin^2 2x}$

5　Simplify the following.

(a) $\dfrac{\sin x}{1 + \cot^2 x}$

(b) $\cos\theta\sqrt{1 + \tan^2\theta}$

6　(a) Show that $\cot\theta = \dfrac{\cos\theta}{\sin\theta}$ and that $\cot\theta\sec\theta = \mathrm{cosec}\,\theta$.

(b) Given $\tan\theta = 3$, find $\cot\theta$, $\sec\theta$ and $\mathrm{cosec}\,\theta$.

7　Show that $\tan(x + \frac{1}{4}\pi) = \dfrac{1 + \tan x}{1 - \tan x}$ and $\cot(x + \frac{1}{4}\pi) = \dfrac{\cot x - 1}{\cot x + 1}$.

After working through this chapter you should

1　be able to apply all the standard trigonometric formulas and techniques to the radian mode sine and cosine functions.

2　know that

$$\dfrac{-\pi}{2} \leqslant \sin^{-1} x \leqslant \dfrac{\pi}{2}, \quad 0 \leqslant \cos^{-1} x \leqslant \pi, \quad \dfrac{-\pi}{2} < \tan^{-1} x < \dfrac{\pi}{2}$$

3　be able to differentiate circular functions, knowing that

$$\dfrac{\mathrm{d}}{\mathrm{d}x}(a\sin bx) = ab\cos bx \quad \text{and} \quad \dfrac{\mathrm{d}}{\mathrm{d}x}(a\cos bx) = -ab\sin bx$$

and be able to use these results in models of periodic motion

4　know the definitions

$$\mathrm{cosec}\,\theta = \dfrac{1}{\sin\theta}, \qquad \sec\theta = \dfrac{1}{\cos\theta}, \qquad \cot\theta = \dfrac{1}{\tan\theta}$$

and be able to sketch their graphs.

5　know and be able to use the identities

$$1 + \tan^2\theta = \sec^2\theta \qquad \text{and} \qquad 1 + \cot^2\theta = \mathrm{cosec}^2\,\theta$$

5 Proof

A Introduction

Proof has been described as the very essence of mathematics. It gives permanence to a result or theorem. It is proof that distinguishes mathematics from most other fields of human endeavour. It is an area of mathematics where great creativity, elegance and beauty can be displayed. Some of the great proofs, for example those devised by the Greek mathematicians, are still regarded as classics. Euclid's proof of the theorem of Pythagoras, and his proof that there are infinitely many prime numbers, are of great beauty, demonstrate conciseness, creativity and elegance, and have not been improved upon. There is no doubt about the theorems they prove – they are permanent, fixed for all time.

A major reason for studying mathematics is to understand something of proof. Proof provides a framework within which you are able to present an argument logically, with clarity and precision, whether within mathematics or more generally.

Proof is often complicated. Disproof, however, is often a very short and simple matter, as the following example shows.

Suppose that a friend, having tried many particular pentagons, is convinced that no pentagon will tessellate. To refute this generalisation, all you have to do is produce a single **counter-example**, i.e. find a pentagon that will tessellate.

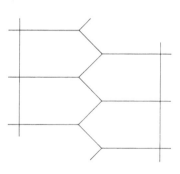

An excellent book, which explores many of the great theorems of mathematics, is *Journey Through Genius* by William Dunham (John Wiley, 1990; ISBN 0 471 50030 5).

Exercise A (answers p. 140)

1 Disprove, by finding a suitable counter-example, the statement
$$x^2 > y^2 \implies x > y$$

2 If two lines are perpendicular to a third line then they must be parallel to each other – true or false?

3 $1 = 0^2 + 1^2, 5 = 1^2 + 2^2, 9 = 0^2 + 3^2, ..., 97 = 4^2 + 9^2$

All numbers of the form $(4n + 1)$ may be expressed as a sum of two squares – true or false?

4 Find the first four terms, t_1, t_2, t_3 and t_4 for the sequence defined by
$$t_n = (n-1)(n-2)(n-3)(n-4) + n$$
What might you expect t_5 to be? Is it?

B Making a proof (answers p. 139)

In the previous section, you considered several conjectures which could be *disproved* by finding counter-examples.

1D When you have a conjecture of your own, how can you be sure that no-one will be able to find a counter-example?

Simply spotting a pattern is not the end of a mathematical investigation. You then need *either* to look for a convincing reason for the pattern *or* to find a counter-example.

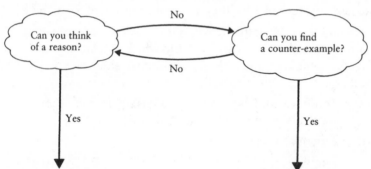

Write out the reason so as to convince someone else. The written reasoning is called a **proof**.

Further investigation is needed so that you can make another conjecture.

The real challenge of a mathematical investigation is to break out of the potentially endless 'no–no' cycle of not being able to find *either* a convincing reason *or* a counter-example!

Amassing particular cases, no matter how many, does not establish a general result. To complete your investigation you must normally find convincing reasons for any patterns or results you have discovered.

Example 1

Prove that
$(1 + 2 + 3 + \ldots + n)^2 = 1^3 + 2^3 + 3^3 + \ldots + n^3$.

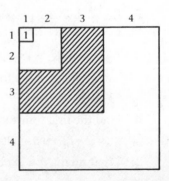

Solution

Building up the left side of the equation above by adding 'shells' provides a geometrical approach.

2 Verify that the L-shaped shells have areas 8, 27 and 64 square units respectively.

The diagram demonstrates that
$$(1 + 2 + 3 + 4)^2 = 1^3 + 2^3 + 3^3 + 4^3$$
You need to show that, in general, the kth shell has area k^3. For this, use the result
$$1 + 2 + 3 + \dots + (k-1) = \tfrac{1}{2}k(k-1)$$

For instance, as you can see in the top diagram, the fourth shell has an 'inside arm' measurement of
$1 + 2 + 3 = \tfrac{1}{2} \times 4 \times 3$.

The kth shell looks like this when divided into three parts.

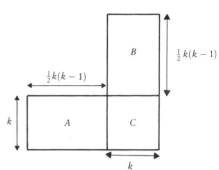

3   Find areas A, B and C and show that $A + B + C = k^3$.

The area of a square of side $(1 + 2 + \dots + n)$ is the sum of the areas of n shells. So

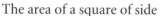

$$(1 + 2 + \dots + n)^2 = 1^3 + 2^3 + \dots + n^3$$

and the proof is complete.

$k^2(k-1) + k^2$

$= k^3 - k^2 + k^2$

$= k^3$

The next example illustrates a very powerful and useful method of proof known as **proof by contradiction**. It has been used by mathematicians for centuries and is at the heart of many classic and beautiful proofs.

Example 2

Prove that the product of two positive integers whose sum is 1001 cannot be divided by 1001.

Solution

Let the two numbers be n and m.
You want to prove that nm is *not* divisible by 1001.
The essence of this proof is to suppose nm *is* divisible by 1001 and to show that this leads to a **contradiction**.
Suppose nm is divisible by 1001, i.e. $nm = 1001k$ (k being a positive integer)

$nm = 1001k$

$\qquad = 7 \times 11 \times 13k$

$\Rightarrow \quad n$ (or m or both) has a factor of 7.

But $n + m = 1001$ (given)

$n + m = 7 \times 11 \times 13$

$\Rightarrow \qquad n + m$ has a factor of 7.

4   Explain why this means that *both* n and m have a factor of 7.
An identical argument applies to 11 and 13.
So n and m have factors of 7, 11 and 13.

5 Explain why this means that both m and n are greater than or equal to 1001.

Since $n \geqslant 1001$ and $m \geqslant 1001$ we have $n + m \geqslant 2002$.
So, *if nm is* divisible by 1001, then $n + m$ must be *greater* than 1001.
But $n + m = 1001$ (given) and so the product nm *cannot* be divisible by 1001 if $n + m = 1001$.

Exercise B (answers p. 140)

1 (a) Explain why $2n$ is always even for all integer values of n.

(b) Write down a number, in terms of n, which you know is odd. Explain *how* you know.

(c) 'The sum of three consecutive odd numbers is always divisible by 3.' Check this conjecture by considering a number of cases. Prove that the statement is true.

2 Take any two-digit number, reverse its digits and add to the original number. The result will always be divisible by 11.

For example:

$$\begin{array}{r} 34 \\ +43 \\ \hline 77 \end{array} = 11 \times 7$$

A convincing explanation might start by letting the two digits be a and b, so that the original number is $10a + b$.

(a) Write down the value of the 'reversed' number.

(b) Find the sum of the numbers and show that the sum *is* always divisible by 11..

(c) Discover if the rule applies to three- or four-digit numbers. Explain your findings.

3 A neat party trick is the rule for multiplication by 11, illustrated on the right for $11 \times 321 = 3531$.

For 11×1325 you can therefore proceed by

$$11 \times 1 \quad 3 \quad 2 \quad 5 = 14\,575$$

(a) Check that this method always seems to work.

(b) Using the method of expressing a two-digit number used in question 2 (i.e. 'ab' $= 10a + b$), explain how this method for multiplying by 11 works.

(c) Explain carefully how the method works for 11×392.

4   What is wrong with the following demonstration that the area of an
8×8 square is the same as the area of a 5×13 rectangle?

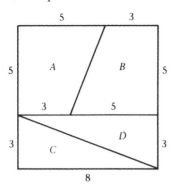

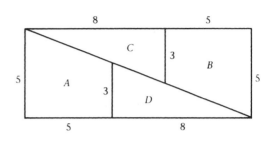

5   (a)   Prove that the sum of two consecutive odd numbers is divisible
by 4.

(b)   Prove that the sum of n consecutive odd numbers is divisible by n
if n is odd, and by $2n$ if n is even.

6E   Using the method of 'proof by contradiction', show that $\sqrt{2}$ is an
irrational number (i.e. it cannot be written as $\dfrac{a}{b}$, where a and b are
whole numbers).

C   Fermat and proof

In question 3 of exercise A you may have discovered that 21 cannot be
expressed as the sum of two squares. The seventeenth-century amateur
mathematician Pierre de Fermat (1601–1665) studied a refinement of
the conjecture that you looked at in exercise A.

All primes of the form $(4n + 1)$ can be expressed as the sum of
two squares.

Of his attempts to prove this conjecture, Fermat wrote (*Diophantus*,
page 268):

'when I had to prove that every prime number of the form
$(4n + 1)$ is made up of two squares, I found myself in a pretty fix.'

Fermat was in the 'no–no' cycle. However,

'But at last a certain reflection many times repeated gave me the
necessary light, and affirmative questions yielded to my method,
with the aid of some new principles by which sheer necessity
compelled me to supplement it.'

Another famous problem is known as 'Fermat's last theorem'. The
problem is to prove that there are no positive integers x, y, z such that,
for some integer m greater than 2,

$$x^m + y^m = z^m$$

There are certainly positive integers satisfying $x^2 + y^2 = z^2$.

$$x = 3, y = 4, z = 5 \qquad \text{and} \qquad x = 5, y = 12, z = 13$$

are well-known cases. Fermat's theorem is that $x^3 + y^3 = z^3$, $x^4 + y^4 = z^4$, and so on, *cannot* be solved for positive integers x, y and z.

Of this problem, Fermat wrote (*Diophantus*, page 145):

> 'I have discovered a truly marvellous proof of this, which however the margin is not large enough to contain.'

Although it was demonstrated for many values of *m*, the full result remained unproved from Fermat's time and was regarded as one of the great unsolved problems of mathematics until, in 1993, it was announced that a complete (and very long) proof had been made by Professor Andrew Wiles of Princeton University, USA. The story does not end even here, however; a tiny but crucial gap in the proof, unnoticed until after the announcement, took a further year's work to repair and the proof is now accepted as correct.

However, other attempts on this problem have stimulated many important advances in number theory. When you are in the 'no–no' cycle, the ideas you think of and try may be far more important than any eventual solution to the problem!

You may feel that proof is not really a part of problem-solving as such. After all, you may argue, the problem has really been solved when you reach the point of 'knowing', and proving is then no more than icing on the cake. The trouble is that you often do not 'know' until a proof has been found.

The following problem illustrates this point.

How many regions are formed when *n* points on the circumference of a circle are joined?

It can be tackled step by step as follows:

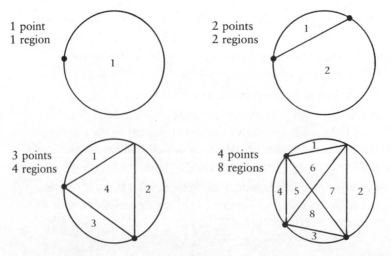

1 point
1 region

2 points
2 regions

3 points
4 regions

4 points
8 regions

Exercise C (answers p. 141)

1   Tabulate the information from the foot of p. 50, guess a pattern and write a general formula based on your conjecture.

2   Check your formula in the cases $n = 5$ and $n = 6$.

   You must draw the diagram for $n = 6$ *very* carefully if you are not to miscount the number of regions. To obtain the greatest number of regions for $n = 6$, you must not draw, for example, a regular hexagon.

3   At this stage, after a recount, your investigation will need to take a fresh direction. Extend your table up to 7 points.

4   Make a table of differences.

5   Make a revised conjecture.

6   Find the first 7 terms of the sequence given by

$$u_n = \frac{1}{24} n(n-1)(n-2)(n-3) + \frac{1}{2} n(n-1) + 1$$

   What does this prove?

D   **Prime number formulas** (answers p. 141)

   Here is another extended example.

   Many quadratic formulas generate long strings of prime numbers. The formula $n^2 - n + 41$ is a much-quoted example.

   First conjecture $n^2 - n + 41$ is always prime.

1   Test the conjecture for values of n up to 10.

   The conjecture is true for all values of n up to and including 40. However, when $n = 41$, $n^2 - n + 41 = 41^2$; when $n = 42$, $n^2 - n + 41 = 41 \times 43$.

2   Find another value of n for which $n^2 - n + 41$ is divisible by 41.

   Second conjecture No quadratic expression in n is prime for all integral values of n.

3   Write down various quadratic expressions in n, for example
   $$n^2 + 7n + 5, \quad n^2 - 1, \quad 3n^2 + 2$$
   Can you always find a value of n for which the expression is not prime?

   It is likely that the more quadratic expressions you try, the more you will become convinced of the truth of the second conjecture. But, as you know, it is not sufficient simply to try lots of examples – you may miss the one example which turns out to be a counter-example!

   This is the exciting phase of the solution of a mathematical problem where all sorts of ideas must be tried out as you search for either a convincing proof or a counter-example. Two attempts at proof are given below.

First attempted proof

The general quadratic is of the form $an^2 + bn + c$.

Putting $n = c$ gives $ac^2 + bc + c = c(ac + b + 1)$, which is not prime because it is divisible by both $ac + b + 1$ and c. Therefore no quadratic expression in n can be prime for all integral values of n.

4   Check over the 'proof' above carefully. Which particular cases spoil the 'proof'?

Second attempted proof ('by contradiction')

Suppose $an^2 + bn + c$ to be prime for all integers n. In particular, for $n = 1$, $a + b + c$ must be a prime. Let $a + b + c = p$.

For $n = 1 + p$,

$$an^2 + bn + c = a(p + 1)^2 + b(p + 1) + c$$
$$= ap^2 + 2ap + bp + a + b + c$$
$$= ap^2 + 2ap + bp + p$$

$an^2 + bn + c$ is therefore $(ap + 2a + b + 1)p$.

5   Find a similar expression for $an^2 + bn + c$ when $n = 1 + 2p$.

$an^2 + bn + c$ is divisible by p when $n = 1$, $n = 1 + p$ and $n = 1 + 2p$. If it is prime for each of these values then $an^2 + bn + c$ must equal p itself and we would have three points on a quadratic graph as shown.

This is not possible for a quadratic.

So $an^2 + bn + c$ is *not* prime for at least one of these three values.

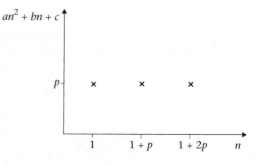

There may be some points on which you are still not convinced. If so, first try to fill in the necessary details yourself and then discuss the unclear points with fellow students and your teacher. Do not be convinced too easily!

E Differentiation from first principles (answers p. 142)

In the development of mathematics, advances are often made through conjecture based on limited evidence, with proof (or disproof) following much later. Calculus has been introduced in this way and we are now ready to put it on a sounder footing.

So far it has been based upon the idea of local straightness. When you zoom in at a point on a locally straight curve, the curve appears to be a straight line and this enables you to find the gradient.

However, zooming in does not always make a curve appear straight. From a spaceship, the Earth appears to have a smooth, spherical surface, but from a closer vantage point, enormous imperfections in the surface are apparent.

1 Use a graph plotter to plot the graph of $y = x + \dfrac{1}{1000}\sin(1000x)$.

Investigate what happens as you zoom in on any point of the graph.

To be able to differentiate a function you require the graph of the function to be locally straight, but so far you have no way of knowing whether a graph *really is* locally straight.

For example, in the question above, the appearance of the graph changed dramatically as you zoomed in at a chosen point. So you cannot be totally sure whether or not the appearance would change again if you zoomed in further.

A central aspect of mathematics concerns giving rigorous arguments to prove results indisputably. It seems that you would have to zoom in forever in order to confirm that graphs of relations such as $y = \sin x$ or $y = x^2$ really *are* locally straight. We now consider the mathematical technique for doing this.

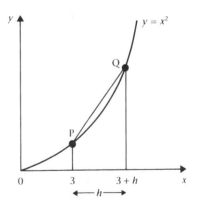

To be able to find the numerical gradient of $y = x^2$ at the point $(3, 9)$ you have previously considered the gradients of lines joining $(3, 9)$ to nearby points on the graph.

2D P is the point $(3, 3^2)$ and Q has x-coordinate $3 + h$.

(a) What is the y-coordinate of Q?

(b) What is the difference between the y-coordinates of Q and P?

(c) Find the gradient of PQ. (Simplify the expression as far as possible.)

(d) As h becomes smaller and smaller, what happens to the value of the gradient?

(e) What is the advantage of using the letter h rather than a small numerical value?

Making the value of h smaller and smaller is termed 'letting h tend to zero' and the notation for this is

$$h \longrightarrow 0$$

Finding the value of $6 + h$ as h tends to zero is termed 'finding the limit of $6 + h$ as h tends to zero' and the notation for this is

$$\lim_{h \to 0} (6 + h)$$

The limit of $6 + h$ as h tends to zero is

$$\lim_{h \to 0} (6 + h) = 6$$

This idea is explored in the questions which follow.

3 Evaluate these.   (a) $\lim_{h \to 0} (5h - 2)$ (b) $\lim_{h \to 0} (3 + 2h)$

Limits can be obtained for h tending to values other than 0.

The limit of $\dfrac{h(h - 2)}{h - 2}$ as h tends to 2 is written as $\lim_{h \to 2} \dfrac{h(h - 2)}{h - 2}$.

This limit *cannot* be evaluated simply by putting h equal to 2, because $\frac{0}{0}$ is undefined. However, for $h \neq 2$, the factor $h - 2$ can be cancelled.

$$\lim_{h \to 2} \frac{h(h - 2)}{h - 2} = \lim_{h \to 2} h = 2$$

4 Use this method to evaluate these.

(a) $\lim_{h \to 0} \dfrac{h(h + 2)}{h}$ (b) $\lim_{h \to 0} \dfrac{5h^2 - 2h}{h}$ (c) $\lim_{h \to 0} \dfrac{4h^2 - h^3}{h}$

(d) $\lim_{h \to 2} \dfrac{(h - 2)(h + 2)}{h - 2}$ (e) $\lim_{h \to -3} \dfrac{2h^2 - 18}{h + 3}$

5 Use a calculator or computer to investigate numerically these limits.

(a) $\lim_{h \to 0} \dfrac{\sin h}{h}$ (b) $\lim_{h \to 0} \dfrac{\cos h - 1}{h}$ (c) $\lim_{h \to 0} \dfrac{e^h - 1}{h}$

You have found a number of limits of the type

$$\lim_{h \to 0} 2(h + 3) = 6$$

A limit of the form

$$\lim_{h \to 0} \frac{3 + h}{2 + h} = \frac{3}{2}$$

can be found simply by substituting zero for h in both numerator and denominator. However, this method cannot be applied if the denominator is zero when h is zero.

Example 3

Find $\lim\limits_{h \to 0} \dfrac{4h - h^3}{9h + h^2}$.

Solution

For $\quad h \neq 0, \dfrac{4h - h^3}{9h + h^2} = \dfrac{(4 - h^2)h}{(9 + h)h} = \dfrac{4 - h^2}{9 + h}$

$$\Rightarrow \lim\limits_{h \to 0} \dfrac{4h - h^3}{9h + h^2} = \dfrac{4}{9}$$

The notation developed for limits can be used to give a general definition for the gradient of the graph of a function.

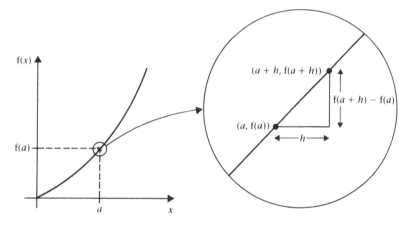

The gradient of the graph of the function f at the point $(a, f(a))$ is given by

$$f'(a) = \lim\limits_{h \to 0} \dfrac{f(a + h) - f(a)}{h}$$

(If the limit does not exist, then the function is *not* locally straight and does not have a gradient at $x = a$.)

The theory of limits is complicated and there is no room to take it further in this text. The results of question 5 in this section, for example, are plausible but have not been proved.

Finding a gradient by means of the limit is called **differentiating from first principles**.

Example 4

Differentiate $y = 3x^2 - 4x$ at $(3, 15)$ from first principles.

Solution

$$
\begin{aligned}
f(3 + h) &= 3(3 + h)^2 - 4(3 + h) \\
&= 3(9 + 6h + h^2) - 12 - 4h \\
&= 15 + 14h + 3h^2
\end{aligned}
$$

The gradient is $\displaystyle\lim_{h \to 0} \frac{\cancel{15} + 14h + 3h^2 - \cancel{15}}{h} = \lim_{h \to 0}(14 + 3h) = 14$

For any function f, a general formula for $f'(x)$ can be found from first principles using the definition

$$
f'(x) = \lim_{h \to 0} \frac{f(x + h) - f(x)}{h}
$$

Example 5

If $y = x^2$, find $\dfrac{dy}{dx}$ from first principles.

Solution

$$
\begin{aligned}
\frac{dy}{dx} &= \lim_{h \to 0} \frac{(x + h)^2 - x^2}{h} \\
&= \lim_{h \to 0} \frac{\cancel{x^2} + 2xh + h^2 - \cancel{x^2}}{h} = \lim_{h \to 0}(2x + h) = 2x
\end{aligned}
$$

Example 6

If $y = \dfrac{1}{x}$, find $\dfrac{dy}{dx}$ from first principles.

Solution

$$
\begin{aligned}
\frac{dy}{dx} &= \lim_{h \to 0} \frac{\dfrac{1}{x + h} - \dfrac{1}{x}}{h} \\
&= \lim_{h \to 0} \frac{x - (x + h)}{hx(x + h)} \\
&= \lim_{h \to 0} \frac{-h}{hx(x + h)} = \lim_{h \to 0} \frac{-1}{x(x + h)} = -\frac{1}{x^2}
\end{aligned}
$$

$$
y = \frac{1}{x} \implies \frac{dy}{dx} = -\frac{1}{x^2}
$$

The method of differentiating from first principles is important, since it is the way in which mathematicians have proved the derivatives of basic functions. It can also be used to prove the correctness of the various rules of differentiation.

Exercise E (answers p. 142)

1   Suppose $y = 3x^2$.

(a) Find the gradient at $(1, 3)$ from first principles.

(b) Find a general formula for $\dfrac{dy}{dx}$ from first principles.

2   Differentiate $5x^2 + 3x$ with respect to x, from first principles.

3   Differentiate $4x^2 - 2x + 7$ with respect to x, from first principles.

4   Differentiate x^3 from first principles.

5E   Show, from first principles, that if $y = \dfrac{1}{2t+5}$ then $\dfrac{dy}{dt} = \dfrac{-2}{(2t+5)^2}$.

6   What are the first two terms of the expansions of the following?

(a) $(x+h)^5$ (b) $(x+h)^9$ (c) $(x+h)^n$, where n is a positive integer

Deduce that $\dfrac{d}{dx}(x^n) = nx^{n-1}$.

7E   Use first principles to find the derivative with respect to x of $\sin x$. (You can assume the limits obtained numerically earlier in this chapter.)

After working through this chapter you should

1   be aware that a general result cannot be established simply by considering a large number of particular cases

2   appreciate that mathematical advances sometimes occur when mathematicians have been unable to find either a proof or a counter-example

3   be more difficult to convince

4   be better at convincing others by improving the standards of rigour in your arguments

5   appreciate that you need the algebraic limit process to determine whether the graph of a function really is locally straight

6   understand the notation $\lim\limits_{h \to 0} f(h)$

7   be able to evaluate simple limits

8   know how to obtain derivatives from first principles using the expression $\lim\limits_{h \to 0} \dfrac{f(x+h) - f(x)}{h}$.

6 The chain rule

A Functions of functions (answers p. 143)

You already know how to differentiate polynomial functions such as $x^3 + 2x^2 - 3$ and other simple functions such as $\sin x$ and e^x. Here we extend these methods to more complicated functions. We consider **composite functions**, which you can think of as functions of other functions. Previously you have used function notation to represent such relationships.

Example 1

If $f(x) = 3x + 7$ and $g(x) = x^3$, find $fg(x)$ and $gf(x)$.

Solution

$$fg(x) = f(x^3)$$
$$= 3x^3 + 7$$
$$gf(x) = g(3x + 7)$$
$$= (3x + 7)^3$$

We now examine the rates of change of composite functions. Initially, only linear relationships will be considered.

1D

(a) A rod with initial temperature 50 °C is being heated so that its temperature increases by 2 °C per minute. What is C, the temperature in degrees celsius, after t minutes?

(b) To convert from degrees celsius to degrees fahrenheit, multiply by 1.8 and add on 32. Express F, the temperature in degrees fahrenheit after t minutes, in terms of C and then in terms of t.

(c) What are $\dfrac{dF}{dt}$, $\dfrac{dF}{dC}$ and $\dfrac{dC}{dt}$? Can you find a connection between these rates of change? Think of other examples which involve two linear functions and see if there is a similar relationship.

If z is a function of y and y is a function of x, then the following relationship is easy to prove for linear functions such as $z = my + c$ and $y = nx + d$.

$$\frac{dz}{dx} = \frac{dz}{dy} \times \frac{dy}{dx}$$

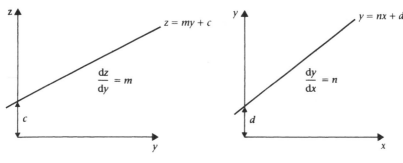

Then $\qquad z = m(nx + d) + c$

$\qquad \Rightarrow \qquad z = mnx + md + c$

$\qquad \Rightarrow \qquad \dfrac{dz}{dx} = mn$

and so $\qquad \dfrac{dz}{dx} = \dfrac{dz}{dy} \times \dfrac{dy}{dx}$

This relationship is called the **chain rule**.

If z is a linear function of y and y is a linear function of x, then to find $\dfrac{dz}{dx}$ it is not in fact necessary to first express z in terms of x. This would be an especially useful result if the chain rule were true for non-linear functions as well.

2   You have seen that the chain rule holds for linear functions. Why might you expect it to hold more generally?

For example, $y = \sin x^3$ is a composite of the locally straight functions $y = \sin u$ and $u = x^3$.

If the chain rule does work for non-linear functions then

$\qquad \dfrac{dy}{dx} = \dfrac{dy}{du} \times \dfrac{du}{dx} \qquad$ where $\qquad \dfrac{dy}{du} = \cos u \qquad$ and $\qquad \dfrac{du}{dx} = 3x^2$

$\qquad \Rightarrow \qquad \dfrac{dy}{dx} = (\cos u) \times (3x^2)$

$\qquad\qquad\qquad = (\cos x^3) \times (3x^2)$

$\qquad\qquad\qquad = 3x^2 \cos x^3$

The example above shows that, if the chain rule works, then

$\qquad f(x) = \sin x^3 \quad \Rightarrow \quad f'(x) = 3x^2 \cos x^3$

You can check this for any particular value of x by using a numerical method for differentiating the function and comparing it with the above formula for the derivative. Alternatively, you could use a graphical calculator or a computer to numerically differentiate the function for several different values of x and then plot the $(x, f'(x))$ points as a graph. You can then superimpose $y = 3x^2 \cos x^3$ and check that the graphs are the same.

3 Assume that the chain rule holds for any locally straight functions and use it to find $\dfrac{dy}{dx}$ for the following.

(a) $y = u^3$ and $u = \sin x$ (i.e. $y = \sin^3 x$)

(b) $y = e^u$ and $u = x^2$

(c) $y = u^2$ and $u = e^x$

4 Check the answers you have obtained for question 3 by a numerical method. (When you check (a), remember to use radian mode.)

Example 2

Water being poured into a paddling pool spreads at such a rate that the area in square metres covered after t minutes is $S = (5 + 4t)^2$.

(a) Find the rate at which the area is increasing after 2 minutes by multiplying out $(5 + 4t)^2$ and differentiating with respect to t.

(b) Alternatively, let $R = 5 + 4t$ so that $S = R^2$. Find $\dfrac{dS}{dt}$ by considering $\dfrac{dS}{dR} \times \dfrac{dR}{dt}$. Check that your results agree.

Solution

(a) $S = 25 + 40t + 16t^2$

$\Rightarrow \quad \dfrac{dS}{dt} = 40 + 32t$

When $t = 2$, $\dfrac{dS}{dt} = 104$

(b) $\dfrac{dS}{dR} = 2R, \qquad \dfrac{dR}{dt} = 4$

$\Rightarrow \quad \dfrac{dS}{dt} = \dfrac{dS}{dR} \times \dfrac{dR}{dt} = 2R \times 4 = 8R = 8(5 + 4t) = 40 + 32t$

When $t = 2$, $R = 13$ and so $\dfrac{dS}{dt} = 104$.

Exercise A (answers p. 143)

1 $S = (3 + t^2)^2$

(a) If you put $R = 3 + t^2$ it follows that $S = R^2$.

Write down $\dfrac{dR}{dt}$ and $\dfrac{dS}{dR}$ and so work out $\dfrac{dS}{dt}$.

(b) Work out $\dfrac{dS}{dt}$ by multiplying out $(3 + t^2)^2$ and check that your answer agrees with part (a).

2 Find $\dfrac{dy}{dx}$ for each of the following by

(a) using the chain rule and

(b) multiplying out the brackets.

(i) $y = (x + 1)^2$ (ii) $y = (2x - 1)^2$ (iii) $y = (x^2 - 2)^2$

Show that your answers agree in each case.

3 You may feel that using the chain rule is not really worthwhile for differentiating $(3 + t^2)^2$. Which method would you prefer to use to find $\dfrac{dS}{dt}$ if $S = (5 + 4t)^3$?

Work out $\dfrac{dS}{dt}$ by your chosen method.

4 Work out $\dfrac{dS}{dt}$ if $S = (4 + 3t^2)^3$.

5 You have already discovered that the derivative of $\sin 2x$ is $2 \cos 2x$.

It is possible to obtain this result using the chain rule and making a substitution for $2x$.

If $u = 2x$, then $y = \sin u$. Write down $\dfrac{dy}{du}$ and $\dfrac{du}{dx}$ and so find $\dfrac{dy}{dx}$.

6 Use the chain rule to show that the derivative of $\cos 3x$ is $-3 \sin 3x$.

7 Use the chain rule to obtain an expression for the derivative of $\sin ax$, where a is any constant.

B Differentiating by inspection

Expressions such as $(x^2 + 3x)^4$ and $\sin(x^2)$ can be differentiated rapidly once the stages of their composition have been recognised.

For example, to differentiate $(x^2 + 3x)^4$, let $y = u^4$, where $u = x^2 + 3x$.

Then $\dfrac{dy}{dx} = \dfrac{dy}{du} \times \dfrac{du}{dx}$.

The derivative is therefore

$$4(x^2 + 3x)^3 \times (\text{derivative of } x^2 + 3x) = 4(2x + 3)(x^2 + 3x)^3$$

To differentiate $\sin(x^2)$, let $y = \sin u$, where $u = x^2$.

The derivative is therefore

$$\cos(x^2) \times (\text{derivative of } x^2) = 2x \cos(x^2)$$

Example 3

Find $\dfrac{dy}{dx}$ for the following.

(a) $y = e^{(x^2+1)}$ (b) $y = \ln(3x^2 + 1)$

Solution

(a) $y = e^{(x^2+1)}$ is a composite function of the two locally straight
     functions $y = e^u$ and $u = x^2 + 1$. Using the chain rule,

$$\frac{dy}{dx} = \frac{dy}{du} \times \frac{du}{dx}$$
$$= e^u \times 2x$$
$$\Rightarrow \quad \frac{dy}{dx} = 2x\, e^{x^2+1}$$

(b) $y = \ln(3x^2 + 1)$

    Let $y = \ln u$ where $u = 3x^2 + 1$

$$\frac{dy}{dx} = \frac{dy}{du} \times \frac{du}{dx}$$
$$= \frac{1}{u} \times 6x$$
$$\Rightarrow \quad \frac{dy}{dx} = \frac{6x}{3x^2 + 1}$$

Exercise B (answers p. 144)

1   Find $\dfrac{dy}{dx}$ for each of the following. You do not need to multiply out the
   brackets in your answers.

   (a) $y = (x^2 + 3)^4$ (b) $y = (5 + 2x)^5$
   (c) $y = (2x^2 - 3x)^3$ (d) $y = (x^3 - 3x^2)^4$

2   Differentiate each of the following. Hence find the gradient of each
   graph at the point $(0, 1)$.

   (a) $y = \cos x^2$ (b) $y = \sin 2x + 1$ (c) $y = e^{3x}$

3   Differentiate these.

   (a) $\cos x^3$ (b) $\sin^3 x$ (c) $2\cos^4 x$ (d) $\sin^2 x$
   (e) e^{x^2} (f) $3\cos 2x$ (g) $2(x^2 + 1)^3$

4 A balloon is inflated at a rate of 200 cm^3 per second.

   After t seconds, when the balloon has radius r cm and volume V cm^3, the following formulas apply.

   $$V = 200t \qquad \text{and} \qquad V = \tfrac{4}{3}\pi r^3$$

   (a) Write down $\dfrac{dV}{dt}$ and $\dfrac{dV}{dr}$.

   (b) By the chain rule, $\dfrac{dV}{dt} = \dfrac{dV}{dr} \times \dfrac{dr}{dt}$.

   Use this to work out an expression for $\dfrac{dr}{dt}$ and so find the rate at which the radius is changing when $t = 1$.

5 When a hot-air balloon is being inflated, the balloonist finds that a good rule of thumb is that after t minutes the radius, r metres, is given by $r = 3 + 0.04t^2$. The balloon can be assumed to be roughly spherical.

   (a) Work out expressions for $\dfrac{dr}{dt}$ and for $\dfrac{dV}{dr}$.

   (b) Combine these two expressions to find $\dfrac{dV}{dt}$.

   (c) How fast is the volume increasing after 2 minutes?

6 An ice cube is melting, and at time t hours it has the form of a cube of side x cm and volume V cm^3.

   (a) Find $\dfrac{dV}{dx}$ in terms of x.

   (b) If $x = 4 - 0.5t$, write down $\dfrac{dx}{dt}$ and so find $\dfrac{dV}{dt}$.

   (c) At what rate is the volume changing when $t = 2$?

7 Differentiate these.

   (a) $\sin^2 2x$ (b) $3\cos^2 4x$ (c) $e^{\cos x}$

   (d) $(e^x)^4$ (e) e^{-3x} (f) $(e^{x^2} - 3x)^4$

8 Use the chain rule to differentiate these.

   (a) $\cos^2 x + \sin^2 x$ (b) $\cos^2 x - \sin^2 x$ (c) $1 - 2\sin^2 x$

   Comment on your answers.

C Applications to integration (answers p. 144)

The derivative of $\sin 2x$ is $2\cos 2x$. It follows that

$$\int 2\cos 2x \, dx = \sin 2x + c$$

and

$$\int \cos 2x \, dx = \tfrac{1}{2}\sin 2x + c$$

Being able to differentiate using the chain rule greatly increases the number of functions you are able to integrate. You need to know what type of integral function you are looking for.

1D   How can you find $\displaystyle\int_1^2 (5x-3)^3 \, dx$?

Example 4

Find $\displaystyle\int_0^1 (2x-1)^4 \, dx$.

Solution

First, try differentiating $(2x-1)^5$.

$$y = (2x-1)^5 \Rightarrow \frac{dy}{dx} = 5(2x-1)^4 \times 2 = 10(2x-1)^4$$

So

$$\int_0^1 10(2x-1)^4 \, dx = \Big[(2x-1)^5\Big]_0^1$$

$$\Rightarrow \int_0^1 (2x-1)^4 \, dx = \tfrac{1}{10}\Big[(2x-1)^5\Big]_0^1$$

$$= \tfrac{1}{10}\Big[1^5 - (-1)^5\Big] = 0.2$$

Exercise C (answers p. 145)

1 Write down the integrals of these.

(a) $\cos 3x$ (b) $\sin \tfrac{1}{2}x$ (c) $2 \sin 5x$ (d) e^{2x} (e) $(4x+2)^6$

2 Find these.

(a) $\displaystyle\int_1^2 e^{0.5x} \, dx$ (b) $\displaystyle\int_{-1}^0 \sin 2x \, dx$

(c) $\displaystyle\int_0^2 3 \cos \tfrac{1}{2} x \, dx$ (d) $\displaystyle\int_0^1 (2x+3)^2 \, dx$

3 Work out the coordinates of the points A, B and C and then evaluate the shaded areas.

(a)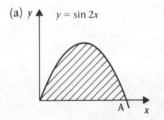

(b)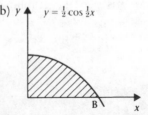

(c)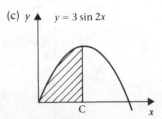

4E If $y = (x^2 + 7)^4$, then $\dfrac{dy}{dx} = 8x(x^2 + 7)^3$.

Check if it is true that

$$\int (x^2 + 7)^3 \, dx = \frac{1}{8x} (x^2 + 7)^4 + c$$

Try to explain what you find.

5E Some of these functions can be integrated by the methods of this section. Integrate as many of them as possible.

(a) $\cos \frac{1}{2}x$ (b) $e^{2.5x}$ (c) $(x^2 - 3)^3$

(d) $(5x + 3)^4$ (e) $\sin 5x$ (f) $\sin x^3$

6E Since $\dfrac{d}{dx} (\sin x^2) = 2x \cos x^2$, $\int x \cos x^2 \, dx = \frac{1}{2} \sin x^2 + c$

Find the following integrals.

(a) $\displaystyle\int x \sin x^2 \, dx$ (b) $\displaystyle\int x^2 \, e^{x^3} \, dx$ (c) $\displaystyle\int 2x(2x^2 + 1)^4 \, dx$

7E Use the identity $\cos 2x \equiv 1 - 2 \sin^2 x$ to find $\displaystyle\int_0^1 \sin^2 x \, dx$.

D Inverse functions and x^n (answers p. 145)

You have proved the result for differentiating x^2 but not for the inverse of this function, $\sqrt{x}$. The chain rule enables you to find the derivative in such cases, using the fact that

$$\frac{dx}{dy} \times \frac{dy}{dx} = 1$$

1D (a) If y is a function of x, explain why $\dfrac{dx}{dy} \times \dfrac{dy}{dx} = 1$ and $\dfrac{dx}{dy} = 1 \div \dfrac{dy}{dx}$.

(b) What connection is there between this result and the chain rule?

The derivatives of a function and its inverse are related by the identity $\dfrac{dy}{dx} = 1 \div \dfrac{dx}{dy}$.

The fact that if $y = x^n$ then $\dfrac{dy}{dx} = nx^{n-1}$ for all rational values of n should be familiar. You have seen how to prove this from first principles when n is a positive integer and in the last chapter the result was also proved for $n = -1$. The chain rule enables you to provide proofs for other values of n.

Example 5

Find the derivative of $y = \sqrt{x}$.

Solution

$$x = y^2$$

$$\Rightarrow \quad \frac{dx}{dy} = 2y \Rightarrow \frac{dy}{dx} = \frac{1}{2y} = \frac{1}{2\sqrt{x}} \text{ or } \frac{dy}{dx} = \frac{1}{2}x^{-\frac{1}{2}}$$

Exercise D (answers p. 146)

1   Obtain $\dfrac{dy}{dx}$ for $y = x^{-4} = \dfrac{1}{x^4}$ by writing $y = u^4$ where $u = \dfrac{1}{x}$.

2   Obtain $\dfrac{dy}{dx}$ for $y = \sqrt[4]{x} = x^{\frac{1}{4}}$ by writing $x = y^4$.

3   If $y = \ln x$, then $x = e^y$. Write down $\dfrac{dx}{dy}$ and use this to find $\dfrac{dy}{dx}$.

Hence explain why the derivative of $\ln x$ is $\dfrac{1}{x}$.

4   Use the chain rule to find the derivative of $\ln 2x$. (Start by putting $u = 2x$.)

5   (a) Work out the derivatives of $\ln 3x$ and $\ln 5x$.

(b) What is the derivative of $\ln ax$, where a is any constant?

(c) Use the laws of logarithms to explain the above result.

6   Differentiate these.

(a) $\ln x^2$ (b) $\ln(\sin x)$ (c) $\ln(x + 2)^3$

7   Use the chain rule to prove that $\dfrac{d}{dx}(x^n) = nx^{n-1}$

(a) when $n = \dfrac{1}{q}$ and q is a positive integer,

(b) when $n = \dfrac{p}{q}$ and p, q are integers with $q > 0$.

8   Find $f'(4)$ given that $f(x)$ is equal to the following.

(a) $\dfrac{1}{\sqrt{x}} = x^{-\frac{1}{2}}$ (b) $\dfrac{1}{x^4} = x^{-4}$ (c) $x + \dfrac{4}{x}$

(d) $e^{\frac{1}{4}x}$ (e) $\ln(x - 3)$ (f) $\sin \pi x$

9   Differentiate these.

(a) $\dfrac{1}{\sin x}$ (b) $\sec x$

10 Find the turning points on the graphs of the following. Decide whether they are maximum or minimum points.

(a) $y = (x-3)\sqrt{x}$ (b) $y = x + \dfrac{4}{x^2}$

(c) $y = \dfrac{1}{x^2 - 4x + 5}$ (d) $y = 3x - \ln x$

11 If $y = \sin^{-1} x$, then $x = \sin y$.

(a) Explain why, for $-1 < x < 1$, $\cos y > 0$.

(b) Hence explain why the derivative of $\sin^{-1} x$ is $\dfrac{1}{\sqrt{1-x^2}}$ for $-1 < x < 1$.

12 Differentiate these.

(a) $\cos^{-1} x$ (b) $\sin^{-1} \frac{1}{8}x$

After working through this chapter you should

1 be able to differentiate functions of functions such as $(3x^2 + 5)^3$ and $\sin^2 x$

2 know how to use the chain rule to solve problems involving rates of change

3 know how to differentiate inverse functions using the fact that
$$\frac{dx}{dy} = 1 \div \frac{dy}{dx}$$

7 Algebra and functions

A Remainders (answers p. 146)

An algebraic fraction is said to be a 'proper' fraction if the degree of the numerator is less than the degree of the denominator. For example,

$\dfrac{x+3}{x^2-5}$ is a proper fraction, but $\dfrac{x+7}{3x-5}$ is an improper fraction.

The improper fraction $\frac{7}{5}$ can be written $\dfrac{5+2}{5} = 1\frac{2}{5}$. Similarly, the improper fraction $\dfrac{x^2-3x+4}{x-5}$ may be written

$$\frac{x(x-5)+5x-3x+4}{x-5} = \frac{x(x-5)}{x-5} + \frac{2x+4}{x-5}$$

$$= x + \frac{2(x-5)+10+4}{x-5}$$

$$= x + \frac{2(x-5)}{x-5} + \frac{14}{x-5}$$

$$= x + 2 + \frac{14}{x-5}$$

Alternatively, you can use the long division method shown in *Methods*, taking extra care over the remainder at each step.

Example 1

Find the quotient and remainder when $x^3 - 3x + 30$ is divided by $x - 4$.

Solution

$$
\begin{array}{r}
x^2 \quad + \quad 4x \quad + \quad 13 \qquad\qquad\qquad \\
x-4\,\overline{)\;x^3 \qquad\qquad -\quad 3x \quad - \quad 30} \\
\underline{x^3 \quad - \quad 4x^2} \qquad\qquad\qquad\qquad \\
4x^2 \quad - \quad 3x \qquad\qquad \\
\underline{4x^2 \quad - \quad 16x} \qquad\qquad \\
13x \quad - \quad 30 \\
\underline{13x \quad - \quad 52} \\
22
\end{array}
$$

Note the space left for the x^2 column. This corresponds to a zero in an ordinary long division.

The quotient is $x^2 + 4x + 13$ and the remainder is 22.

In other words, $\dfrac{x^3 - 3x + 30}{x-4} = x^2 + 4x + 13 + \dfrac{22}{x-4}$.

The remainder theorem

You already know that if a polynomial P(x) can be divided by $x - a$ exactly (i.e. $(x - a)$ is a factor of P(x)) then P(a) = 0. (This is the converse of the factor theorem.) A more general result can sometimes be useful, where $x - a$ is not a factor of P(x).

1 Consider the polynomial $P(x) = x^3 + 3x^2 - 6x + 5$.

    (a) Divide P(x) by $x - 2$ to give a quotient Q(x) and a remainder R.

    (b) Evaluate P(2).

2 Now consider the polynomial $P(x) = x^4$.

    (a) Divide P(x) by $x + 3$ to give a quotient Q(x) and a remainder R.

    (b) Evaluate P(−3).

3D | What do you notice? Make up your own polynomial and divide it by a linear factor to check your conjecture.

---

4 (a) If $P(x) = (x - 4)(x^3 + 3x - 5) + 6$, explain why P(4) = 6.

    (b) More generally, if $P(x) = (x - a)Q(x) + R$, explain why P(a) = R.

In question 4(b) you proved this fact:

> When P(x) is divided by $(x - a)$ the remainder is P(a).
> This is known as the **remainder theorem**.

Note that the remainder theorem gives us only the remainder; if we need the quotient then we have to do the long division. However, the result can be used as a useful check.

5 Explain how the factor theorem follows easily from the remainder theorem.

Exercise A (answers p. 146)

1 Find the quotient and remainder when $2x^3 - 3x^2 - 4x - 5$ is divided by $x - 3$.

2 Find the remainder in the following cases.

    (a) $x^4 - 3x^3 + 7x - 8$ is divided by $x - 2$

    (b) $x^3 - 5x^2 + 3x + 2$ is divided by $x + 3$

3 $x^3 - 3x^2 + c$ has a remainder of 2 when divided by $x - 2$. Find c.

4 If $\dfrac{5x - 2}{2x + 1} = a + \dfrac{b}{2x + 1}$, find a and b.

5 Write $\dfrac{3x^2 - 2x + 1}{x + 1}$ in the form $ax + b + \dfrac{c}{x + 1}$.

6   Make up your own polynomials of degree 4 and 5 and divide them by
      $x + 3$ and $x - 2$. Use the remainder theorem to check your answers.

B   Rational functions (answers p. 147)

Graphs of rational functions (proper and improper algebraic
fractions) will bring to your attention some general ideas. As an

example, consider $y = \dfrac{x^2 + 2x - 3}{x - 2}$.

1   Obtain the graph from a graph plotter. On a sketch, label important
      features. What happens when $x = 2$? Obtain approximate values of y
      when (a) $x = 2.01$, (b) $x = 1.99$.

The function is not defined for $x = 2$. The denominator of the fraction
equals 0 and division by 0 is not defined. On the graph there can be no
y-value when $x = 2$, and the graph will have a break. Such a break is
called a **discontinuity**.

2   Write the equation in the form $y = x + 4 + \dfrac{a}{x - 2}$. Draw the line
      $y = x + 4$ on your sketch. Is the graph above or below $y = x + 4$ when
      (a) $x = 100$, (b) $x = -100$?

3   Find where the graph crosses the coordinate axes and mark these
      values on your sketch.

In the graph of $y = \dfrac{x^2 + 2x - 3}{x - 2}$, the lines $x = 2$ and $y = x + 4$ are called

asymptotes to the curve. As the graph 'goes off the page', it
approaches these lines but never meets them.

Sometimes a graph plotter can produce a misleading picture when a
graph has discontinuities. It is important to be able to work out what
the graph should look like without the aid of a plotter.

> When sketching the graph of a function, it is helpful to consider
> the following.
>
> (a)   Is the graph related to a standard graph by means of a
>   simple transformation?
>
> (b)   Are there values of x for which the function is undefined?
>   Given a value of x at which the graph is discontinuous, is y
>   positive or negative each side of the vertical asymptote?
>
> (c)   How does the graph behave for large values of x, both
>   positive and negative?
>
> (d)   Where does the graph cut the axes?

Example 2

Sketch the graph of $y = \dfrac{x+1}{x+2}$.

Solution

(a) The equation may be written $y = 1 - \dfrac{1}{x+2}$.

(b) There is a discontinuity at $x - 2$. Just to the right of the vertical asymptote $x = -2$, $\dfrac{1}{x+2}$ is large and positive, so y is large and negative (e.g. $x = -1.99$ gives $y = -99$). Just to the left of $x = -2$, y is large and positive.

(c) When x is large and positive, $\dfrac{1}{x+2}$ is small and positive and y is a little less than 1 (e.g. $x = 100$ gives $y \approx 0.99$). When x is large and negative, y is just greater than 1. The line $y = 1$ is a horizontal asymptote.

(d) $y = 0$ when $x = -1$. This is shown by the function in its original form. When $x = 0$, $y = \frac{1}{2}$.

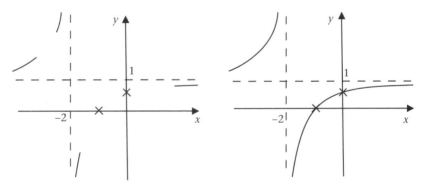

The information from (b), (c) and (d) is shown on the first diagram. It is not difficult to complete the graph, as shown in the second diagram.

It is the graph of $y = \dfrac{1}{x}$, reflected then translated.

Exercise B (answers p. 147)

Graphical calculators should not be used for these questions.

1 Using the suggestions on the previous page, and rearranging the equation as a quotient and remainder when possible, sketch the graphs of the following.

(a) $y = \dfrac{1}{x-2}$ (b) $y = \dfrac{x}{x-2}$ (c) $y = \dfrac{1}{2-x}$

(d) $y = \dfrac{x+2}{x-2}$ (e) $y = \dfrac{3(x-2)}{x+1}$ (f) $y = \dfrac{1-2x}{1+x}$

2 Sketch the graphs of the following.

(a) $\dfrac{x}{x+1}$ (b) $\dfrac{x^2}{x+1}$ (c) $\dfrac{x}{(x+1)(x-2)}$

(d) $\dfrac{x+2}{x^2-x-2}$ (e) $\dfrac{(x+1)(x-2)}{(x-3)}$ (f) $\dfrac{x^2+5x+6}{x^2-x-2}$

(g) $\dfrac{x}{x^2-1}$ (h) $x+\dfrac{1}{x}$ (i) $\dfrac{1}{(x-3)^2}$

3 Sketch the graphs of the following.

(a) $y = \dfrac{x}{x^2-4}$ (b) $y = \dfrac{x}{x^2+4}$ (c) $y = \dfrac{x+4}{x^2}$

4 A person who wishes to walk 20 km in 4 hours proposes to walk half the distance at v km h^{-1} and the remainder at u km h^{-1}. Show that $\dfrac{10}{v} + \dfrac{10}{u} = 4$, and hence that $v = \dfrac{5u}{2u-5}$. Sketch the graph of v as a function of u, and comment on the result.

5 The total resistance R ohms of two resistors of R_1 and R_2 ohms in parallel is given by $\dfrac{1}{R} = \dfrac{1}{R_1} + \dfrac{1}{R_2}$. Sketch a graph of R as a function of R_1, assuming that R_2 is fixed. Comment on the physical significance of very small and very large values of R_1.

C Inequalities (answers p. 148)

Inequalities involving rational functions bring out some useful general points.

1 Solve the equation $\dfrac{x+1}{x+2} = -1$.

2 Use the sketch graph from example 2 to solve $\dfrac{x+1}{x+2} > -1$.

Why is it untrue that $\dfrac{x+1}{x+2} > -1 \Rightarrow x+1 > -(x+2)$?

You know that you have to be careful when multiplying an inequality by a negative number.

Example 3

Solve $\dfrac{x+1}{x+2} > -1$ algebraically.

Solution

You need to separate your workings into two different scenarios.

EITHER $x+2>0$ and $x+1>-(x+2)$ **OR** $x+2<0$ and $x+1<-(x+2)$

$x>-2$ and $2x>-3$ $x<-2$ and $2x<-3$

$x>-2$ and $x>-1\frac{1}{2}$ $x<-2$ and $x<-1\frac{1}{2}$

$x>-1\frac{1}{2}$ $x<-2$

The values of x giving the bold part of the graph make up the complete solution set of the inequality.

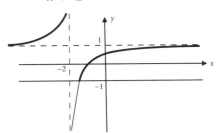

Exercise C (answers p. 148)

1 (a) Solve the equation $\dfrac{x}{x-4} = 2$.

   (b) Solve the inequality $\dfrac{x}{x-4} > 2$ algebraically.

   (c) Confirm your answer to (b) with a sketch graph.

2 Solve these.

   (a) $\dfrac{3x-9}{x-5} < 1$ (b) $\dfrac{4x+1}{x+2} > 3$

   (c) $\dfrac{2x+3}{4x-11} > 9$ (d) $\dfrac{3x-1}{2x+2} < 3$

3 (a) Sketch the graph of $y = \dfrac{x}{(x+3)(x+2)}$ and list the asymptotes. You may use a graph plotter.

   (b) Solve the equation $\dfrac{x}{(x+3)(x+2)} = -2$.

   (c) Solve the inequality $\dfrac{x}{(x+3)(x+2)} > -2$.

4 Solve these.

   (a) $\dfrac{(x+3)(x+2)}{x+1} > 0$ (b) $\dfrac{(x+3)(x+2)}{x+1} = 6$ (c) $\dfrac{(x+3)(x+2)}{x+1} > 6$

5E Solve $\dfrac{x^2 - 3x - 4}{x^2 + 3x - 10} < 1$.

D Quadratic equations (answers p. 148)

You know from factorising quadratics that a quadratic equation can be written in the form

$$x^2 - (\text{sum of roots})x + (\text{product of roots}) = 0$$

The coefficient of x^2 in a quadratic equation may not be 1. For example, the general equation could be

$$ax^2 + bx + c = 0$$

In this case we can divide through by a to give

$$x^2 + \frac{b}{a}x + \frac{c}{a} = 0$$

> If the roots of the equation are α and β, then
>
> $$\alpha + \beta = -\frac{b}{a} \qquad \text{and} \qquad \alpha\beta = \frac{c}{a}$$

1 Write down the quadratic equation with roots α and β in factorised form.
Multiply out the brackets and equate coefficients to confirm the above result.

If the roots α and β are small integers, you can solve the equation quickly in your head. Sometimes, though, you want to find a related equation, where perhaps the roots are double those of the original equation. If the quadratic can be factorised this is simple enough. It is, though, possible to find the new equation *without* solving the original.
Consider the equation $x^2 + 5x + 3 = 0$. Let the roots of the equation be α and β.

2 Write down the value of $\alpha\beta$ and $\alpha + \beta$.
The roots of a second equation are 2α and 2β.

3 Write down the value of $2\alpha + 2\beta$ and $2\alpha \times 2\beta$.

4 Explain why the second equation is $x^2 + 10x + 12 = 0$

Once you know the values of $\alpha + \beta$ and $\alpha\beta$, it is possible to find the sum and product of many pairs of related roots.

Example 4

Express the following in terms of $\alpha + \beta$ and $\alpha\beta$.
(a) $\alpha^2 + \beta^2$ (b) $(\alpha + 1)(\beta + 1)$

Solution

(a) $(\alpha + \beta)^2 = \alpha^2 + 2\alpha\beta + \beta^2$
  $\Rightarrow \quad \alpha^2 + \beta^2 = (\alpha + \beta)^2 - 2\alpha\beta$

(b) $(\alpha + 1)(\beta + 1) = \alpha\beta + (\alpha + \beta) + 1$

Example 5

The roots of the equation $2x^2 - 3x + 4 = 0$ are α and β. Find the quadratic equation with roots $\dfrac{1}{\alpha}$ and $\dfrac{1}{\beta}$.

Solution

$$2x^2 - 3x + 4 = 0 \qquad \Longrightarrow \qquad x^2 - \tfrac{3}{2}x + 2 = 0$$

So $\qquad \alpha + \beta = \tfrac{3}{2} \qquad$ and $\qquad \alpha\beta = 2$

The sum of the new roots is $\dfrac{1}{\alpha} + \dfrac{1}{\beta}$ | The product of the new roots is $\dfrac{1}{\alpha} \times \dfrac{1}{\beta}$

$$= \frac{\beta + \alpha}{\alpha\beta} \qquad\qquad\qquad\qquad\qquad = \frac{1}{\alpha\beta}$$

$$= \tfrac{3}{2} \div 2 \qquad\qquad\qquad\qquad\qquad\quad = \tfrac{1}{2}$$

$$= \tfrac{3}{4}$$

The new equation is $\qquad\qquad x^2 - \tfrac{3}{4}x + \tfrac{1}{2} = 0$

or $\qquad\qquad\qquad\qquad\qquad 4x^2 - 3x + 2 = 0$

Exercise D (answers p. 149)

1 The quadratic equation $x^2 + 4x - 7 = 0$ has roots α and β. Find the equations with the following roots.

(a) α^2 and β^2 (b) $(\alpha - 1)$ and $(\beta - 1)$

2 The quadratic equation $x^2 - 5x + 8 = 0$ has roots α and β. Find the equations with the following roots.

(a) 2α and 2β (b) $\dfrac{\alpha}{\beta}$ and $\dfrac{\beta}{\alpha}$ (c) $-\alpha$ and $-\beta$

3 The roots of $x^2 - kx + 3 = 0$ differ by 3. Find the value of k.

After working through this chapter you should

1 know the remainder theorem, i.e. that the remainder when a polynomial $P(x)$ is divided by $(x - a)$ is $P(a)$

2 be able to sketch graphs of rational functions with or without a graph plotter

3 be able to solve inequalities like $\dfrac{2x + 5}{x - 3} < 4$ algebraically and graphically

4 know the relation between the roots and the coefficients of a quadratic equation and use it to solve problems.

8 Differentiation

A The product rule (answers p. 149)

It is always possible to estimate numerically the gradient at any point of a locally straight curve and you also know how to work out the gradients of many such curves by differentiation.

1D The diagrams below show three curves with their tangents at $x = 1$, $x = 1.5$ and $x = 2$ respectively. In two cases you should be able to work out an algebraic expression for $\dfrac{dy}{dx}$ and so find the equation of the tangent. In the other case you will only be able to find the gradient of the tangent by a numerical method. In which case must you use a numerical method?

Think of some other functions for which you do not yet know how to work out a derivative. What sorts of function are they?

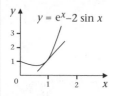

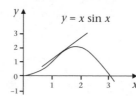

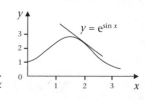

You know how to deal with functions of functions (such as $\sin x^2$) by using the chain rule.

You also know that, to differentiate compound functions which have been obtained by addition or subtraction (such as $x^2 - \sin x$), you merely add or subtract the separate derivatives.

It is unfortunate that derivatives of products (such as $x \sin x$) cannot be dealt with by multiplying the separate derivatives.

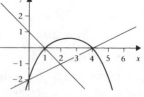

The diagram shows the graphs of the two linear functions $y = 1 - x$ and $y = \frac{1}{2}x - 2$, together with the graph of their product, $y = (1 - x)(\frac{1}{2}x - 2)$. It is clear that the two linear graphs have gradients -1 and $\frac{1}{2}$ respectively for any value of x. However, the gradient of the product graph is changing and so cannot have the value $-1 \times \frac{1}{2} = -\frac{1}{2}$ for every value of x.

You could, of course, differentiate the product function by first multiplying out the brackets, but this method will be lengthy for functions like $(2 + 3x)^2(3 - 2x)^3$ and it is not possible to 'multiply out' a product like $x \sin x$. It would therefore be very useful to find a formula for the derivative of a product.

Example 1

Let $y = uv$, where $u = ax + b$ and $v = cx + d$.

Work out $\dfrac{dy}{dx}$ and show that it is equal to $u\dfrac{dv}{dx} + v\dfrac{du}{dx}$.

Solution

$$y = (ax + b)(cx + d) = acx^2 + adx + bcx + bd$$

$$\frac{dy}{dx} = 2acx + ad + bc$$

$$u\frac{dv}{dx} + v\frac{du}{dx} = (ax + b)c + (cx + d)a = 2acx + ad + bc$$

So, for a function $y = uv$, where u and v are linear functions of x,

$$\frac{dy}{dx} = v\frac{du}{dx} + u\frac{dv}{dx}$$

This rule is called the **product rule**. It would be of limited use if it could only be used for products of linear functions. Here, we consider its use for other functions.

Any function which is differentiable has a graph which is locally straight. Since the product rule can be proved to be true for products of linear functions, you would expect the rule to be true for any two differentiable functions.

The following questions provide some evidence that the product rule works for any two differentiable functions.

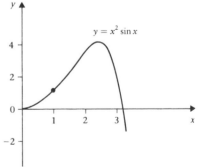

2 (a) Use the product rule to find the gradient of $y = x^2 \sin x$ at $x = 1$ and check that your answer seems reasonable in view of the shape of the graph of $y = x^2 \sin x$.

   (b) Use a numerical method to evaluate the gradient of $y = x^2 \sin x$ at $x = 1$ and check that it agrees with your answer to (a).

3 (a) Use the product rule to obtain the equation of the gradient graph for $y = uv$ where $u = \cos\frac{1}{2}x$ and $v = 4x - \frac{1}{2}x^2$.

   (b) Use a program for numerical gradients to check your answer to (a).

4 Repeat question 3 for any two functions you choose.

5 (a) x^5 can be written as $x^3 \times x^2$.

Use the product rule with $u = x^3$ and $v = x^2$ and check that you do obtain the derivative of x^5.

(b) Write x^8 as a product in at least two different ways. In each case, differentiate using the product rule and check that you obtain $8x^7$.

(c) $x^{a+b} = x^a \times x^b$

Differentiate $x^a \times x^b$ using the product rule. Do you obtain the expected answer?

You have seen some evidence that the product rule holds for any 'well-behaved' function.

6D What do you understand by the term 'well-behaved'?

An outline of a proof of the product rule is in section E.

> The product rule holds for general functions u and v.
>
> $$\frac{d}{dx}(uv) = u\frac{dv}{dx} + v\frac{du}{dx}$$

It is important to be clear about which part you are using as u and which as v, and to set your working out carefully.

Example 2

Differentiate $y = \sin x \cos x$ with respect to x.

Solution

$$u = \sin x \qquad\qquad v = \cos x$$

$$\frac{du}{dx} = \cos x \qquad\qquad \frac{dv}{dx} = -\sin x$$

$$\frac{d(uv)}{dx} = u\frac{dv}{dx} + v\frac{du}{dx}$$

$$= \sin x \times -\sin x + \cos x \times \cos x$$

$$= \cos^2 x - \sin^2 x$$

Notice that the original function can be written as $\frac{1}{2}\sin 2x$ and its derivative as $\cos 2x$.

Exercise A (answers p. 149)

1 Differentiate each of the following (i) by the product rule and (ii) after multiplying out the brackets; check that your answers agree.

(a) $y = x(x^2 + 1)$ (b) $y = x(x - 5)^2$

(c) $y = (x + 1)(2x - 3)^2$ (d) $y = (x^3 - x)(x^3 + x)$

2 Use the product rule to work out the derivatives of the following.

(a) $e^x \sin x$ (b) $x^2 e^x$ (c) $x^3 \cos x$ (d) $x\sqrt{2x+3}$

(e) $x^2 \sqrt{x}$ (f) $(x^2 + 2x + 2)e^{-x}$

3 Work out the gradients of the following.

(a) the tangent to $y = x^3 e^x$ at $x = 2$

(b) the tangent to $y = 2x^2 e^x$ at $x = 1$

4 Use the product rule to differentiate $x \sin x$ and hence work out the equation of the tangent at $x = 1.5$ on the graph of $y = x \sin x$. (Work to 2 significant figures.)

5 A rectangle on a computer screen has width w, height h and area A. w and h are programmed to be functions of time, t.

(a) (i) If $w = t^2$ and $h = \sin t$, use the product rule to find $\dfrac{dA}{dt}$ and so work out the rate at which the area of the rectangle is increasing when $t = 1$.

(ii) What is happening to the area when $t = 2.5$?

(b) (i) If $w = \sin t$ and $h = \cos t$, how fast is the area increasing when $t = 0.5$?

(ii) At what value of t does the area of this rectangle first stop increasing?

6 Find the equation of the tangent to the graph of $y = 0.25x\, e^x$ at the point where $x = 1$. (Work to 2 decimal places.)

7 Differentiate $x\, e^x$ and so work out the coordinates of the turning point on the graph of $y = x\, e^x$.

8 (a) Differentiate $x^2 e^x$ and explain how this shows that the graph of $y = x^2 e^x$ must have a stationary point at $(0, 0)$.

(b) How do you know that there is only one other stationary point on the graph? Work out the coordinates of this stationary point.

9 (a) Let $y = uv$, where $u = x$ and $v = \dfrac{1}{x}$.

It follows that $y = x \times \dfrac{1}{x} = 1$ and $\dfrac{dy}{dx} = 0$.

But $\dfrac{dy}{dx} = v\dfrac{du}{dx} + u\dfrac{dv}{dx}$.

Use the above to find $\dfrac{dv}{dx}$. Hence show that the derivative of $\dfrac{1}{x}$ is $-\dfrac{1}{x^2}$.

(b) Show that the answer $\dfrac{dv}{dx} = -\dfrac{1}{x^2}$ agrees with the one obtained by using the nx^{n-1} rule.

10E Show that there is a stationary point on the curve $y = x \sin x$ when $x + \tan x = 0$. Show graphically that $x + \tan x = 0$ has three solutions in the interval $-\pi \leqslant x \leqslant \pi$.

One of these three solutions should be obvious. Use any method you wish to find the other two solutions and so work out the coordinates of the stationary points of $y = x \sin x$ for $-\pi \leqslant x \leqslant \pi$.

B Product rule and chain rule

It is very important to be clear when you need to use the chain rule and when you need to use the product rule.

$e^x \sin x$ means $e^x \times \sin x$, so two simple functions are being multiplied together and the product rule is needed.

$e^{\sin x}$ is a composite function $fg(x)$ where $g(x) = \sin x$ and $f(x) = e^x$, so the chain rule is needed.

It is sometimes necessary to use both rules.

Example 3

Find $\dfrac{dy}{dx}$ where $y = e^{2x} \sin 0.5x$.

Solution

$y = uv$, where

$$u = e^{2x} \qquad \text{and} \qquad v = \sin 0.5x$$

By the chain rule, $\dfrac{du}{dx} = 2e^{2x}$ and $\dfrac{dv}{dx} = 0.5 \cos 0.5x$

By the product rule, $\dfrac{dy}{dx} = v\dfrac{du}{dx} + u\dfrac{dv}{dx}$

So $\dfrac{dy}{dx} = \sin 0.5x \times 2e^{2x} + e^{2x} \times 0.5 \cos 0.5x$

Or $\dfrac{dy}{dx} = e^{2x}(2 \sin 0.5x + 0.5 \cos 0.5x)$

Exercise B (answers p. 150)

1 Let $u = (2x - 3)^2$ and $v = (3x + 7)^5$.

(a) Differentiate u using the chain rule.

(b) Differentiate v using the chain rule.

(c) Use the product rule and your answers to (a) and (b) to differentiate $y = (2x - 3)^2(3x + 7)^5$.

2 Let $u = \cos^2 x$ and $v = \sin 5x$.

(a) Differentiate u.

(b) Differentiate v.

(c) Use the product rule to differentiate $y = \cos^2 x \sin 5x$.

3 Differentiate these products, using both the chain rule and the product rule. Set out your working as in example 3.

(a) $2e^{3x} \sin 2x$ (b) $e^{2x} \cos 3x$ (c) $e^{x^2} \sin 4x$

4 Use the product rule or the chain rule or both in order to differentiate the following functions.

(a) $\ln(x^2 + 1)$ (b) $x \ln x$ (c) $x \sin^2 x$

(d) $x \sin x^2$ (e) $(x + \sin x)^2$ (f) $e^x \cos x + x \sin x$

(g) $(2x + 3)^{-1}$ (h) $x^2 e^{3x}$

5 Find the x-coordinates of any turning points on the graphs of the following. Use a graph plotter to confirm your answers.

(a) $y = x(x - 5)^2$ (b) $y = (2x + 1)(x - 3)^4$ (c) $y = x e^{-x}$

(d) $y = x^2 e^{-x}$ (e) $y = x\sqrt{2x + 5}$ (f) $y = x\sqrt{2x - 5}$

6 Work out the gradient of each of these graphs at $x = 2$.

(a)

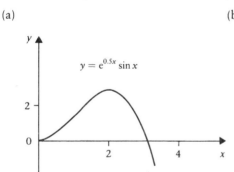

$y = e^{0.5x} \sin x$

(b)

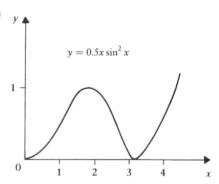

$y = 0.5x \sin^2 x$

7 The tip of a tuning fork moves so that its distance in centimetres from a central position is given by

$$s = 0.4 \sin 512\pi t, \quad \text{where } t \text{ is the time in seconds}$$

(a) What are the displacement and the velocity of the tip of the tuning fork after 1 second?

(b) How many vibrations per second does the fork make?

8 Differentiate $\dfrac{x + 2}{x + 1}$ by writing the function as $(x + 2)(x + 1)^{-1}$.

C Differentiating quotients (answers p. 151)

When tackling exercise B, you probably found the derivative of $\dfrac{x+2}{x+1}$ to be

$$(x+1)^{-1} + -1(x+1)^{-2}(x+2)$$

You may have rearranged the answer as $\dfrac{1}{x+1} - \dfrac{x+2}{(x+1)^2}$.

This is still not a very neat answer, and it can be simplified further.

$$\frac{(x+1)-(x+2)}{(x+1)^2} = \frac{-1}{(x+1)^2}$$

It is possible to differentiate any quotient by rewriting the function with negative indices and using the product rule, but the process of writing the answer in a neat form is tedious. It is therefore worthwhile to try to find a formula for the derivative of a quotient.

1   $y = \dfrac{x}{\sin x} = x(\sin x)^{-1}$

Show that $\dfrac{dy}{dx} = \dfrac{\sin x - x \cos x}{\sin^2 x}$.

Alternatively, $\dfrac{x}{\sin x}$ can be differentiated by considering it as $\dfrac{u}{v}$ instead of as uv.

$$u = x, \quad v = \sin x, \quad \frac{du}{dx} = 1 \quad \text{and} \quad \frac{dv}{dx} = \cos x$$

So $\dfrac{dy}{dx} = \dfrac{v\dfrac{du}{dx} - u\dfrac{dv}{dx}}{v^2}$ (1)

2   (a) Differentiate $\dfrac{e^x}{\sin x}$ by writing the function as $e^x(\sin x)^{-1}$.

Check that the answer agrees with the one you would obtain by using formula (1).

   (b) Repeat part (a) for any quotient of your choice.

3   Formula (1) is called the **quotient rule** and it is true for any quotient $\dfrac{u}{v}$, where u and v are differentiable functions of x. Here is the start of a proof of the rule.

$$y = \frac{u}{v} = uv^{-1}$$

So, by the product rule,

$$\frac{dy}{dx} = v^{-1}\frac{du}{dx} + u\frac{d(v^{-1})}{dx}$$

Use the chain rule to work out $\dfrac{d(v^{-1})}{dx}$ and so complete the proof.

> **The quotient rule**
>
> If $y = \dfrac{u}{v}$, where u and v are functions of x, then $\dfrac{dy}{dx} = \dfrac{v\dfrac{du}{dx} - u\dfrac{dv}{dx}}{v^2}$

Example 4

(a) Use the quotient rule to differentiate $\dfrac{x^2}{2x+3}$.

(b) Show that the function has a local maximum at $x = -3$.

Solution

(a) $y = \dfrac{u}{v}$, where $u = x^2$ and $v = 2x + 3$

$$\frac{dy}{dx} = \frac{v\dfrac{du}{dx} - u\dfrac{dv}{dx}}{v^2} = \frac{2x(2x+3) - 2x^2}{(2x+3)^2} = \frac{2x^2 + 6x}{(2x+3)^2} = \frac{2x(x+3)}{(2x+3)^2}$$

(b) At stationary points, $\dfrac{dy}{dx} = 0$

$$x(x+3) = 0$$

$$\Rightarrow x = 0 \qquad \text{or} \qquad x = -3$$

There are stationary points at $(0, 0)$ and $(-3, -3)$.

Examine the nature of the stationary point at $x = -3$.

When x is just less than -3 (say -3.1), $\dfrac{dy}{dx}$ is positive.

When x is just greater than -3 (say -2.9), $\dfrac{dy}{dx}$ is negative.

So $(-3, -3)$ is a local maximum.

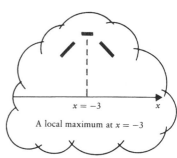

$x = -3$

A local maximum at $x = -3$

Exercise C (answers p. 151)

1 Differentiate these.

(a) $\dfrac{\sin x}{x}$ (b) $\dfrac{x}{e^x}$ (c) $\dfrac{e^x}{\sin x}$ (d) $\dfrac{e^{3x}}{\sin 2x}$

2 Work out the gradients of the following.

(a) $y = \dfrac{\sin x}{e^x}$ at $x = -1$ (b) $y = \dfrac{e^{2x}}{x^2}$ at $x = 0.8$

Use a graph plotter to check that your answers look reasonable.

3 You can differentiate $\dfrac{1}{2x+3} = (2x+3)^{-1}$ by using either the quotient rule or the chain rule. Work out the derivative using each method in turn. Which method do you prefer?

4 (a) The graph of $y = \dfrac{x}{1+x^2}$ has a local minimum and a local maximum.

   Work out the coordinates of these points, showing clearly how you know which is the maximum and which is the minimum.

   (b) Repeat (a) for $y = \dfrac{x^2}{x+4}$.

5 Find the maximum and minimum points (if any) on the graphs of these.

   (a) $y = \dfrac{x}{(x-2)^2}$ (b) $y = \dfrac{x}{x^2-4}$ (c) $y = \dfrac{x}{x^2+4}$

   (d) $y = \dfrac{x^2+2x+8}{x-2}$ (e) $y = \dfrac{2x+7}{x^2+2x-3}$

6 (a) Use the quotient rule to differentiate $\tan x = \dfrac{\sin x}{\cos x}$.

   (b) Show that $y = \tan^{-1} x \Rightarrow \dfrac{dy}{dx} = \dfrac{1}{1+x^2}$ by first writing $x = \tan y$.

7 Work out the derivative of $\cot x$ by first writing the following.

   (a) $\cot x = \dfrac{\cos x}{\sin x}$ (b) $\cot x = \dfrac{1}{\tan x}$

   (c) Check that your answers to parts (a) and (b) are consistent by writing each one in as simple a form as you can.

8 You know that $\sec x = \dfrac{1}{\cos x}$. Show that $\dfrac{d}{dx}(\sec x) = \sec x \tan x$ using
   (a) the chain rule, (b) the quotient rule.
   Find a similar result for $\dfrac{d}{dx}(\operatorname{cosec} x)$.

9E The first part of an alternative proof of the quotient rule, assuming that the product rule is true, is given below. Try to complete the proof.

   $y = \dfrac{u}{v}$ where u and v are functions of x.

   Then $u = vy$.

   By the product rule, $\dfrac{du}{dx} = \ldots$

In this chapter and earlier ones, a number of results connecting tan, cot, sec and cosec have been found.

$$\tan^2 x + 1 = \sec^2 x \qquad 1 + \cot^2 x = \cosec^2 x$$

y	$\tan x$	$\cot x$	$\sec x$	$\cosec x$
$\dfrac{dy}{dx}$	$\sec^2 x$	$-\cosec^2 x$	$\sec x \tan x$	$-\cosec x \cot x$

D Differentiation practice

You are now able to differentiate a wide variety of functions, but you need to practise using your skills and, importantly, choosing which technique to use. In some of the later questions you will need to rearrange the function first.

Example 5

If $x^2 + y^2 = 25$, find $\dfrac{dy}{dx}$ at $(4, 3)$.

Solution

First rearrange the function in the form $y = \sqrt{25 - x^2}$ or $y = (25 - x^2)^{\frac{1}{2}}$.

Now, using the chain rule,

$$\frac{dy}{dx} = \tfrac{1}{2}(25 - x^2)^{-\frac{1}{2}} \times (-2x)$$

$$= -x(25 - x^2)^{-\frac{1}{2}}$$

$$= \frac{-x}{\sqrt{25 - x^2}}$$

When $x = 4$, $\dfrac{dy}{dx} = -\dfrac{4}{3}$.

Since the graph is a circle, the answer can be obtained easily without differentiation (see Chapter 2). Note that the function used describes just the upper semicircle.

Exercise D (answers p. 152)

1   Use the chain rule to differentiate the following; then check your answers by applying an addition formula to y and differentiating each term separately.

(a) $y = \cos(3x + 2)$ (b) $y = \cos(4x - 1)$ (c) $y = \sin(5x - 11)$

2 Differentiate these.

(a) $\sin^2 x$ (b) $\sin(x^2)$ (c) $\cos^3 x$ (d) $\cos^2(3x)$

3 Use the chain rule to differentiate the following.

(a) $(3x+5)^2$ (b) $\sin 4x$ (c) $6x^{\frac{1}{2}}$

(d) $\sqrt{2x-7}$ (e) $4\cos(2x-7)$ (f) $3(x^2-5)^{-\frac{1}{2}}$

(g) $\cos^2 x$ (h) $\cos^2 5x$ (i) $\sqrt{x^2-3x}$

(j) $x+\sqrt{x^2+1}$ (k) $\dfrac{1}{(3x+4)^3}$

4 Use the product and quotient rules to differentiate the following.

(a) $3x^2(2x-1)$ (b) $2x\cos x$ (c) $x(x+5)^3$

(d) $\dfrac{3x+2}{4x-1}$ (e) $\dfrac{\cos 3x}{x}$ (f) $(2x+1)\sin 3x$

(g) $x^2\tan 2x$ (h) $\sin 3x\cos 4x$ (i) $\sin^2 x\cos x$

5 Differentiate these.

(a) $\tan\frac{1}{2}x$ (b) $\cot 3x$ (c) $1+\tan^2 x$

(d) $\sec^2 x$ (e) $\tan^{-1}\frac{1}{3}x$

6 Use the quotient rule to find $\dfrac{dy}{dx}$ given $y = \dfrac{\sin x}{1+\cos x}$. Show that y can be written as $\tan\frac{1}{2}x$ and $\dfrac{dy}{dx}$ as $\frac{1}{2}\sec^2\frac{1}{2}x$.

7 Find $\dfrac{dy}{dx}$ for the following.

(a) $y = \dfrac{1}{x^2}$ (b) $y = \dfrac{1}{2x+5}$ (c) $y = \sqrt{5x}$

(d) $y = (2x^2-3)^3$ (e) $y = x(2x-3)^4$ (f) $y = x^4(2x-3)$

(g) $y = \dfrac{4+x}{\sqrt{x}}$ (h) $y = \dfrac{\sqrt{x}}{4+x}$ (i) $y = 3\cos 4x$

(j) $y = \sin^2 6x$ (k) $y = \ln 4x$ (l) $y = e^{2x}\sin\frac{1}{2}x$

(m) $y = \dfrac{\sin x}{\cos 2x}$ (n) $x^2-y^3 = 12$ (o) $e^{3x}y = x^2$

8 Sketch the graph of $y = x + \dfrac{2}{2x+1}$ and determine the coordinates of the maximum and minimum points.

9E (a) Given that $y = \dfrac{\cos x}{1-\sin x}$, find $\dfrac{dy}{dx}$ and verify that $\cos x\dfrac{dy}{dx} = y$.

(b) Show that $\dfrac{\cos x}{1-\sin x} = \sec x + \tan x$ and hence verify your answer to (a).

10E Differentiate (a) ln sin x,   (b) ln cos x,   (c) ln sec x

Simplify your answers and use them to evaluate $\int_0^{\frac{1}{4}\pi} \tan x \, dx$.

11E Show that $\dfrac{d}{dx}(\ln \tan x) = 2 \operatorname{cosec} 2x$.

E Proving the product rule

Let u and v be general well-behaved functions of x. Then

$$\frac{d(uv)}{dx} = \lim_{h \to 0} \frac{u(x+h)v(x+h) - u(x)v(x)}{h}$$

$$= \lim_{h \to 0} \frac{u(x+h)v(x+h) + [-u(x)v(x+h) + u(x)v(x+h)] - u(x)v(x)}{h}$$

(putting in a pair of terms which cancel each other out)

$$= \lim_{h \to 0} \left[\frac{u(x+h) - u(x)}{h} \times v(x+h) + u(x) \times \frac{v(x+h) - v(x)}{h} \right]$$

At this point the argument skates over thin ice with regard to the use of limits. However, providing everything is sufficiently well behaved:

$$\frac{d(uv)}{dx} = \left[\lim_{h \to 0} \frac{u(x+h) - (x)}{h} \right] \times \lim_{h \to 0} (v(x+h)) + u(x) \times \left[\lim_{h \to 0} \frac{v(x+h) - v(x)}{h} \right]$$

$$= \frac{du}{dx} v + u \frac{dv}{dx}$$

After working through this chapter you should

1 know how to differentiate products and quotients using the two rules

- Product rule

$$\frac{d}{dx}(uv) = v \frac{du}{dx} + u \frac{dv}{dx}$$

- Quotient rule

$$\frac{d}{dx}\left(\frac{u}{v}\right) = \frac{v \dfrac{du}{dx} - u \dfrac{dv}{dx}}{v^2}$$

2 understand the importance of approaching differentiation systematically and recognise when to use the chain rule and when to use the product rule.

9 Numerical methods

A Numerical integration (answers p. 153)

With the techniques now at your disposal, it is possible to differentiate any combination of standard functions, however complicated. But integration is much more difficult and even quite simple-looking integrals may be impossible to evaluate by exact methods. An example is

$$\int \frac{\sin x}{x+1}\,dx$$

Consequently, it is useful to develop approximate methods which can give sufficiently accurate answers to definite integrals. You have already met the mid-ordinate rule.

1 The rate at which water was flowing into a stream was measured at hourly intervals with the following results.

Time	12:30 p.m.	1:30 p.m.	2:30 p.m.	3:30 p.m.	4:30 p.m.	5:30 p.m.
Rate (m^3 min^{-1})	5	9.5	12	9.5	7	6.5

(a) Draw the (time, rate of flow) graph for times from 12 noon to 6 p.m. What does the area under the graph represent?

(b) Use the mid-ordinate rule to estimate the volume of water flowing into the stream between 12 noon and 6 p.m.

(c) Draw this estimated area on your graph.

(d) Do you think your answer over-estimates or under-estimates the actual flow?

We now consider an alternative numerical method, known as the **trapezium rule**.

The trapezium rule uses a series of trapezia to estimate the area under a graph.

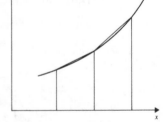

2 Suppose the readings of the rates of flow considered in question 1 were taken at different times, with results as follows.

Time	12 noon	1 p.m.	2 p.m.	3 p.m.	4 p.m.	5 p.m.	6 p.m.
Rate (m^3 min^{-1})	4	7	11.5	11	8	6.5	6

Draw the (time, rate of flow) graph for times from 12 noon to 6 p.m. Although the graph is obviously curved, you can approximate it with a series of six straight-line segments by joining the known points on the graph. In this model of the flow you assume that the rate of flow increases or decreases uniformly during each 1-hour interval.

3 Superimpose this model as a graph on the (time, rate of flow) graph you have just drawn.

4 Use the model to estimate the volume of water passing into the stream in the hour.

5 Does the model over-estimate or under-estimate the actual flow?

Example 1

Depth readings are taken across a river of width 20 metres. Depths at various distances from the left bank are shown in the table.

Distance (m)	0	2	4	6	8	10	12	14	16	18	20
Depth (m)	0	0.2	1	2	3.1	3.8	3.8	3.9	3.5	2.9	0

Estimate the cross-sectional area using

(a) the mid-ordinate rule with 5 strips,

(b) the trapezium rule with 5 strips.

Solution

(a) Mid-ordinate rule

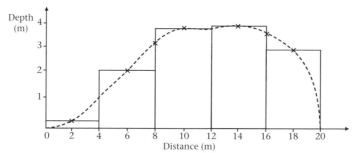

$$\text{Area} = 4 \times 0.2 + 4 \times 2 + 4 \times 3.8 + 4 \times 3.9 + 4 \times 2.9 = 51.2$$

(b) Trapezium rule

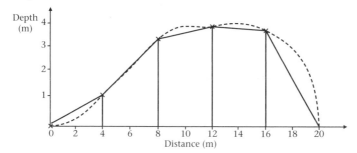

$$\text{Area} = \tfrac{1}{2} \times 4 \times (0 + 1) + \tfrac{1}{2} \times 4 \times (1 + 3.1) + \tfrac{1}{2} \times 4 \times (3.1 + 3.8)$$
$$+ \tfrac{1}{2} \times 4 \times (3.8 + 3.5) + \tfrac{1}{2} \times 4 \times (3.5 + 0) = 45.6$$

Here, the trapezium rule under-estimates the area while the mid-ordinate rule over-estimates the area. The actual area is somewhere between the two values calculated.

With the data given, the graph could be approximated by 10 trapezia instead of 5. The area is then 48.4.

Exercise A (answers p. 153)

1 A geologist does a survey of stalactites and stalagmites in a cave. In order to estimate their volumes, she measures their circumferences at different points along their lengths.

Her measurements for one particular stalagmite are shown in the following table.

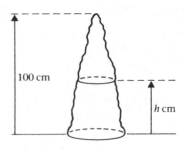

Height (cm)	10	30	50	70	90
Circumference (cm)	50	40	30	20	10

(a) Estimate the cross-sectional area of the stalagmite at each height and draw a graph which shows how the cross-sectional area changes with the height of the stalagmite. What assumptions have you made?

(b) Use the mid-ordinate rule to estimate the area under the graph. What does this area represent?

2 A train is travelling at 20 m s^{-1} when the brakes are applied; t seconds later the speed of the train is given by $20 - 0.2t^2 \text{ m s}^{-1}$. Sketch the (time, speed) graph and use the trapezium rule, with two-second intervals, to estimate the distance travelled by the train before it comes to rest.

3 (a) Sketch the graph of $y = \ln x$ and shade the area represented by the integral $\displaystyle\int_{1}^{2} \ln x \, dx$.

(b) Find the approximate value using the trapezium rule with 4 strips.

B Increasing the accuracy (answers p. 154)

Example 2

Consider the function $y = \sqrt{4 - x^2}$.

(a) Draw a diagram to illustrate the area represented by $\displaystyle\int_{0}^{2} \sqrt{4 - x^2} \, dx$.

(b) What is the precise value of this integral?

(c) Use the mid-ordinate rule with two strips to estimate this integral.

Solution

(a) The shaded area under the graph of $y = \sqrt{4 - x^2}$ is one quarter of the area of the circle with equation $x^2 + y^2 = 4$. The radius is 2.

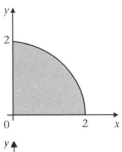

(b) The area of the circle is 4π. So $\int_0^2 \sqrt{4 - x^2}\, dx = \pi$.

(c) When $x = 0.5$, $y = \sqrt{3.75} = 1.936$ (to 4 s.f.)
When $x = 1.5$, $y = \sqrt{1.75} = 1.323$ (to 4 s.f.)

$$\int_0^2 \sqrt{4 - x^2}\, dx \approx (1 \times 1.936) + (1 \times 1.323)$$

$$\approx 3.26 \text{ (to 3 s.f.)}$$

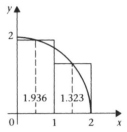

You can see that the mid-ordinate rule with just two strips has given an answer about 4% greater than the correct area. You can improve this by using more (thinner) strips.

Now use ten strips.
The diagram shows only a few.

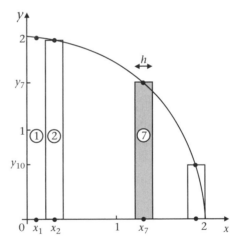

1D

(a) What are the values of the following?
  (i)   the width, h, of each strip
  (ii) x_1, y_1, x_2 and y_2
  (iii) the areas of strips ① and ②

(b) Copy and complete the table below for the areas of each strip.

Strip	1	2	3	4	5	6	7	8	9	10
Area			0.3873	0.3747	0.3572	0.3341		0.2646	0.2107	

(c) Find the total area and its percentage error as an estimate of π.

To get a very accurate estimate of the integral you might have to use a very large number of strips. Making a large number of routine calculations is a task well-suited to a programmable calculator, computer or spreadsheet.

The mid-ordinate rule

Consider the area represented by the integral $\int_a^b f(x)\,dx$ to be split up

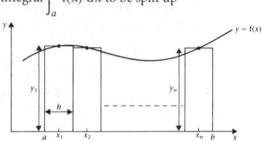

into n strips of equal width, h. Using the mid-ordinate rule to approximate the integral, the area of the first strip would be calculated as hy_1, the second strip would be hy_2, and so on.

2 (a) Express h in terms of a, b and n.

(b) Express x_1 in terms of a and h.

(c) By how much do you increase x each time you move up a strip?

3 (a) Use the mid-ordinate rule to evaluate $\int_0^2 \sqrt{4 - x^2}\,dx$ with

(i) 10 strips   (ii) 20 strips   (iii) 40 strips   (iv) 80 strips

and so on. Compare each of your estimates with an accurate value for π, and comment on how the error changes as you increase the number of strips.

(b) Approximately how many strips do you need to estimate π to an accuracy of 4 decimal places?

The trapezium rule

Again, consider the area represented by $\int_a^b f(x)\,dx$ to be split up into n strips of equal width, h. Using the trapezium rule, the area of the first strip would be $\tfrac{1}{2}h(y_0 + y_1)$, the area of the second strip would be $\tfrac{1}{2}h(y_1 + y_2)$, and so on.

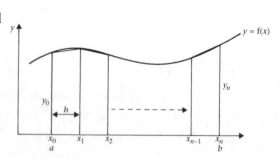

4 Derive a formula for the total area of the n strips shown.

5 Repeat question 3(a) for the trapezium rule, using a programmable calculator or computer.

The trapezium and the mid-ordinate rules with n strips both involve the sum of areas.

The mid-ordinate rule

$$\int_a^b f(x)\, dx \approx \sum_{r=1}^{n} hy_r$$

where

$$h = \frac{b-a}{n}$$
$$x_1 = a + \tfrac{1}{2}h$$
$$x_{r+1} = x_r + h$$
$$y_r = f(x_r)$$

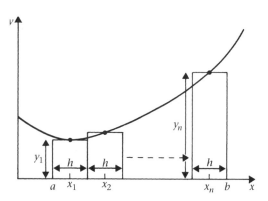

The trapezium rule

$$\int_a^b f(x)\, dx \approx \sum_{r=1}^{n} \tfrac{1}{2}h(y_{r-1} + y_r)$$

where

$$h = \frac{b-a}{n}$$
$$x_0 = a$$
$$x_{r+1} = x_r + h$$
$$y_r = f(x_r)$$

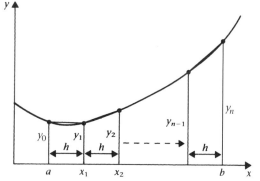

The two rules can be summarised as follows.

The mid-ordinate rule

$$\int_a^b y\, dx \approx hy_1 + hy_2 + hy_3 + \ldots + hy_n = h(y_1 + y_2 + \ldots + y_n)$$

The trapezium rule

$$\int_a^b y\, dx \approx \tfrac{1}{2}h(y_0 + y_1) + \tfrac{1}{2}h(y_1 + y_2) + \ldots + \tfrac{1}{2}h(y_{n-1} + y_n)$$
$$= \tfrac{1}{2}h(y_0 + 2y_1 + 2y_2 + \ldots + y_n)$$

As you take more and more strips, the area estimate given by either the trapezium or the mid-ordinate rule will become closer and closer to the true value, at least for all locally straight graphs.

For the graph of $y = \sqrt{4 - x^2}$ you may have noticed that the trapezium rule consistently under-estimates the true area whereas the mid-ordinate rule always over-estimates it.

The trapezium rule approximates a graph with a series of chords and it is easy to tell whether it will over- or under-estimate the area.

Over-estimate   Under-estimate

To predict if the mid-ordinate rule will over- or under-estimate an area, it is helpful to think of it as producing trapezia rather than rectangles!

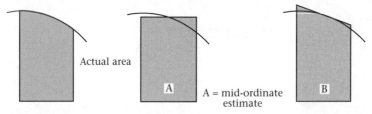

Actual area

A   A = mid-ordinate estimate   B

The area of trapezium B is precisely the same as the area of rectangle A.

Thus, you can think of the mid-ordinate rule as approximating a graph with a series of tangents to the graph.

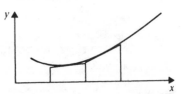

Exercise B (answers p. 154)

1   State, where it is clear, whether a mid-ordinate rule estimate of each of the following areas will be too large or too small.

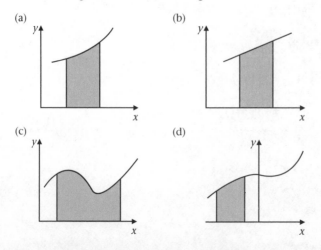

(a)   (b)
(c)   (d)

2 Repeat question 1 for the trapezium rule.

3 Find an approximate value for $\displaystyle\int_1^2 \frac{1}{x}\,dx$

(a) by the mid-ordinate rule,

(b) by the trapezium rule.

Use five strips in each case. Compare with the correct value.

4 Find the approximate values of the following.

(a) $\displaystyle\int_{-1}^1 \frac{1}{1+x^2}\,dx$ (b) $\displaystyle\int_{-3}^0 2^x\,dx$ (c) $\displaystyle\int_{-1}^1 e^{-\frac{1}{2}x^2}\,dx$

C The Newton–Raphson method (answers p. 154)

You solved some equations by iterative methods in Chapter 1. Sometimes you got divergent sequences and sometimes the convergence was very slow.

A contemporary and colleague of Isaac Newton, Joseph Raphson (1648–1715), developed a variation using tangents to a curve which solves virtually any equation quickly and reliably.

All iterative methods require a first approximation to a root, which will normally be obtained by doing a quick sketch of the graph. The method can be illustrated by looking at a specific problem, such as solving $x^2 - 3 \sin x = 0$.

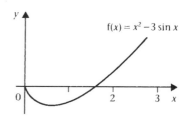

From the graph, it can be seen that $x = 2$ is a reasonable first approximation to the root.

By enlarging the region around the root it can be seen that a better approximation can be found where the tangent at $x = 2$ cuts the x-axis.

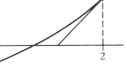

At $x = 2$, $f(2) = 4 - 3 \sin 2 = 1.27$ and, since $f'(x) = 2x - 3 \cos x$, the gradient of the tangent is $f'(2) = 4 - 3 \cos 2 = 5.25$.

The equation of the tangent is given by:

$$\frac{y - 1.27}{x - 2} = 5.25$$

$$\Rightarrow \quad y - 1.27 = 5.25(x - 2)$$

$$\Rightarrow \quad y = 5.25x - 9.23$$

The tangent meets the x-axis where $5.25x - 9.23 = 0$. This gives $x = 1.76$.

This method will generalise to give a formula for the improved approximation.

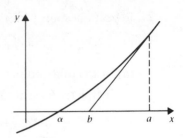

Suppose the equation to be solved is $f(x) = 0$ and the root you are trying to find is α.

Suppose that $x = a$ is the first guess and the tangent at $x = a$ crosses the x-axis at $x = b$.

1D Show that $f'(a) = \dfrac{f(a)}{a - b}$ and hence that $b = a - \dfrac{f(a)}{f'(a)}$.

You have seen that, if $x = a$ is an approximation to the solution of $f(x) = 0$, then $b = a - \dfrac{f(a)}{f'(a)}$ appears to be a better approximation.

You can now use this 'improved guess' as the starting value in the process and hence obtain a value for x which is even closer to the root. So if you repeat the process several times you can get closer and closer to the solution of $f(x) = 0$.

2   The equation $x^2 - 3 \sin x = 0$ has a solution near $x = 2$.

(a) If $f(x) = x^2 - 3 \sin x$, write down $f'(x)$.

(b) Show that the formula $b = a - \dfrac{f(a)}{f'(a)}$ with $a = 2$ gives $b = 1.76$, to 3 significant figures.

(c) Taking your improved approximation in (b) as your new value for a, find a new approximation. Give your answer to 5 significant figures.

3

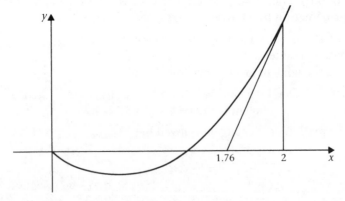

The diagram shows how the second approximation, 1.76, is obtained geometrically from the first approximation, $a = 2$. Copy the diagram and show how the third approximation can be constructed.

The Newton–Raphson process can be repeated as often as necessary. It generates an iterative sequence, $x_1, x_2, x_3, x_4, \ldots, x_n$, and the equation

$$b = a - \frac{f(a)}{f'(a)}$$

can be written as

$$x_{n+1} = x_n - \frac{f(x_n)}{f'(x_n)}$$

In practice, not all equations are of the form $f(x) = 0$. Sometimes an equation will take the form

$$h(x) = g(x)$$

Such an equation can always be rearranged into the form

$$h(x) - g(x) = 0$$

and so the problem becomes one of finding the zero of the function $h(x) - g(x)$.

Example 3

Solve $\sin 2x = x^2$.

Solution

(Note that you must work in radians here.)

This equation cannot be solved algebraically, so a numerical method must be used.

The sketch shows that there are two solutions.

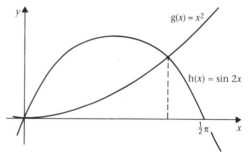

$x = 0$ is one solution, and the other is somewhere between $x = 0$ and $x = \frac{1}{2}\pi$.

This suggests a possible value of $x_1 = 1$.

The equation can be expressed in the form $f(x) = 0$ by writing

$$x^2 - \sin 2x = 0$$

Then $f(x) = x^2 - \sin 2x$ and $f'(x) = 2x - 2\cos 2x$.

Hence the iteration formula will be

$$x_{n+1} = x_n - \frac{x_n^2 - \sin 2x_n}{2x_n - 2\cos 2x_n}$$

Taking $x_1 = 1$, then $x_2 = 0.967\ 976$, $x_3 = 0.966\ 878$, $x_4 = 0.966\ 877$ and $x_5 = 0.966\ 877$. Since x_4 and x_5 agree to 6 decimal places, you can conclude that $x = 0.966\ 877$ to 6 decimal places.

The Newton–Raphson method is usually extremely efficient. You will often find that if x_1 is accurate to 1 decimal place, then x_2 is accurate to 2 decimal places, x_3 to 4 decimal places, x_4 to 8 decimal places and x_5 to 16 decimal places!

The Newton–Raphson method gives a sequence of numbers $x_1, x_2, x_3, \ldots$, which converges to a zero of a function f(x). For a starting value x_1

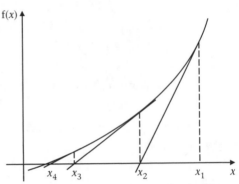

$$x_2 = x_1 - \frac{f(x_1)}{f'(x_1)}$$

$$x_3 = x_2 - \frac{f(x_2)}{f'(x_2)}$$

$\ldots$

The general iterative formula is

$$x_{n+1} = x_n - \frac{f(x_n)}{f'(x_n)}$$

Exercise C (answers p. 155)

1 (a) For f(x) = $x^3 - 3x + 1$, write down f'(x) and hence give the Newton–Raphson formula.

(b) Use the graph below to write down approximate roots for $x^3 - 3x + 1 = 0$.

(c) Use the Newton–Raphson method to find the greatest and least roots to 3 significant figures.

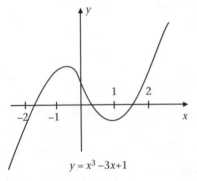

$y = x^3 - 3x + 1$

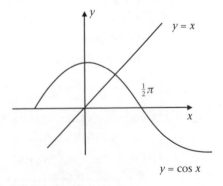

$y = \cos x$

2 The graphs of $y = \cos x$ and $y = x$ intersect where $x \approx 0.7$ (see above). Find this value (correct to 3 s.f.) by using the Newton–Raphson method with f(x) = $x - \cos x$.

3 Find (to 4 s.f.) the root of the equation $x^3 + 4x = 40$.

4 Use the Newton–Raphson method to find the positive root of
$$x^3 + 10x^2 - 73 = 0$$
taking (a) $x = 2$ as the first approximation, (b) $x = 3$ as the first approximation.

5 Find the positive solution of $e^{2x} = 3 \cos x$ correct to 6 decimal places.

6 A circular disc, centre O, is divided by a straight cut AB so that the smaller area ACB is $\frac{1}{10}$ the area of the whole circle.

Show that, if angle AOB $= \theta$ radians, then
$\theta - \frac{1}{5}\pi = \sin \theta$.

Solve the equation and find θ correct to 3 decimal places.

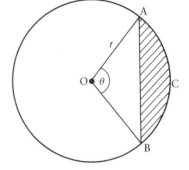

7 Two circles of radius r intersect as shown.

The angle subtended by the common chord at the centre of each circle is 2θ.

(a) Find an expression for the shaded area in terms of r and θ.

(b) If the shaded area is equal to $\frac{1}{4}$ of the area of one of the two circles, show that $8\theta - 4 \sin 2\theta = \pi$ and hence find θ to 4 decimal places.

8 A biologist is investigating models for the growth of a population of bacteria. Model A predicts that the population will be $5000(e^{0.1t} - 1)$ after t hours. Model B predicts that it will be $700(1 + 0.06t)$.

(a) Which model predicts the larger population:
    (i) in the short term,   (ii) in the long term?

(b) At what time do both models predict the same population?

9 Obtain the smallest positive root of each of the following equations to 4 significant figures.

(a) $\tan \theta + \sin \theta = 0.5$ (b) $\sin \theta = \cos^3 \theta$

(c) $2 \sin \theta + \sin 2\theta = \cos \theta$

10 Find both roots of $x^2 - 6x + 4e^{-x} = 0$ to 4 significant figures.

11

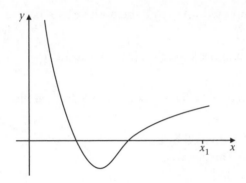

Copy the diagram and draw tangents to show how to construct the approximations x_2, x_3, from the starting value of x_1 given.

Why is Newton–Raphson not appropriate in this case?

12E (a) Use a computer or calculator with function
$f(x) = 30 - 15x - 2x^2 + x^3$ and $x_1 = 5$ to solve the equation
$30 - 15x - 2x^2 + x^3 = 0$.

(b) Do other starting values work? Can you find any that do not?
What happens if $x_1 = 3$, 3.1, 2.8, 2.9?

(c) What range of starting values converges to the root $x = 2$?

(d) What happens when   (i) $x_1 = -0.68$ (ii) $x_1 = -0.69$?

(e) Change the function and solve $5 \cos x - x = 0$ with starting values
(i) $x_1 = -1$ (ii) $x_1 = -0.5$ (iii) $x_1 = -7$ (iv) $x_1 = -6.5$
Comment on your results.

(f) Change the function to $2\sqrt{x} - 1 = 0$. Can you find a suitable
starting point?

After working through this chapter you should

1   understand the mid-ordinate and trapezium rules for estimating
areas and evaluating integrals approximately

2   know the Newton–Raphson method for solving equations.

10 Applications of integration

A Volumes of revolution (answers p. 156)

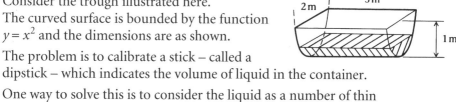

Consider the trough illustrated here.
The curved surface is bounded by the function
$y = x^2$ and the dimensions are as shown.

The problem is to calibrate a stick – called a
dipstick – which indicates the volume of liquid in the container.

One way to solve this is to consider the liquid as a number of thin
horizontal slabs, each of thickness δh.

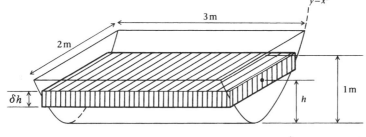

The width of a slab at distance h from the
bottom will be $2\sqrt{h}$, ...

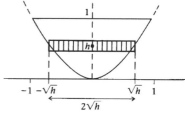

the horizontal cross-sectional area will
be $6\sqrt{h}$, ...

and the volume of the slab will therefore
be $6\sqrt{h}\,\delta h$.

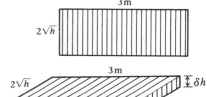

The total volume of the container will be the sum of the volumes of
the thin slabs.

$$\sum 6\sqrt{h}\,\delta h$$

In the limit as $\delta h \to 0$, the exact volume is

$$V = \int_0^1 6\sqrt{h}\,dh$$

$$= \left[4h^{\frac{3}{2}} \right]_0^1$$

$$= 4 \text{ m}^3 \text{ (or 4000 litres)}$$

The (h, V) graph for the container is as shown.

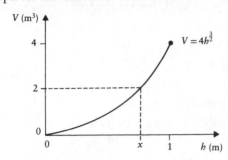

The container is half full at a height x as shown on the graph.

$$V = 4h^{\frac{3}{2}} = 2$$
$$\implies \quad h^{\frac{3}{2}} = \tfrac{1}{2}$$
$$h = (\tfrac{1}{2})^{\frac{2}{3}} \approx 0.63 \text{ m}$$

1   At what depth will the container be
   (a) a quarter full,   (b) three-quarters full?

Another container is shown below.

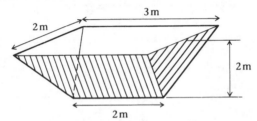

2   Explain why a thin slab at height h will have the dimensions shown below.

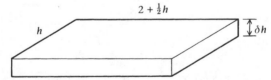

3   Calculate the volume of the container and sketch the (h, V) graph.

4   For what value of h is the container half full?

5   The depth of liquid in the container increases from 1.1 m to 1.4 m. What is the increase in volume?

Whenever the horizontal cross-sectional area of a solid can be expressed as a function of the vertical height, then the volume of the solid can be calculated.

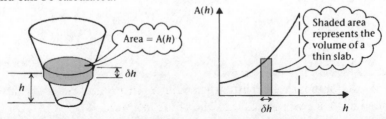

> If $A(h)$ is the cross-sectional area of a solid at height h then the volume is given by
>
> $$V = \int A(h)\, \mathrm{d}h$$

Example 1

A container and a horizontal cross-section are shown below. The depth of liquid increases from $h = 0.6$ m to $h = 1.2$ m. Calculate the increase in volume.

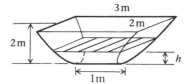
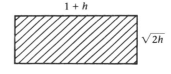

Solution

The horizontal cross-sectional area at depth h is
$(1 + h)\sqrt{2h} = \sqrt{2}(h^{0.5} + h^{1.5})$ m^2.

$$\int_{0.6}^{1.2} (1 + h)\sqrt{2h}\, \mathrm{d}h = \sqrt{2} \int_{0.6}^{1.2} (h^{0.5} + h^{1.5})\, \mathrm{d}h$$

$$= \sqrt{2}\left[\tfrac{2}{3}h^{1.5} + \tfrac{2}{5}h^{2.5} \right]_{0.6}^{1.2}$$

$$= 1.536 \text{ m}^3 \text{ (or 1536 litres)}$$

6 Calculate the volume of the container.

You can apply these ideas when finding the volumes of shapes which are formed by rotating areas. For example, a solid with the same shape as a wine glass can be produced by spinning the area between the graph of $y = x^2$, the line $y = 4$ and the y-axis about the y-axis.

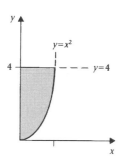

The horizontal cross-sectional areas you would use to calculate the volume of the glass are particularly simple, as they are all circles. Solids formed in such a way are called **solids of revolution**.

7   The graph of $y = x^2$ for $0 \leqslant x \leqslant 2$ is rotated about the x-axis.

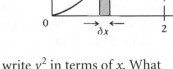

(a) Explain why the volume obtained by rotating the shaded strip is approximately $\pi y^2 \, \delta x$.

(b) If you consider the area as being made up of a large number of thin strips of this kind, the volume is

$$\int_0^2 \pi y^2 \, dx$$

To be able to integrate this you must write y^2 in terms of x. What will this give?

(c) Evaluate the volume.

8   Work out the volumes obtained by rotating each of these shaded areas about the x-axis.

(a)

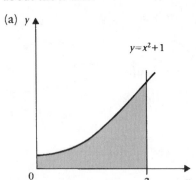

(b)

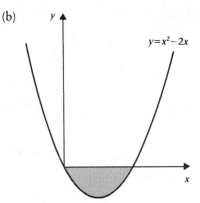

9   Work out the volume obtained by rotating $y = x^2$ for $0 \leqslant y \leqslant 4$ about the y-axis.

Work as in question 7 by first writing down the volume obtained by rotating the shaded strip about the y-axis.

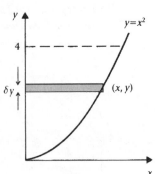

10   Work out the volume obtained by rotating the area bounded by the curve $y = \dfrac{1}{x}$, the y-axis and the lines $y = 1$ and $y = 2$ about the y-axis. (First draw a sketch to show the area being rotated.)

11D | The two shaded areas shown on the graph are equal.

Would you expect the volume generated by rotating area A about the x-axis to be the same as that obtained by rotating B about the y-axis?

Justify your answer.

If the area between $y = f(x)$ and the x-axis for $a < x < b$ is rotated about the x-axis, then the solid formed will have volume

$$V = \pi \int_a^b y^2 \, dx$$

Similarly, if the area between $y = f(x)$ and the y-axis for $c < y < d$ is rotated about the y-axis, then the solid formed will have volume

$$V = \pi \int_c^d x^2 \, dy$$

Example 2

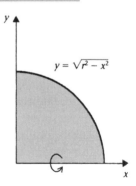

The shaded area shown is part of a circle with centre at the origin and radius r.

Rotate this area about the x-axis and hence prove that the volume of a sphere is given by the formula
$$V = \tfrac{4}{3}\pi r^3$$

Solution

The solid generated will be a hemisphere and its volume is

$$V = \pi \int_0^r y^2 \, dx$$

But $y^2 = r^2 - x^2$

$$\Rightarrow \quad V = \int_0^r r^2 - x^2 \, dx$$

$$= \pi \left[r^2 x - \tfrac{1}{3}x^3 \right]_0^r$$

$$= \tfrac{2}{3}\pi r^3$$

The volume of a sphere is twice the volume of a hemisphere and so the formula is proved.

Exercise A (answers p. 157)

1 Find the volume formed when the area between the curve $y = x^2$, the x-axis and the lines $x = 1$ and $x = 2$ is rotated about the x-axis.

2 The region between the curve $y = 2 - x^2$ and the x- and y-axes is rotated about

(a) the y-axis,   (b) the x-axis.

Find the volumes of the solids formed.

3 Calculate the volumes formed by rotating about the x-axis the areas bounded by

(a) the lines $y = x$, $x = 1$, $x = 2$ and the x-axis

(b) $y = x$ and $y = x^2$

(c) $y = x - x^2$ and $y = 0$

4 Find the points of intersection of the curve $y = x(4 - x)$ and the line $y = 2x$. Find the volume generated when the area enclosed between the curve and the line is rotated through 2π radians about the x-axis.

5 Find an approximation to the volume of the solid of revolution formed when the graph of $y = \tan x$ from $x = 0$ to $x = 1$ is rotated about the x-axis. Use the mid-ordinate or trapezium rule to evaluate the required integral.

B Integration by inspection (answers p. 158)

You have now used integration to find areas and volumes. You also know that to integrate a function you only need to find a function whose derivative is the original function. Unfortunately, this is far from simple in practice, as many functions *cannot* be integrated algebraically. Definite integrals can always be evaluated numerically, but having an algebraic solution is often more convenient and may even be essential in obtaining a complete solution to a problem. When integrating, it is important to know how to choose the best method.

Example 3

Find $\displaystyle\int (\sin 3x - x^2)\, dx$.

Solution

Always try to integrate by inspection first, since this is likely to give the answer more quickly.

$$\int (\sin 3x - x^2)\, dx = -\tfrac{1}{3}\cos 3x - \tfrac{1}{3}x^3 + c$$

Example 4

Find $\displaystyle\int (x^5 - 3x^2)(4x^3 - 3)\,dx$.

Solution

In some cases it is necessary to multiply out brackets first.

$$\int (x^5 - 3x^2)(4x^3 - 3)\,dx = \int (4x^8 - 15x^5 + 9x^2)\,dx$$

$$= \tfrac{4}{9}x^9 - \tfrac{15}{6}x^6 + 3x^3 + c$$

To integrate a function by inspection, you must first think of a function which is likely to differentiate to the original function. You then compare the derived function with the function you want and make any small adjustment as necessary.

Example 5

Find $\displaystyle\int x\,e^{3x^2}\,dx$.

Solution

Differentiating the function e^{3x^2} seems to be a sensible starting point.

$$\frac{d}{dx}(e^{3x^2}) = 6x\,e^{3x^2} \implies \frac{d}{dx}(\tfrac{1}{6}e^{3x^2}) = x\,e^{3x^2}$$

$$\implies \int x\,e^{3x^2}\,dx = \tfrac{1}{6}e^{3x^2} + c$$

1D What functions might you try to differentiate to solve the following integrals?
Find the integrals where possible.

(a) $\displaystyle\int x\cos x^2\,dx$ (b) $\displaystyle\int x\cos 2x\,dx$

(c) $\displaystyle\int \cos 2x\,dx$ (d) $\displaystyle\int \cos x^2\,dx$

The questions above illustrate the difficulty of integration compared with differentiation. In (a) and (b) the function being integrated is the product of two functions. (a) looks more complicated, but proves to be an easy 'backward' chain rule, while (b) requires the product rule and some very clear thinking. (c) and (d) both look straightforward, but (d) cannot be integrated algebraically.

Exercise B (answers p. 158)

1   Find the following.

(a) $\displaystyle\int \cos 3x \, dx$

(b) $\displaystyle\int (x+2)(x-2) \, dx$

(c) $\displaystyle\int e^{5x} \, dx$

(d) $\displaystyle\int \frac{1}{x} \, dx$

2   Write down the derivatives of these.

(a) $\sin x^3$

(b) $\cos 2x^2$

(c) $(x^2 - 3)^3$

3   Use your answers to question 2 to write down the integrals of the following.

(a) $x^2 \cos x^3$

(b) $x \sin 2x^2$

(c) $x(x^2 - 3)^2$

4   The nose-cone of a rocket is obtained by rotating the area between the graph of $y = 3(1 - x^2)$ and the axes about the y-axis.

(a) Draw a sketch showing the area being rotated.

(b) Calculate the volume of the nose-cone.

5   (a) Sketch the parabolas $y^2 = 4x$ and $y^2 = 5x - 4$ on the same axes and find their points of intersection.

(b) A bowl is made by rotating the area enclosed by the curves about the x-axis. Find the volume of the material used to make the bowl.

6   (a) Find the values of the solids formed when the following are rotated about the x-axis.

(i) $y = 2e^{-x}$ for $-1 \leqslant x \leqslant 1$

(ii) $y = \dfrac{2}{\sqrt{x}}$ for $1 \leqslant x \leqslant 4$

(iii) $y = x + \dfrac{1}{x}$ for $\frac{1}{2} \leqslant x \leqslant 2$

(b) Find the volumes of the solids formed when the following are rotated about the y-axis.

(i) $y = \ln(1 + x)$ for $0 \leqslant y \leqslant 2$

(ii) $y = \dfrac{2}{1 + x^2}$ for $1 \leqslant y \leqslant 2$

(iii) $x^2 + y^2 = 25$ for $3 \leqslant y \leqslant 5$

C Integrating trigonometric functions (answers p. 159)

You have seen that not all functions can be integrated algebraically. However, many functions which may look impossible to integrate *can* be integrated if they are first rewritten. The trigonometric identities developed in Chapter 3 are particularly useful.

The following identities are the addition formulas, developed in Chapter 3.

$\sin(A + B) = \sin A \cos B + \cos A \sin B$ ①

$\sin(A - B) = \sin A \cos B - \cos A \sin B$ ②

$\cos(A + B) = \cos A \cos B - \sin A \sin B$ ③

$\cos(A - B) = \cos A \cos B + \sin A \sin B$ ④

These may be used to prove other useful results.

1D Show how you can use the addition formulas to prove the sum and difference formulas.

(a) $2 \cos A \cos B = \cos(A + B) + \cos(A - B)$

(b) $2 \sin A \sin B = -\cos(A + B) + \cos(A - B)$

(c) $2 \sin A \cos B = \sin(A + B) + \sin(A - B)$

2 Use the sum and difference formulas to prove the following.

(a) $2 \cos^2 x = 1 + \cos 2x$

(b) $2 \sin^2 x = 1 - \cos 2x$

(c) $2 \sin x \cos x = \sin 2x$

All of these results, especially the double angle results, are useful in integration.

Example 6

Find $\int \cos^2 x \, dx$.

Solution

The identity $2 \cos^2 x - 1 = \cos 2x$ can be written as $\cos^2 x = \frac{1}{2} + \frac{1}{2} \cos 2x$

$$\Rightarrow \int \cos^2 x \, dx = \int (\tfrac{1}{2} + \tfrac{1}{2} \cos 2x) \, dx$$

$$= \tfrac{1}{2} x + \tfrac{1}{4} \sin 2x + c$$

Example 7

Find $\displaystyle\int \sin 5x \cos 2x \, dx$.

Solution

Using the identity $2 \sin A \cos B = \sin(A + B) + \sin(A - B)$,

$$\int \sin 5x \cos 2x \, dx = \int (\tfrac{1}{2} \sin 7x + \tfrac{1}{2} \sin 3x) \, dx$$

$$= -\tfrac{1}{14} \cos 7x - \tfrac{1}{6} \cos 3x + c$$

Exercise C (answers p. 159)

1   Find the following.

(a) $\displaystyle\int \sin x \cos x \, dx$ (b) $\displaystyle\int \sin 3x \cos 2x \, dx$ (c) $\displaystyle\int \sin x \cos 3x \, dx$

2   Find the following.

(a) $\displaystyle\int \cos 5x \cos x \, dx$ (b) $\displaystyle\int \sin 3x \sin 2x \, dx$ (c) $\displaystyle\int \sin x \sin 4x \, dx$

3   Find $\displaystyle\int_0^{\frac{1}{4}\pi} \cos^2 x \, dx$.

4   Calculate the volume generated by
    rotating the shaded area about the x-axis.

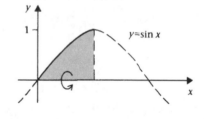

5E Find $\displaystyle\int_0^{\frac{1}{6}\pi} \sin^4 x \, dx$.

(Hint: double angle formulas must be used twice.)

D   Two further integrals

Two important integrals arise from experience of differentiating
inverse functions. In Chapter 6, $\sin^{-1} x$ was differentiated to give
$\dfrac{1}{\sqrt{1 - x^2}}$. In Chapter 8, $\tan^{-1} x$ was differentiated to give $\dfrac{1}{1 + x^2}$.

Similar work gives the following more general results for any non-zero
constant a.

$$\int \frac{1}{\sqrt{a^2 - x^2}} \, dx = \sin^{-1}\left(\frac{x}{a}\right) + c$$

$$\int \frac{1}{a^2 + x^2} \, dx = \frac{1}{a} \tan^{-1}\left(\frac{x}{a}\right) + c$$

Exercise D (answers p. 160)

1   Work out $\displaystyle\int_0^4 \frac{1}{9+x^2}\,dx$ to 3 significant figures using

(a) the trapezium rule with 4 strips, (b) integration.

2   Repeat question 1 for the integral $\displaystyle\int_0^1 \frac{1}{\sqrt{4-x^2}}\,dx$.

3   (a) Obtain values to 3 significant figures of $\displaystyle\int_{-3}^3 \frac{1}{1+x^2}\,dx$ and $\displaystyle\int_{-10}^{10} \frac{1}{1+x^2}\,dx$.

(b) What is the limit of $\displaystyle\int_{-n}^{n} \frac{1}{1+x^2}\,dx$ as n tends to infinity? Illustrate with a sketch graph.

After working through this chapter you should

1   know how to use integration to calculate a volume by

● integrating a cross-sectional area with respect to height,

$$V = \int A(h)\,dh$$

● rotating an area about the x-axis, $V = \pi \displaystyle\int y^2\,dx$

● rotating an area about the y-axis, $V = \pi \displaystyle\int x^2\,dy$

2   know how to integrate a function by inspection

3   know how to use trigonometric identities to rewrite an expression so that it can be integrated by inspection.

11 More integration techniques

A Integration by parts (answers p. 160)

You know that not all functions can be integrated using exact methods and that those that can are not always straightforward. The first technique you should try when searching for an algebraic solution is 'trial and improvement' or 'inspection'. Think of a function which looks as though it might differentiate to the function you need to integrate, then differentiate it and make adjustments as necessary (for example, multiply or divide by a constant). We now develop some standard techniques which often prove useful when 'trial and improvement' fails.

The formula for the product rule for differentiation can be rearranged into a form which is helpful when integrating certain functions.

$$\frac{d}{dx}(uv) = v\frac{du}{dx} + u\frac{dv}{dx} \Rightarrow uv = \int v\frac{du}{dx}dx + \int u\frac{dv}{dx}dx$$

$$\Rightarrow \int u\frac{dv}{dx}dx = uv - \int v\frac{du}{dx}dx$$

This is called the formula for **integration by parts**. It provides an efficient method for integrating some products of functions.

Example 1

Find $\int x\cos 2x\,dx$.

Solution

Let $u = x$, so $\frac{du}{dx} = 1$.

Let $\frac{dv}{dx} = \cos 2x$, so $v = \frac{1}{2}\sin 2x$.

$$\int x\cos 2x\,dx = \frac{1}{2}x\sin 2x - \int \frac{1}{2}\sin 2x\,dx$$

$$= \frac{1}{2}x\sin 2x + \frac{1}{4}\cos 2x + c$$

Integration by parts

$$\int u\frac{dv}{dx}dx = uv - \int v\frac{du}{dx}dx$$

Integration by parts is only applicable to functions written as the *product* of two functions. When using the formula, always start by deciding which part of the product should be u and which should be $\dfrac{dv}{dx}$. Then write down $\dfrac{du}{dx}$ and v. Only when you have the functions u, v, $\dfrac{du}{dx}$ and $\dfrac{dv}{dx}$ clearly written down can you be reasonably sure of substituting correctly into the formula.

1D (a) What happens if, in example 1, you let $u = \cos 2x$ and $\dfrac{dv}{dx} = x$?

(b) What happens if you use integration by parts to find
$$\int x \cos x^2 \, dx\,?$$

Integration by parts will not always prove successful for functions written as the product of two functions. Experience will help you decide when this method will work. The method works for all the functions in the next exercise.

Exercise A (answers p. 160)

1 Find these.

(a) $\displaystyle\int x\,e^x \, dx$ (b) $\displaystyle\int x\,e^{3x} \, dx$ (c) $\displaystyle\int x\,e^{ax} \, dx$

2 Find the following.

(a) $\displaystyle\int x \cos x \, dx$ (b) $\displaystyle\int x \cos 3x \, dx$ (c) $\displaystyle\int x \cos ax \, dx$

3 Use integration by parts twice to evaluate these.

(a) $\displaystyle\int x^2\,e^x \, dx$ (b) $\displaystyle\int x^2 \sin x \, dx$

4 Work out each of these definite integrals. Sketch diagrams to show the areas you have found and check that your answers seem reasonable.

(a) $\displaystyle\int_{-1}^{0} x \sin 2x \, dx$ (b) $\displaystyle\int_{-3}^{0} 2x\,e^{0.5x} \, dx$

5E (a) Find $\displaystyle\int x^2 \ln x \, dx$ using integration by parts with $u = \ln x$, $\dfrac{dv}{dx} = x^2$.

(b) Show that $\dfrac{d}{dx}(x \ln x - x) = \ln x$.

(c) Find $\displaystyle\int x^2 \ln x \, dx$ using integration by parts with $u = x^2$, $\dfrac{dv}{dx} = \ln x$.

B Change of variable in integration (answers p. 161)

Another useful technique of integration can be obtained from the chain rule for differentiation. Essentially this involves replacing a complicated integral with variable x by a simpler one involving a related variable u.

The chain rule has been expressed as $\dfrac{dy}{dx} = \dfrac{dy}{du} \times \dfrac{du}{dx}$.

It can be written in another way as $\dfrac{dy}{du} = \dfrac{dy}{dx} \times \dfrac{dx}{du}$.

Both forms are helpful.

1D If $\dfrac{dy}{dx} = \dfrac{x}{\sqrt{x^2 + 1}}$ and $u = x^2 + 1$, write down an expression for $\dfrac{du}{dx}$ and hence find $\dfrac{dy}{du}$ (a) in terms of x, (b) in terms of u.

Example 2

If $\dfrac{dy}{dx} = x^2(2x + 3)^4$ and $u = 2x + 3$, find $\dfrac{dy}{du}$ in terms of u.

Solution

Since $\dfrac{du}{dx} = 2$, the chain rule gives $x^2(2x + 3)^4 = \dfrac{dy}{du} \times 2$

So $\dfrac{dy}{du} = \tfrac{1}{2}x^2(2x + 3)^4$

Now $u = 2x + 3 \Rightarrow x = \tfrac{1}{2}(u - 3) \Rightarrow x^2 = \tfrac{1}{4}(u^2 - 6u + 9)$

giving $\dfrac{dy}{du} = \tfrac{1}{8}(u^2 - 6u + 9)u^4 = \tfrac{1}{8}u^6 - \tfrac{3}{4}u^5 + \tfrac{9}{8}u^4$.

Exercise B (answers p. 161)

In each question, $\dfrac{dy}{dx}$ is given in terms of x, and a substitution formula is given. In each case find $\dfrac{dy}{du}$ (a) in terms of x, (b) in terms of u.

1 $\dfrac{dy}{dx} = 4x(2x + 1)^3, \quad u = 2x + 1$

2 $\dfrac{dy}{dx} = x\sqrt{\tfrac{1}{2}x + 1}, \quad u = \tfrac{1}{2}x + 1$

3 $\dfrac{dy}{dx} = x\sqrt{\tfrac{1}{2}x + 1}, \quad x = 2u^2 - 2$

4 $\dfrac{dy}{dx} = \sin^3 x \cos x, \quad u = \sin x$

5 $\dfrac{dy}{dx} = \dfrac{x}{(1 + x^2)^2}, \quad u = 1 + x^2$

6 $\dfrac{dy}{dx} = \sqrt{1 - x^2}, \quad u = 1 - x^2$

C Integration by substitution

In exercise B, you started with $\dfrac{dy}{dx}$ in terms of x and transformed the

equation into one for $\dfrac{dy}{du}$ in terms of u. In question 6 this does not

help since the new function cannot be integrated. But it does help

whenever the expression for $\dfrac{dy}{du}$ can be integrated.

Example 2 solution, continued

$\dfrac{dy}{dx} = x^2(2x + 3)^4$ has been transformed to $\dfrac{dy}{du} = \tfrac{1}{8}u^6 - \tfrac{3}{4}u^5 + \tfrac{9}{8}u^4$.

It follows that $y = \tfrac{1}{56}u^7 - \tfrac{1}{8}u^6 + \tfrac{9}{40}u^5 + c$.

In terms of x, this gives

$\displaystyle\int x^2(2x + 3)^4 \, dx = \tfrac{1}{56}(2x + 3)^7 - \tfrac{1}{8}(2x + 3)^6 + \tfrac{9}{40}(2x + 3)^5 + c$

The way we write out the complete process may be streamlined.

$$\frac{dy}{du} = \frac{dy}{dx} \times \frac{dx}{du} \implies y = \int \frac{dy}{dx} \times \frac{dx}{du} \, du \quad \text{but } y = \int \frac{dy}{dx} \, dx$$

> The variable of the integral can be changed from x to u by
>
> replacing 'dx' by '$\dfrac{dx}{du} \, du$'.

Example 3

Find $y = \int x \cos(3x^2 + 5)\, dx$.

Solution

$$u = 3x^2 + 5 \implies \frac{du}{dx} = 6x \qquad \text{This gives } \frac{dx}{du} = \frac{1}{6x}.$$

$$\implies y = \int x \cos(3x^2 + 5) \frac{1}{6x}\, du \qquad \text{Replacing } dx \text{ by } \frac{dx}{du}\, du.$$

$$\implies y = \frac{1}{6} \int \cos(3x^2 + 5)\, du \qquad \text{This cannot be solved as it stands. You must express the integral entirely in terms of the new variable } u.$$

$$\implies y = \frac{1}{6} \int \cos u\, du \quad \text{and so} \quad y = \tfrac{1}{6} \sin u + c = \tfrac{1}{6} \sin(3x^2 + 5) + c$$

You may have been able to solve the integral in this example by inspection. While using substitution is not wrong in such a case, it is unnecessarily complicated. Substitution only works for some functions and even then it is sometimes no more than a rather slow method for finding integrals which can be found by inspection. However, there are many cases where it considerably simplifies the integral.

It is important to choose the right substitution when using this method of integration. All the integrals in the exercise below lend themselves to integration by substitution, although you may feel that some of them could be done by inspection. Others respond equally well to integration by parts.

Remember that, whatever substitution you make, your final solution must be in terms of the original variable.

Exercise C (answers p. 161)

1   Evaluate the following integrals by using the suggested substitution.

(a) $\int (x + 3)^5\, dx$ (let $u = x + 3$)   (b) $\int x(2x - 5)^6\, dx$ (let $u = 2x - 5$)

(c) $\int x^2(x - 2)^7\, dx$ (let $u = x - 2$)   (d) $\int x(x^2 - 4)^8\, dx$ (let $u = x^2 - 4$)

(e) $\int x^2\sqrt{x^3 - 2}\, dx$ (let $u = x^3 - 2$)

2   Integrate the following functions using the suggested substitutions.

(a) $\sin^2 x \cos x$ (let $u = \sin x$)   (b) $\cos^2 x \sin x$ (let $u = \cos x$)

3 Integrate the following functions using a suitable substitution.

(a) $x^2\sqrt{x^3 + 3}$ (b) $x(x - 3)^5$ (c) $x\sqrt{x - 2}$

(d) $\cos x \sin^3 x$ (e) $\cos^5 x \sin x$ (f) $\dfrac{x}{(x + 2)^3}$

4 Evaluate $\displaystyle\int_0^2 x^2(x - 1)^6 \, dx$.

5 Evaluate $\displaystyle\int x(2x + 1)^3 \, dx$

(a) using integration by parts, (b) using the substitution $u = 2x + 1$. Show that the two answers are consistent.

D Definite integrals (answers p. 162)

In exercise C you probably found $\displaystyle\int_0^2 x^2(x - 1)^6 \, dx$ by converting back to x before evaluating the limits. There is a more elegant way of evaluating a definite integral, and that is to substitute the limits at the same time as you substitute the function.

Example 4

Evaluate $\displaystyle\int_0^2 x^3(x^2 + 5)^4 \, dx$.

Solution

Start by writing the integral, emphasising that the limits are values of x.

$$I = \int_{x=0}^{x=2} x^3(x^2 + 5)^4 \, dx$$

Let $u = x^2 + 5$. Then $\dfrac{du}{dx} = 2x$.

This gives $\quad \dfrac{dx}{du} = \dfrac{1}{2x}$

$$\implies \quad I = \int_{x=0}^{x=2} x^3(x^2 + 5)\frac{1}{2x} \, du \quad \text{replacing } dx \text{ by } \frac{dx}{du} \, du$$

$$= \int_{x=0}^{x=2} \tfrac{1}{2}x^2(x^2 + 5)^4 \, du \qquad .$$

Now make the substitutions:

$$u = x^2 + 5 \implies x^2 = u - 5$$

$$x = 0 \implies u = 5$$

$$x = 2 \implies u = 9$$

$$I = \int_{u=5}^{u=9} \tfrac{1}{2}(u-5)u^4 \, du$$

$$= \int_{u=5}^{u=9} \tfrac{1}{2}(u^5 - 5u^4) \, du$$

$$= \tfrac{1}{2}\left[\tfrac{1}{6}u^6 - u^5 \right]_5^9$$

$$= \tfrac{1}{2}[(\tfrac{1}{6}\times 9^6 - 9^5) - (\tfrac{1}{6}\times 5^6 - 5^5)]$$

$$= \frac{180\,272}{12} = 15\,022\tfrac{3}{4}$$

1   Evaluate $\displaystyle\int_0^2 x^2(x-1)^6 \, dx$ by this method and check that you get the same answer as before.

Exercise D (answers p. 162)

1   Using the suggested substitutions, integrate the following.

(a) $\displaystyle\int_1^3 x(x-1)^4 \, dx$, $u = x - 1$ (b) $\displaystyle\int_0^2 2x\sqrt{1+x} \, dx$, $u = 1 + x$

(c) $\displaystyle\int_0^4 (1+x)\sqrt{3x+1} \, dx$, $u = 3x+1$ (d) $\displaystyle\int_0^2 \frac{1-x}{(1+x)^4} \, dx$, $u = 1 + x$

E   Integrating $\dfrac{1}{x}$ (answers p. 162)

You know that $\dfrac{d}{dx}(\ln x) = \dfrac{1}{x}$; it follows that

$$\int_a^b \frac{1}{x} \, dx = \left[\ln x \right]_a^b = \ln b - \ln a$$

This is correct for positive a and b; negative values, however, present a problem.

$$\int_{-2}^{-\frac{1}{2}} \frac{1}{x} \, dx \neq \ln(-\tfrac{1}{2}) - \ln(-2)$$

since $\ln x$ is only defined for $x > 0$. Check that your calculator shows an error if you enter $\ln(-2)$.

The integral has a meaning and the symmetry of the $\dfrac{1}{x}$ graph gives

$$\int_{-2}^{-\frac{1}{2}} \frac{1}{x} \, dx = -\int_{\frac{1}{2}}^2 \frac{1}{x} \, dx = -(\ln 2 - \ln \tfrac{1}{2}) = \ln \tfrac{1}{2} - \ln 2$$

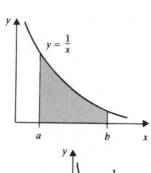

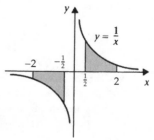

Notice that this is $\left[\ln|x|\right]_{-2}^{-\frac{1}{2}}$.

In general, we have $\displaystyle\int_a^b \frac{1}{x}\,dx = \left[\ln|x|\right]_a^b = \ln|b| - \ln|a|$ *for a, b ≠ 0 and*

both positive or both negative.

Any integral where *a, b* have opposite signs like

$\displaystyle\int_{-1}^2 \frac{1}{x}\,dx$ cannot be evaluated because it

consists of two parts, both infinite in area.
A function can only be integrated if it is
continuous over the interval of the integration.

An important generalisation follows.

1 Use the substitution $u = 3x^2 + 1$ to evaluate $\displaystyle\int \frac{6x}{3x^2+1}\,dx$.

Any integral of the form $\displaystyle\int \frac{f'(x)}{f(x)}\,dx$ can be reduced to the form $\displaystyle\int \frac{1}{u}\,du$

by the substitution $u = f(x)$.

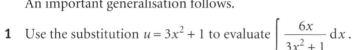

If the graph of $f(x)$ is continuous (between *a* and *b*) then

$$\int \frac{f'(x)}{f(x)}\,dx = \ln|f(x)| + c \qquad \text{or} \qquad \int_a^b \frac{f'(x)}{f(x)}\,dx = \left[\ln|f(x)|\right]_a^b$$

where $|f(x)|$ denotes the absolute value of $f(x)$.

Sometimes the integral needs to be rewritten slightly to be in the
correct form, as in the following example.

Example 5

Find   (a) $\displaystyle\int \frac{3}{2x-5}\,dx$ (b) $\displaystyle\int \frac{x}{1+x^2}\,dx$ (c) $\displaystyle\int \tan x\,dx$

Solution

(a) $\displaystyle\int \frac{3}{2x-5}\,dx = \frac{3}{2}\int \frac{2}{2x-5}\,dx = \frac{3}{2}\ln|2x-5| + c$

(b) $\displaystyle\int \frac{x}{1+x^2}\,dx = \frac{1}{2}\int \frac{2x}{1+x^2}\,dx = \frac{1}{2}\ln|x^2+1| + c$

(c) $\displaystyle\int \tan x\,dx = \int \frac{\sin x}{\cos x}\,dx = -\int \frac{(-\sin x)}{\cos x}\,dx = -\ln|\cos x| + c$

In (b), the modulus signs are unnecessary since $x^2 + 1$ is always
positive.

Exercise E (answers p. 162)

1 Find   (a) $\displaystyle\int \frac{3}{x-2}\,dx$ (b) $\displaystyle\int \frac{6}{2x+7}\,dx$ (c) $\displaystyle\int \frac{1}{3x-1}\,dx$

2 Evaluate   (a) $\displaystyle\int_{1}^{2} \frac{2}{3x-2}\,dx$ (b) $\displaystyle\int_{-2}^{-1} \frac{2}{3x-2}\,dx$

3 Explain why you cannot evaluate $\displaystyle\int_{1}^{4} \frac{3}{x-2}\,dx$.

4 Show the following.

(a) $\displaystyle\int \tan x\,dx = \ln |\sec x| + c$ (b) $\displaystyle\int \cot x\,dx = \ln |\sin x| + c$

5 Find the following.

(a) $\displaystyle\int \frac{x^2}{4-x^3}\,dx$ (b) $\displaystyle\int \frac{2x}{3+x^2}\,dx$

(c) $\displaystyle\int \frac{1}{x\ln x}\,dx$ (d) $\displaystyle\int \frac{\sin x}{1+\cos x}\,dx$

6 Write $\ln\left|\dfrac{x-1}{x+1}\right|$ as $\ln|x-1| - \ln|x+1|$ and then differentiate. Hence

show that $\displaystyle\int \frac{1}{x^2-1}\,dx = \frac{1}{2}\ln\left|\frac{x-1}{x+1}\right| + c$.

7 (a) Show that $\displaystyle\int \frac{1}{x^2-a^2}\,dx = \frac{1}{2a}\ln\left|\frac{x-a}{x+a}\right| + c$.

(b) Show that $\displaystyle\int_{2}^{3} \frac{1}{x^2-16}\,dx = -\frac{1}{8}\ln \frac{7}{3}$.

(c) Compare your answer to (b) with that given by the mid-ordinate rule with 5 strips. Work to 4 decimal places.

8 A solid of revolution is formed by rotating the region under the graph

of $y = \dfrac{1}{\sqrt{1-x^2}}$ between $x = -\frac{1}{2}$ and $x = \frac{1}{2}$ about the x-axis.

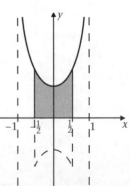

(a) Find the area of the region (shown shaded in the diagram).

(b) Find the volume of the solid.

(c) Do quick rough checks to show that your answers are reasonable.

F Integration practice

As with differentiation, you can now integrate a wide variety of functions, but you again need practice in using your skills and choosing which technique to use.

Here are some standard results (in which $a > 0$ and the constant of integration has been omitted) together with a few examples where integrals can be done by inspection.

$f(x)$	$\int f(x)\,dx$
$x^n (n \neq -1)$	$\dfrac{1}{n+1} x^{n+1}$
$\dfrac{1}{x}$	$\ln|x|$
e^x	e^x
$\sin x$	$-\cos x$
$\cos x$	$\sin x$
$\tan x$	$-\ln|\cos x|$
$\dfrac{1}{\sqrt{a^2 - x^2}}$	$\sin^{-1}\left(\dfrac{x}{a}\right)$
$\dfrac{1}{a^2 + x^2}$	$\dfrac{1}{a} \tan^{-1}\left(\dfrac{x}{a}\right)$
$\dfrac{1}{x^2 - a^2}$	$\dfrac{1}{2a} \ln\left|\dfrac{x-a}{x+a}\right|$
$(2x+7)^4$	$\frac{1}{10}(2x+7)^5$
$x(x^2 - 3)^6$	$\frac{1}{14}(x^2 - 3)^7$
$2e^{5x}$	$\frac{2}{5}e^{5x}$
$3\cos 4x$	$\frac{3}{4}\sin 4x$
$\dfrac{x+1}{x^2 + 2x - 5}$	$\frac{1}{2}\ln|x^2 + 2x - 5|$

Exercise F (answers p. 163)

Integrate the following.

1 $\dfrac{2}{3x+1}$ **2** $(1-5x)^3$ **3** $2x(1-x^2)^3$

4 $x(1-5x)^3$ **5** $(e^{2x}-3)^2$ **6** $\dfrac{1}{4+x^2}$

7 $\dfrac{x}{4+x^2}$ **8** $\dfrac{x}{\sqrt{4+x^2}}$ **9** $\dfrac{x}{(4+x^2)^2}$

10 $x^2\sin x$ **11** $x\,e^{-3x}$ **12** $\dfrac{x}{\sqrt{3-x}}$

13 $\tan 5x$ **14** $\cos^2\tfrac{1}{2}x$ **15** $(\cos x+\sin x)^2$

16 $\dfrac{x}{(x-9)^2}$ **17** $\dfrac{x}{x^2-9}$ **18** $\dfrac{9}{x^2-9}$

19 $\dfrac{2x+3}{x^2-9}$ **20** $\dfrac{3}{\sqrt{9-x^2}}$ **21** $\dfrac{3x}{\sqrt{9-x^2}}$

After working through this chapter you should

1   understand how to use the technique of integration by parts

2   know how integration by parts and the product rule for differentiation are related

3   understand how to use the technique of substitution for integration

4   know how integration by substitution and the chain rule for differentiation are related

5   understand why it is necessary to use the absolute value of the function in the result

$$\int \frac{f'(x)}{f(x)}\,dx = \ln|\,f(x)\,| + c$$

6   be familiar with the standard integrals listed in section F.

Answers

1 Iterative processes

A Inductive definition (p. 1)

1. (a) $u_1 = 1$, $u_4 = 19$

   (b) $u_5 = 25$, $u_5 = u_4 + 6$

   (c) $u_{i+1} = u_i + 6$

2. (a) 14, 23, 32, 41

   (b) $t_{20} = 5 + (19 \times 9) = 175$

3. (a) $u_1 = -5$, $u_2 = -7$, $u_3 = -9$, $u_4 = -11$,
   $u_5 = -13$
   $u_{20} = -5 + (19 \times 2) = 33$

   (b) $u_1 = 2$, $u_2 = 3 \times 2 = 6$, $u_3 = 3 \times 6 = 18$,
   $u_4 = 3 \times 18 = 54$, $u_5 = 3 \times 54 = 162$
   $u_{20} = 3^{19} \times 2 \approx 2.3 \times 10^9$

   Note how *multiplying* by 3 gives a
   rapid increase in magnitude.

   (c) $u_1 = 2$, $u_2 = -4$, $u_3 = 8$, $u_4 = -16$,
   $u_5 = 32$
   $u_{20} = -2^{19} \times 2 = -2^{20} \approx -1.05 \times 10^6$

   (d) $u_1 = 5$, $u_2 = \frac{1}{5}$, $u_3 = 5$, $u_4 = \frac{1}{5}$, $u_5 = 5$,
   $u_{20} = \frac{1}{5}$

   The sequence oscillates.

4E. If $u_1 = u_2 = 1$ the Fibonacci sequence 1, 1,
   2, 3, 5, 8, 13, ... is obtained. Otherwise, a
   similar sequence where each term is the
   sum of the two preceding terms is
   obtained.

5. 0, 2, 6, 12, 20, 30

6. $u_i = i u_{i-1}$

Exercise A (p. 2)

1. $u_1 = 4$, $u_2 = 8$, $u_3 = 16$, $u_4 = 32$, $u_5 = 64$

2. (a) $u_1 = -3$, $u_2 = -2$, $u_3 = \frac{-4}{3}$, $u_4 = \frac{-8}{9}$

   (b) $u_1 = 2$, $u_2 = \frac{1}{4}$, $u_3 = 16$, $u_4 = \frac{1}{256}$

   (c) $u_1 = 1$, $u_2 = -5$, $u_3 = 1$, $u_4 = -5$

3. The sequence is 1, 2, 0.5, 4, 0.125, 32,
   0.0039, 8192.3, ...

   Odd terms approach zero, whilst the even
   terms become very large.

4. (a) $u_1 = 1$, $u_{i+1} = \frac{1}{3} u_i$

   (b) $u_1 = 1$, $u_{i+1} = (-\frac{1}{3}) u_i$

B The general term (p. 3)

1. (a) $s_{50} = 300$

   (b) The inductive method requires every
   term in turn to be calculated, in this
   case a further forty-nine terms!

2. Each term is 1.1 times the previous term, so
   $t_2 = 2 \times 1.1$
   $t_3 = (2 \times 1.1) \times 1.1 = 2 \times 1.1^2$
   $t_4 = (2 \times 1.1 \times 1.1) \times 1.1 = 2 \times 1.1^3$
   To obtain t_n, t_1 must be multiplied by 1.1 a
   total of $n - 1$ times. Therefore,
   $t_n = 2 \times 1.1^{n-1}$.

3. $u_1 = (-1)^1 \frac{1}{1} = -1$, $u_2 = (-1)^2 \frac{1}{4} = \frac{1}{4}$,
   $u_3 = (-1)^3 \frac{1}{9} = -\frac{1}{9}$, $u_4 = (-1)^4 \frac{1}{16} = \frac{1}{16}$ and
   so on.

   The $(-1)^i$ causes the sign to change for
   alternate terms.

4. $u_1 = 0$, $u_2 = 1$, $u_3 = 3$, $u_4 = 6$,
   $u_{i+1} = u_i + i$

5. $u_1 = 1$, $u_2 = 2$, $u_3 = 6$, $u_4 = 24$
   $u_{i+1} = (i+1) u_i$

Exercise B (p. 4)

1. (a) $i = 1$: $u_1 = 3 \times 1 + 2 = 5$
   $i = 2$: $u_2 = 3 \times 2 + 2 = 8$
   $u_3 = 3 \times 3 + 2 = 11$
   $u_4 = 3 \times 4 + 2 = 14$
   $u_5 = 3 \times 5 + 2 = 17$

   (b) $u_1 = 5 \times 2^1 = 10$, $u_2 = 5 \times 2^2 = 20$,
   $u_3 = 5 \times 2^3 = 40$, $u_4 = 80$, $u_5 = 160$

   (c) $u_1 = 3 \times 1^2 = 3$, $u_2 = 3 \times 2^2 = 12$,
   $u_3 = 27$, $u_4 = 48$, $u_5 = 75$

   (d) $u_1 = 10 - 1 = 9$, $u_2 = 10 - 2 = 8$, $u_3 = 7$,
   $u_4 = 6$, $u_5 = 5$

   (e) $u_1 = 10 - (\frac{1}{2})^1 = 9\frac{1}{2}$, $u_2 = 10 - (\frac{1}{2})^2 = 9\frac{3}{4}$,
   $u_3 = 9\frac{7}{8}$, $u_4 = 9\frac{15}{16}$, $u_5 = 9\frac{31}{32}$

   (f) $u_1 = 10 + (\frac{1}{2})^1 = 10\frac{1}{2}$, $u_2 = 10 + (\frac{1}{2})^2 = 10\frac{1}{4}$,
   $u_3 = 10\frac{1}{8}$, $u_4 = 10\frac{1}{16}$, $u_5 = 10\frac{1}{32}$

2 (a) (i) $-1, 1, -1, 1, -1$

(ii) $1, -1, 1, -1, 1$

(iii) $-1, 1, -1, 1, -1$

(iv) $-1, 2, -4, 8, -16$

(b) (i) $u_i = 4 \times (-1)^{i+1}$

(ii) $u_i = 4 \times (-1)^i$

3

	5	6	Term 9	100	i
A	14	17	26	299	$3i-1$
B	32	64	512	2^{100}	2^i
C	$\frac{1}{6}$	$\frac{1}{7}$	$\frac{1}{10}$	$\frac{1}{101}$	$\frac{1}{i+1}$
D	-5	6	-9	100	$(-1)^i i$
E	5	-6	9	-100	$(-1)^{i+1} i$
F	10	-12	18	-200	$(-1)^{i+1} 2i$
G	25	-36	81	$-10\,000$	$(-1)^{i+1} i^2$

4 General term is $100 \times 1.2^{n-1}$.
$100 \times 1.2^{n-1} = 900 \Rightarrow n \approx 13$
The surveyor has observed the 13th day of digging.

5 General term is $f_1 \times 1.15^{n-1}$, where f_1 is the initial house price.

$$f_1 \times 1.15^{n-1} = 2f_1 \Rightarrow n = \frac{\ln 2}{\ln 1.15} + 1 = 5.95$$

House prices will double in a little under 6 years.

C Mortgages, loans and depreciation
(p. 5)

			£
1	YEAR ONE:	Initial loan	40 000
		Interest	4 000
		Total debt	44 000
		Repayments 12 @ £395	4 740
		Outstanding balance	39 260
	YEAR TWO:	Loan outstanding	39 260
		Interest	3 926
		Total debt	43 186
		Repayments 12 @ £395	4 740
		Outstanding balance	38 446

2 (a) $L_1 = 40\,000$

(b) $L_{n+1} = L_n \times 1.1 - 4740$

3D L_{20} is negative, so the mortgage will be completed during its 20th year.

4 24 years.

5 After three years the final debt is

$(40\,000 \times 1.1^2 - 4740(1.1 + 1)) \times 1.1 - 4740$
$= 40\,000 \times 1.1^3 - 4740(1.1^2 + 1.1 + 1)$

After four years the final debt is

$(40\,000 \times 1.1^3 - 4740(1.1^2 + 1.1 + 1))$
$\qquad\qquad\qquad \times 1.1 - 4740$
$= 40\,000 \times 1.1^4 - 4740(1.1^3 + 1.1^2 + 1.1 + 1)$

6 (a) $\sum_{i=1}^{n} 1.1^{i-1}$ is a geometric progression (G.P.) with first term 1 and common ratio 1.1. The sum of n terms of this G.P. is

$$1 \times \frac{1.1^n - 1}{1.1 - 1} = \frac{1.1^n - 1}{1.1 - 1}$$

(b) $40\,000 \times 1.1^n - 4740 \times \dfrac{1.1^n - 1}{0.1}$

$= 40\,000 \times 1.1^n - 47\,400 \times (1.1^n - 1)$
$= 47\,400 - 7400 \times 1.1^n$

7E Let p be the monthly payment.
After 1 year, the final debt is

$$50\,000 \times 1.11 - 12p$$

After 2 years the final debt is

$$50\,000 \times 1.11^2 - 12p(1.11 + 1)$$

After 3 years the final debt is

$$50\,000 \times 1.11^3 - 12p(1.11^2 + 1.11 + 1)$$

After 25 years the final debt is

$50\,000 \times 1.11^{25} - 12p(1.11^{24}$
$\qquad\qquad + 1.11^{23} + \dots + 1.11 + 1)$

$= 50\,000 \times 1.11^{25} - 12p \sum_{i=1}^{25} 1.1^{i-1}$

$= 50\,000 \times 1.11^{25} - 12p \dfrac{(1.11^{25} - 1)}{0.11}$

Since the debt is reduced to zero,

$50\,000 \times 1.11^{25} - 12p \dfrac{(1.11^{25} - 1)}{0.11} = 0$

$\Rightarrow 50\,000 \times 1.11^{25} = 12p \dfrac{(1.11^{25} - 1)}{0.11}$

$\Rightarrow 5500 \times 1.11^{25} = 12p(1.11^{25} - 1)$

$\Rightarrow \dfrac{5500 \times 1.11^{25}}{12(1.11^{25} - 1)} = p$

$\Rightarrow p = 494.751\,008\,6$

A monthly payment of £494.76 is required.

Exercise C (p. 6)

1 (a) £8695.75

 (b) £3038.59

 (c) $v_n = 0.85^n \times 9995 + 200$
$$\times 0.85^{n-1} + \dots + 200$$
$$= 0.85^n \times 9995 + 200 \sum_{i=1}^{n} 0.85^{i-1}$$
$$= 0.85^n \times 9995 + 200 \frac{(1 - 0.85^n)}{1 - 0.85}$$
$$= 0.85^n \times 9995 + 200 \frac{(1 - 0.85^n)}{0.15}$$
$$= 0.85^n \times 9995 + 4000 \frac{(1 - 0.85^n)}{3}$$

 (d) As $n \to \infty$, $0.85^n \to 0$
$$\Rightarrow v_n \to \frac{4000}{3} = 1333.33$$
The limit is £1333.

2 (a) $u_{n+1} = 1.0075 u_n - 150$

 (b) 30 months

 (c) Final payment
= £150 − £20.35 = £129.65
Total = 29 × £150 + £129.65 = £4479.65

3 $4000 \times 1.0075^{60} - x \sum_{i=1}^{60} 1.0075^{i-1}$
$$= 4000 \times 1.0075^{60} - \frac{x(1.0075^{60} - 1)}{1.0075 - 1}$$

The loan will be repaid at the end of the 60 months, so
$$\frac{x(1.0075^{60} - 1)}{1.0075 - 1} = 4000 \times 1.0075^{60}$$
$$\Rightarrow x(1.0075^{60} - 1) = 30 \times 1.0075^{60}$$
$$\Rightarrow x = \frac{30 \times 1.0075^{60}}{1.0075^{60} - 1} = 83.033\ 420\ 91$$

Her monthly payments need to be £83.04.

D Convergent sequences (p. 7)

1 1.5, 1.6667, 1.6, 1.625, 1.6154

2 1.6190, 1.6176, 1.6182, 1.6180, 1.6181, 1.6180

3 $x = \dfrac{1}{x} + 1 \Rightarrow x^2 = 1 + x \Rightarrow x^2 - x - 1 = 0$

4 $\frac{1}{2}(1 + \sqrt{5}) = 1.618\ 033\ 989$

Exercise D (p. 7)

1 (a) $u_9 = 0.347\ 296\ 699$,
$u_{10} = 0.347\ 296\ 396$

 (b) 0.347 296 (to 6 d.p.)
$x = 0.347\ 296$
$$\Rightarrow x^3 - 3x + 1 \approx 9 \times 10^{-7} \approx 0$$

2 $x = \sqrt{20/x} \Rightarrow x^2 = 20/x \Rightarrow x^3 = 20$
To 5 d.p., $u_9 = 2.715\ 48$, $u_{10} = 2.713\ 89$
$\sqrt[3]{10} = 2.714\ 42$

3 $u_4 = 2.645\ 751\ 312$, $u_5 = 2.645\ 751\ 311$

The sequence converges very rapidly to $\sqrt{7}$. This method for finding square roots was given by the third-century Greek mathematician Heron.

4 6.25, 2.56, 15.26, 0.43

The sequence *diverges*.

E Iterative formulas for solving equations (p. 8)

1D (a) $x_4 = 3.189\ 0(58\ 983)$

 (b) $x_5 = 3.191\ 6(60\ 311)$
$x_6 = 3.192\ 3(41\ 14)$
$x_7 = 3.192\ 5(19\ 281)$
$x_8 = 3.192\ 5(65\ 889)$
$x_9 = 3.192\ 5(78\ 083)$
So the solution is 3.193 to 3 decimal places.
You can stop when two successive terms agree to 4 decimal places.

 (c) There is little point in recording more than 4 or 5 decimal places if only 3 are required in the final answer.

Exercise E (p. 9)

1 (a) $2x^2 = 5x - 1$
$$x^2 = \frac{5x - 1}{2}$$
$$x = \sqrt{\frac{5x - 1}{2}}$$

 (b) $5x = 2x^2 + 1$
$$x = \frac{1 + 2x^2}{5}$$

 (c) $2x^2 = 5x - 1$
$$2x = 5 - \frac{1}{x}$$
$$x = \frac{1}{2}\left(5 - \frac{1}{x}\right)$$

(d) $5x - 2x^2 = 1$

   $x(5 - 2x) = 1$

   $$x = \frac{1}{5 - 2x}$$

(e) Not possible

(f) $2x^2 - 4x - x + 1 = 0$

   $2x^2 - 4x + 1 = x$

2 (a) (i) $x^3 = 10 \Rightarrow x^2 = \dfrac{10}{x}$

   $$\Rightarrow x = \sqrt{\frac{10}{x}}$$

   (ii) $x_1 = 2$, $x_2 = 2.236\,067\,977$,

   $x = 2.15\,443$ to 5 decimal places

   (b) (i) $x^3 = 10 \Rightarrow x^4 = 10x$

   $$\Rightarrow x^2 = \sqrt{10x}$$

   $$\Rightarrow = \sqrt{\sqrt{10x}}$$

   (ii) $x_1 = 2$, $x_2 = 2.114\,742\,527$,

   $x = 2.154\,43$ to 5 decimal places

   In part (b) the convergence to the solution
   is much faster.

3 Using the iterative formula $x_{i+1} = \frac{1}{3}(2^{x_i})$

   $x_1 = 3$

   $x_2 = 2.\dot{6}$

   $x = 0.4578$ to 4 decimal places

4 (a) [3, 4]

   (b) $x^2 - 1 = 6\sqrt{x}$

   $$\Rightarrow x^2 = 6\sqrt{x} + 1$$

   $$\Rightarrow x = \sqrt{6\sqrt{x} + 1}$$

   (c) With $x_1 = 3$, $x_2 = 3.375\,25$ and
   $x = 3.495\,358$ to 6 decimal places.

5 (b) $x^3 + 2x - 1 = 0$

   $$\Rightarrow 2x = 1 - x^3$$

   $$\Rightarrow x = \frac{1}{2}(1 - x^3)$$

   (c) (i) 0.453 40   (ii) 0.453 40

   (d) $x_1 = 2$ gives $x_2 = -3.5$, $x_3 = 21.9$,
   $x_4 = -5278$

   The sequence diverges and $x_1 = 2$ is
   clearly an unsuitable starting value.

6 (b) (i) $x_1 = 0$ would give $\sqrt{\dfrac{-1}{2}}$, which
   cannot be found.

   (ii) $x_1 = 1$ gives 2.280 776 after 27
   iterations.

   $x_1 = 2$ gives 2.280 776 after 24
   iterations.

   $x_1 = 10$ gives 2.280 776 after 30
   iterations.

(c) $x_1 = 1$ gives 2.280 776 after 8
   iterations.

   $x_1 = 2$ gives 2.280 776 after 7
   iterations.

   $x_1 = 10$ gives 2.280 776 after 10
   iterations.

(d) $x_1 = 1$ gives 0.219 224 after 11
   iterations.

   $x_1 = 2$ gives 0.219 224 after 14
   iterations.

   $x_1 = 3$ diverges.

(e) The iterations in (b) and (c) converge
   to the root in the interval [2, 3] but
   not to the root in [0, 1], even with a
   starting value of 1.

   The convergence in (b) is very slow.

   The iteration in (d) will converge to
   the root in [0, 1] but not to the one in
   [2, 3].

F Convergence (p. 10)

1 (a) $\sqrt[3]{8} = 2$ so $\sqrt[3]{10} \approx 2.1$

   (b) $x^3 = 10 \Rightarrow x = \dfrac{10}{x^2}$

$x_1 = 2.1$	$x_2 = 2.267\,57$
$x_3 = 1.944\,81$	$x_4 = 2.6439$
$x_5 = 1.430\,57$	$x_6 = 4.886\,33$
$x_7 = 0.418\,83$	$x_8 = 57.0073$
$x_9 = 0.003\,08$	$x_{10} = 1\,056\,139$

   Odd terms form a subsequence
   tending to zero, but even terms
   increase without limit. Other starting
   values will give a similar pattern. The
   sequence does not converge.

2 (b) (x_1, x_2) is the point on the graph of

   $y = \dfrac{10}{x^2}$ located by moving vertically

   from (x_1, x_1). (x_2, x_2) is the point on
   the line $y = x$ located by moving
   horizontally from (x_1, x_2).

   This method can be continued to
   generate further approximations. It
   can be described geometrically.

   **Move vertically from the line to the
   curve, then move horizontally from
   the curve to the line. Repeat
   indefinitely.**

3 The diagram illustrates that the sequence diverges *away* from the root.

4 (a)

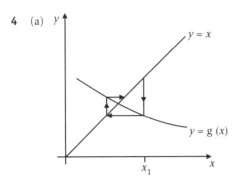

(b) The sequence converges.

5 (a) The sequence converges to the root, whichever side of the root x_1 is on.

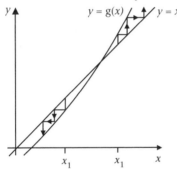

(b) The sequence diverges from the root, whichever side of the root x_1 is on.

6 A cobweb diagram is obtained if $g(x)$ is decreasing and a staircase diagram is obtained if $g(x)$ is increasing.

7 A rearrangement will converge to a root α if $g'(\alpha)$ lies between -1 and $+1$. In practice, since α is unknown, it is necessary to ensure that $g'(\alpha)$ lies between -1 and $+1$ on an interval which contains the root.

8 (a) $x^3 = 10 \Rightarrow x = \dfrac{10}{x^2}$

$\Rightarrow 3x = 2x + \dfrac{10}{x^2}$

$\Rightarrow x = \dfrac{1}{3}\left(2x + \dfrac{10}{x^2}\right)$

(b) The gradient of $y = \dfrac{1}{3}\left(2x + \dfrac{10}{x^2}\right)$ is zero when $x = \sqrt[3]{10}$, so the sequence converges very rapidly. See also exercise D, question 3.

Exercise F (p. 13)

1

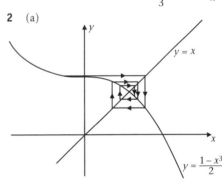

2 (a)

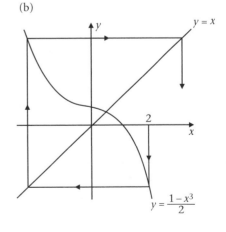

(b)

3 (a) $f'(x) = \dfrac{1}{2x^2}$, $f'(2.28) \approx 0.096$

$g'(x) = \dfrac{4x}{5}$, $g'(0.219) \approx 0.175$

Both the corresponding iterations converge quite rapidly since these gradients are small. The first is quicker, as question 6 did indeed show.

(b) A gradient of 0.55 is acceptable (less than 1) but (for example) 10 steps will only reduce the error by a factor of approximately 0.55^{10}, i.e. 0.0025.

4 (a) $x = \frac{1}{4}e^x \Longrightarrow 4x = e^x \Longrightarrow x = \ln(4x)$

(b) 0.3574, 2.1533

(c)

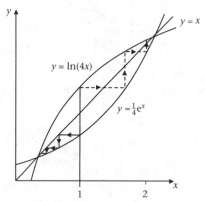

The functions are inverses of each other so the graphs are mirror images in $y = x$.

5 (a) When $t = 8$, $8t = 64$ and $120(1 - e^{-0.1t_i}) = 66$

(b) $t_1 = 8$, $t_{i+1} = 15(1 - e^{-0.1t_i})$ has a limit of 8.74 (to 2 d.p.)

6 Area of sector OACB = $\frac{1}{2}r^2\theta$
Area of triangle AOB = $\frac{1}{2}r^2 \sin\theta$
Area of segment ACB = $\frac{1}{2}r^2\theta - \frac{1}{2}r^2 \sin\theta$,
which equals $\frac{1}{8} \times \pi r^2$.
Hence $\theta = \sin + \frac{1}{4}\pi$.
Try taking $\theta_1 = 2$, $\theta_{i+1} = \sin\theta_i + \frac{1}{4}\pi$.
This gives a convergent sequence with limit 1.766 (to 3 d.p.).

2   Circles, tangents and normals

A   The equation of a circle (p. 15)

1 (a) $\sqrt{3^2 + 3^2} = \sqrt{18}$
(b) 5

2 (a) $(4, 3)$, $(-3, 4)$, $(-5, 0)$
(b) $x^2 + y^2 = 25$

3 (a) All the points
(b) $(x - 2)^2 + (y - 5)^2 = 25^2$

Exercise A (p. 16)

1 Using $x^2 + y^2 = r^2$ the equations are
(a) $x^2 + y^2 = 225$
(b) $x^2 + y^2 = 16$
(c) $x^2 + y^2 = 2.53$ since $2\pi r = 10$, so $r = 1.59$
(d) $x^2 + y^2 = 400$ since the radius is the distance of $(12, 16)$ from the origin

2 Using the formula $(x - a)^2 + (y - b)^2 = r^2$, the equations are
(a) $(x - 1)^2 + (y - 1)^2 = 9$
(b) $(x + 4)^2 + (y - 6)^2 = 64$

3 By Pythagoras' theorem
$(E - 20)^2 + (N - 85)^2 = 18^2$

4 (a) The square of the distance from $(3, 2)$ to $(1, 4)$ is $(3 - 1)^2 + (2 - 4)^2 = 8$
Since $8 < 9$, the (radius)^2, it follows that $(3, 2)$ lies inside the circle.

(b) Outside

5 (a) Radius 2 units, centre $(2, 1)$
(b) Radius 3 units, centre $(1, 0)$
(c) Radius $\frac{1}{4}$ unit, centre $(\frac{1}{2}, -\frac{1}{4})$

6E Suppose the equation is
$(x - a)^2 + (y - b)^2 = r^2$.
Each point which lies on this circle will satisfy the equation.
$$(6 - a)^2 + (9 - b)^2 = r^2$$
$$(13 - a)^2 + (-8 - b)^2 = r^2$$
$$(-4 - a)^2 + (-15 - b)^2 = r^2$$
These simplify to
$$a^2 + b^2 - 12a - 18b + 117 = r^2 \quad ①$$
$$a^2 + b^2 - 26a + 16b + 233 = r^2 \quad ②$$
$$a^2 + b^2 + 8a + 30b + 241 = r^2 \quad ③$$
Eliminating r^2,
$① - ② \Longrightarrow 14a - 34b - 116 = 0$
$③ - ② \Longrightarrow 34a + 14b + 8 = 0$
giving $a = 1$, $b = -3$, $r = 13$
So the centre is $(1, -3)$, radius 13 and equation $(x - 1)^2 + (y + 3)^2 = 169$.

7E Suppose the equation is
$$(x-a)^2 + (y-b)^2 = 100.$$

Since the circle passes through $(10, 9)$ and $(8, -5)$ it follows that
$$(10 - a)^2 + (9 - b)^2 = 100$$
$$(8 - a)^2 + (-5 - b)^2 = 100$$

which become
$$a^2 + b^2 - 20a - 18b + 81 = 0 \quad \text{①}$$
$$a^2 + b^2 - 16a + 10b - 11 = 0 \quad \text{②}$$

First eliminate $a^2 + b^2$ by subtracting ① from ②.
$$4a + 28b = 92$$
i.e. $a = 23 - 7b$

Now substitute for a in ① to obtain a quadratic in b.
$$(23 - 7b)^2 + b^2 - 20(23 - 7b) - 18b + 81 = 0$$
which reduces to $b^2 - 4b + 3 = 0$

Hence $b = 1$ or $b = 3$
If $b = 1$, $a = 16$, and if $b = 3$, $a = 2$

So the two equations are
$$(x - 16)^2 + (y - 1)^2 = 100$$
$$(x - 2)^2 + (y - 3)^2 = 100$$

$(-6, -3)$ lies on the second circle.

B   Intersections of lines and circles
(p.17)

Exercise B (p. 18)

1 (a) $(-1, -2)$, $(3, 6)$;   centre $(5, 0)$,
radius $\sqrt{40}$

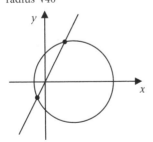

(b) $(1, 3)$, $(3, 1)$;   centre $(0, 0)$,
radius $\sqrt{10}$

(c) $(4, 3)$, $(6, -1)$;   centre $(3, 0)$,
radius $\sqrt{10}$

(d) $(-2, 0)$;   centre $(1, -1)$, radius $\sqrt{10}$.
Equal roots give one point of intersection. The line is the tangent to the circle at $(-2, 0)$.

(e) $(4, 5)$;   centre $(2, 1)$, radius $\sqrt{20}$

2 Eliminating y gives $2x^2 - 10x + 17 = 0$
which has no real roots, so there are no points of intersection.

3 $(\sqrt{2}, 2)$ and $(-\sqrt{2}, 2)$

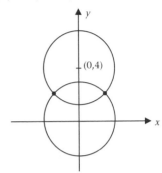

C   Tangents and normals to curves
(p. 18)

1D The gradient is $-\dfrac{1}{g}$.

Exercise C (p. 19)

1 (a) $\dfrac{dy}{dx} = 2 - 2x$

At $(2, 3)$, $\dfrac{dy}{dx} = 2 - 2 \times 2 = -2$

The tangent passes through $(2, 3)$ and has gradient -2. Its equation is therefore $y - 3 = -2(x - 2)$, or $y = -2x + 7$.

(b) $y = 12x - 21$ (c) $y = -8x + 19$

2 $\dfrac{dy}{dx} = 1 + 4x$

When $x = 3$, $\dfrac{dy}{dx} = 13$ and $y = 21$.

The equation of the tangent is
$y - 21 = 13(x - 3)$, or $y = 13x - 18$.

3 (a) $y = x + 5$
(b) $y = -3x + 5$
(c) $y = 5$

4 (a)

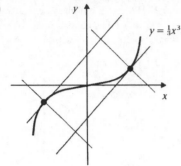

$$y = \tfrac{1}{3}x^3$$

(b) $y = x - \tfrac{2}{3}, \quad y = x + \tfrac{2}{3}$
(c) $y = -x - \tfrac{4}{3}, \quad y = -x + \tfrac{4}{3}$
(d) $(1, \tfrac{1}{3}), (\tfrac{1}{3}, 1), (-1, -\tfrac{1}{3}), (-\tfrac{1}{3}, -1)$
(e) The rectangle has edges of lengths $\tfrac{2}{3}\sqrt{2}$ and $\tfrac{4}{3}\sqrt{2}$. Its area is $\tfrac{16}{9}$ square units.

5 (a) The tangents and normals must have gradients of ± 1. At the corners of the square on $y = x^2$,
$$\frac{dy}{dx} = \pm 1 \implies 2x = \pm 1 \implies x = \pm \tfrac{1}{2}$$
The corners are $(\tfrac{1}{2}, \tfrac{1}{4}), (0, \tfrac{3}{4}), (-\tfrac{1}{2}, \tfrac{1}{4}), (0, -\tfrac{1}{4})$.

(b) The square has edge of length $\tfrac{1}{2}\sqrt{2}$. Its area is therefore $(\tfrac{1}{2}\sqrt{2})^2 = \tfrac{1}{2}$ square unit.

6 The normal has gradient $-\tfrac{1}{2}$ and equation $y = -\tfrac{1}{2}x + \tfrac{3}{2}$. At A,
$$-\tfrac{1}{2}x + \tfrac{3}{2} = x^2 \implies 2x^2 + x - 3 = 0$$
$$\implies x = 1 \text{ or } -\tfrac{3}{2}$$
A has coordinates $(-\tfrac{3}{2}, \tfrac{9}{4})$.

7 $(-3.2, 10.04)$

8 (a) $y = -\tfrac{1}{4}x + 1, \quad y = 4x - 7\tfrac{1}{2}$
(b) $y = \tfrac{1}{6}x + 1\tfrac{1}{2}, \quad y = -6x + 57$
(c) $y = 6, \quad x = 3$
(d) $y = \tfrac{1}{2}x - \tfrac{1}{2}, \quad y = -2x + 2$
(e) $y = 12x - 16, \quad y = -\tfrac{1}{12}x + 8\tfrac{1}{6}$
(f) $x = 12y - 16, \quad x = -\tfrac{1}{12}y + 8\tfrac{1}{6}$

9E The tangent has equation $y = 16x - 27$. It meets the curve where $x^3 + x^2 - 16x + 20 = 0$, which gives $(x - 2)^2(x + 5) = 0$. The point is $(-5, -107)$.

D Tangents and normals to circles
(p. 20)

1 The radius and tangent are perpendicular.

2 The gradient of PC is $\dfrac{7 - 3}{5 - 2} = \dfrac{4}{3}$.

3 The gradient of the tangent is $-\tfrac{3}{4}$.

4 For every point (x, y) on the tangent
$$\frac{y - 7}{x - 5} = -\frac{3}{4}$$
$$\implies 4(y - 7) = -3(x - 5)$$
$$\implies 4y - 28 = -3x + 15$$
$$\implies 4y = -3x + 43$$

Exercise D (p. 21)

1 (a) 10
(b) $4y = -3x + 60, \quad 3y = 4x - 5$

2 $y = 3x + 17, \quad 3y = -x + 11$

3 (a) $(3, 1)$
(b) $y = 2x, \quad 2y = -x + 5$

4 The tangents have equations $y = 7x + 36$ and $y = -x + 12$. They meet at $(-3, 15)$. $AP = BP = \sqrt{200}$

5 (b) The tangent has equation $y = -\tfrac{3}{4}x + 11$ and passes through $(8, 5)$.
(c) Yes. A diagram shows this immediately.
(d) $(8, 0)$

3 Trigonometric functions

A Inverse functions and equations
(p. 23)

1 (a)

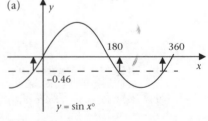

$$y = \sin x^\circ$$

(b) -27.4
(c) $207.4, 332.6$

2 Answered in the text

3 (a) 28.4, 151.6

(b) As in the text

4 73.1, 286.9

5 97.2, 262.8

6 (a) All x except odd multiples of 90°

(b)

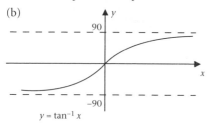

$y = \tan^{-1} x$

Exercise A (p. 25)

1 (a) −348.5, −191.5, 11.5, 168.5

(b) ±107.5, ±252.5

(c) −318.2, −221.8, 41.8, 138.2

(d) ±33.2, ±146.8, ±213.2, ±326.8

2 (a) 15.0, 211.0

(b) 49.9, 152.1, 229.9, 332.1

(c) 94.0

(d) 27.3, 87.3, 147.3, 207.3, 267.3, 327.3

(e) 21.8, 201.8

3

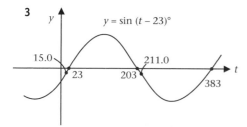

$y = \sin(t - 23)°$

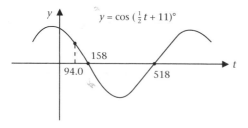

$y = \cos(\frac{1}{2}t + 11)°$

4 (a) 65.5, 114.5, 425.5, 474.5

(b) 3665.5, 3714.5

(c) $360n + 65.5$, $360n + 114.5$

It still applies when n is negative.

5 (a)

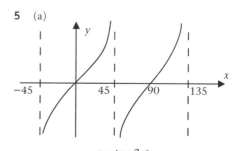

$y = \tan 2x°$

(b)

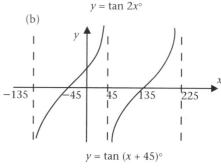

$y = \tan(x + 45)°$

B $r \sin(\theta + a)°$ (p. 25)

1D

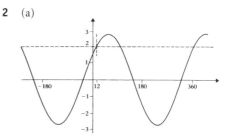

From the diagram,
$a = 1.5 \cos \theta°$
$b = 2.5 \sin \theta°$
So, if the wardrobe is to pass through the doorway, $a + b \leqslant 2$
$\Rightarrow 1.5 \cos \theta° + 2.5 \sin \theta° \leqslant 2$

2 (a)

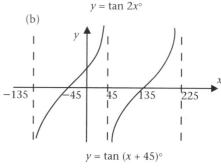

(b) The approximate solution is 10°.
(The value predicted by theory is 12.4°.)

(c) (i) The greatest height above ground is 2.9 m, which occurs at an angle of approximately 60° (59° in theory).

  (ii) The wardrobe may be tipped at any angle between 0° and 12°.

3 (a)

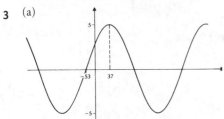

The graph is a phase-shifted sine wave.

(b) $y = 5 \sin(x + 53)°$ since the graph has amplitude 5 and is $y = 5 \sin x°$ translated through $\begin{bmatrix} -53 \\ 0 \end{bmatrix}$.

4

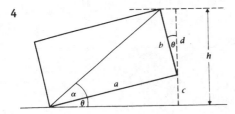

(a) (i) $h = c + d = a \sin \theta° + b \cos \theta°$

  (ii) $\dfrac{h}{r} = \sin(\theta + \alpha)°$
  $$\Rightarrow h = r \sin(\theta + \alpha)°$$

(b) $r^2 = a^2 + b^2$ and $\tan \alpha° = \dfrac{b}{a}$
Thus, you can write $a \sin \theta° + b \cos \theta°$ in the form $r \sin(\theta + \alpha)°$, where $r^2 = a^2 + b^2$ and $\tan \alpha° = \dfrac{b}{a}$.

5 (a) $r = \sqrt{4^2 + 7^2} = 8.06$

  $\tan \alpha° = \dfrac{7}{4} \Rightarrow \alpha = 60.3$

  $\Rightarrow 4 \sin \theta° + 7 \cos \theta°$
  $$= 8.06 \sin(\theta + 60.3)°$$

Exercise B (p. 28)

1 (a) $\sqrt{13} \sin(\theta + 33.7)°$

  (b) 22.6, 90

2 (a) $5 \sin \theta° + 12 \cos \theta° = 13 \sin(\theta + 67.4)°$, which has a maximum value of 13

  (b) 68.8, 336.4

3E (a) $AD = 6 \sin \theta°$, $AB = 8 \cos \theta°$, perimeter $= 12 \sin \theta° + 16 \cos \theta°$

  (b) $12 \sin \theta° + 16 \cos \theta° = 14$
  $$\Rightarrow 3 \sin \theta° + 4 \cos \theta° = 3.5$$

  (c) $\theta = 82.5$ for $0 < \theta < 90$
  The sides have length 5.95 and 1.05.

  (d) Largest perimeter is 20, when $\theta = 36.9$.

4E (a) Centre O, radius $= \sqrt{45}$

  (b) $d = 6 \sin \theta° + 3 \cos \theta°$

  (c) $d = \sqrt{45} \sin(\theta + 26.6)°$

  (d) The maximum distance is $\sqrt{45}$, when $\theta + 26.6 = 90, 270, 450$ etc.
  So $\theta = 63.4, 243.4, 423.4$ etc.

C Addition formulas (p. 29)

1D

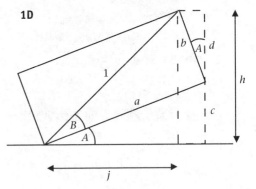

(a) $\sin(A + B) = h = c + d$
  $$= a \sin A + b \cos A$$
  $$= \sin A \cos B + \cos A \sin B,$$
  since $a = \cos B$, $b = \sin B$

(b) Similarly, $\cos(A + B) = j$
  $$= a \cos A - b \sin A$$
  $$= \cos A \cos B - \sin A \sin B$$

(c) Checks are straightforward to make. For example,
  $\sin(25° + 35°) = \sin 60° = 0.866$
  $\sin 25° \cos 35° + \cos 25° \sin 35°$
  $$= 0.423 \times 0.819 + 0.906 \times 0.574$$
  $$= 0.866$$

2D The formulas give

$$\sin 2A = 2 \sin A \cos A$$

$$0 = 0$$

$$\cos 2A = \cos^2 A - \sin^2 A$$

$$1 = \cos^2 A + \sin^2 A$$

From the last two,

$$\cos 2A + 1 = 2 \cos^2 A \text{ and}$$

$$1 - \cos 2A = 2 \sin^2 A,$$

giving $\cos 2A = 2 \cos^2 A - 1 = 1 - 2 \sin^2 A$

Exercise C (p. 31)

1 (a) $\sin(x + 60)° = \sin x° \cos 60°$

$$+ \cos x° \sin 60°$$

$$= \frac{1}{2} \sin x° + \frac{\sqrt{3}}{2} \cos x°$$

2 (a) $\sin(x + 180)° = \sin x° \cos 180°$

$$+ \cos x° \sin 180°$$

$$= -\sin x°$$

(b)

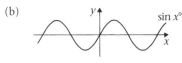

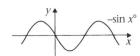

A translation of the sine graph by -180 in the x-direction has the same effect as a reflection in the x-axis.

3 (a) $\cos(A + B) + \cos(A - B)$

$$= \cos A \cos B - \sin A \sin B$$

$$+ \cos A \cos B + \sin A \sin B$$

$$= 2 \cos A \cos B$$

(b) $\cos(A - B) - \cos(A + B) = 2 \sin A \sin B$

4 (a) $\sin(45° + 30°)$

$$= \sin 45° \cos 30° + \cos 45° \sin 30°$$

$$= \frac{1}{\sqrt{2}} \times \frac{\sqrt{3}}{2} + \frac{1}{\sqrt{2}} \times \frac{1}{2}$$

$$= \frac{\sqrt{3} + 1}{2\sqrt{2}}$$

(b) $\sin 15° = \sin(45° - 30°) = \dfrac{\sqrt{3} - 1}{2\sqrt{2}}$

5 $\sin(A + B) = \frac{63}{65}$, $\cos(A + B) = \frac{16}{65}$

6 (a) $\cos 3A$ (b) $\sin 5B$

(c) $\sin 6C$ (d) $\cos B$

(e) $\sin 2A$

7 (a) $(\cos A + \sin A)(\cos B + \sin B)$

$$= \cos A \cos B + \cos A \sin B$$

$$+ \sin A \cos B + \sin A \sin B$$

$$= \sin(A + B) + \cos(A - B)$$

(b) $(\cos A + \sin A)^2 = \sin 2A + 1$, putting $B = A$ in (a)

(c) Easily proved like (a)

(d) $\dfrac{\sin 3A}{\sin A} + \dfrac{\cos 3A}{\cos A}$

$$= \frac{\sin 3A \cos A + \cos 3A \sin A}{\sin A \cos A}$$

$$= \frac{\sin 4A}{\frac{1}{2} \sin 2A}$$

$$= \frac{2 \sin 2A \cos 2A}{\frac{1}{2} \sin 2A}$$

$$= 4 \cos 2A$$

9 (a) $\cos 2A = -\frac{31}{32}$, $\cos \frac{1}{2} A = \pm \frac{3}{4}$

(b) $\cos^2 A = 1 - \sin^2 A = \frac{16}{25}$

$$\Rightarrow \cos A = \pm \frac{4}{5}$$

Then $\sin 2A = \pm \frac{24}{25}$, $\cos 2A = \frac{7}{25}$,

$\sin 4A = \pm \frac{336}{625}$

(c) $\cos 2A = -\frac{1}{2}$, $\cos 4A = -\frac{1}{2}$

It could be that $A = 60°$, $2A = 120°$, $4A = 240°$.

10 (a) 30, 90, 150, 270

(b) $\sin x° = 1$ or $-\frac{1}{2}$; $x = 90, 210, 330$

(c) 120, 240

(d) 0, 180, 210, 330, 360

(e) 0, 45, 135, 180, 225, 315, 360

11 (a) Using $s = \sin x$ and $c = \cos x$,

$$\sin x \cos 2x + \cos x \sin 2x$$

$$= s(1 - 2s^2) + c \times 2sc$$

$$= s - 2s^3 + 2s(1 - s^2)$$

$$= 3s - 4s^3$$

(b) $4 \cos^3 x - 3 \cos x$

D Extending the method for $r\sin(\theta + a)°$ (p. 32)

1 (a)

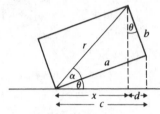

(i) $x = r\cos(\theta + a)°$

(ii) $x = c - d = a\cos\theta° - b\sin\theta°$

(b) $a\cos\theta° - b\sin\theta° = r\cos(\theta + a)°$

2

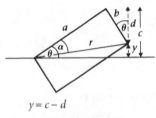

$y = c - d$
$= a\sin\theta° - b\cos\theta°$

Also $y = r\sin(\theta - a)°$

$\Rightarrow a\sin\theta° - b\cos\theta° = r\sin(\theta - a)°$

3

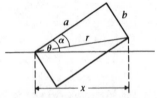

Considering the projections on the x-axis,

$x = a\cos\theta° + b\sin\theta°$

Also $x = r\cos(\theta - a)°$

$\Rightarrow a\cos\theta° + b\sin\theta° = r\cos(\theta - a)°$

4 (a) $r_1 = \sqrt{49 + 16} = \sqrt{65}$
$a_1 = \tan^{-1}\frac{4}{7} = 29.7$

(b) $r_2 = \sqrt{16 + 49} = \sqrt{65}$
$a_2 = \tan^{-1}\frac{7}{4} = 60.3$

(c) You can consider the function either as a sine graph with a phase shift of -29.7 or as a cosine graph of phase shift $+60.3$.

(d) $a_1 + a_2 = 90°$. This relationship may be seen clearly from the triangle below.

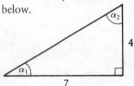

Exercise D (p. 33)

1 (a) $3\sin(\theta + 30)°$ (b) $3\cos(\theta - 60)°$

(c) $3\sin(\theta - 330)°$ (d) $3\cos(\theta + 300)°$

2 (a) $25\cos(\theta - 73.7)°$

(b) $13\sin(\theta + 22.6)°$

(c) $41\sin(\theta - 77.3)°$

(d) $4.47\sin(\theta + 26.6)°$

3 (a) 76.7, 209.6

(b) 38.1, 263.8

(c) 84.0, 345.9

E Formulas for tan (p. 34)

1D (a) $\tan(A + B) = \dfrac{\sin(A + B)}{\cos(A + B)}$

$= \dfrac{\sin A\cos B + \cos A\sin B}{\cos A\cos B - \sin A\sin B}$

$= \dfrac{\tan A + \tan B}{1 - \tan A\tan B},$

dividing each term by $\cos A\cos B$

(b) Replacing B by $-B$ gives

$\tan(A - B) = \dfrac{\tan A - \tan B}{1 + \tan A\tan B}$

Putting $B = A$ gives

$\tan 2A = \dfrac{2\tan A}{1 - \tan^2 A}$

Exercise E (p. 35)

1 (a) $\tan(A + B) = 1$ and
$\tan(26.57 + 18.43)° = \tan 45°$
$= 1$

(b) $\tan(C + D) = -1$ and
$\tan(C + D) = \tan(90° - A + 90° - B)$
$= \tan(180° - A - B)$
$= \tan 135° = -1$

2 $\tan(A + B) = \frac{2}{3}, \tan(A + B + C) = 1$
Hence $A + B + C = 45°$.

3 $\tan 2A = \frac{5}{12}, \tan 4A = \frac{120}{119}$
Hence $4A$ is just greater than $45°$.

4 (a) The graph goes up m for every 1 across, so $\tan A = m$

(b) If $\tan A = 2$ and $\tan B = \frac{1}{3}$,
$\tan(A - B) = 1$.
Hence the angle between the lines is $45°$.

5 Using $t = \tan A$,

$$\frac{2t}{1-t^2} = \frac{3}{4}$$

$$\Rightarrow 3t^2 + 8t - 3 = 0$$

$$\Rightarrow t = \tfrac{1}{3} \text{ or } -3$$

So $\tan A = \tfrac{1}{3}$ or -3

4 Differentiating trigonometric functions

A Radians (p. 36)

Exercise A (p. 36)

1

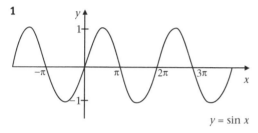

$y = \sin x$

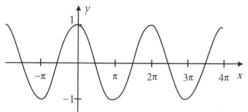

$y = \cos x$

2 (a)

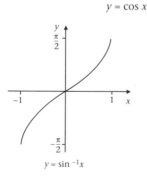

$y = \sin^{-1} x$

(b)

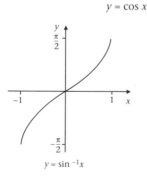

$y = \cos^{-1} x$

(c)

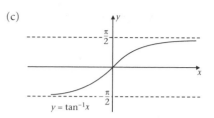

$y = \tan^{-1} x$

$\sin^{-1}$: domain $-1 \leqslant x \leqslant 1$,

range $\dfrac{-\pi}{2} \leqslant \sin^{-1} x \leqslant \dfrac{\pi}{2}$

$\cos^{-1}$: domain $-1 \leqslant x \leqslant 1$,

range $0 \leqslant \cos^{-1} x \leqslant \pi$

$\tan^{-1}$: domain all real x,

range $\dfrac{-\pi}{2} < \tan^{-1} x < \dfrac{\pi}{2}$

3

x	0	$\frac{1}{6}\pi$	$\frac{1}{4}\pi$	$\frac{1}{3}\pi$	$\frac{1}{2}\pi$	$\frac{2}{3}\pi$	$\frac{3}{4}\pi$	$\frac{5}{6}\pi$	π	$\frac{5}{4}\pi$	$\frac{3}{2}\pi$	$\frac{7}{4}\pi$	2π
$\sin x$	0	$\frac{1}{2}$	$\frac{1}{\sqrt{2}}$	$\frac{1}{2}\sqrt{3}$	1	$\frac{1}{2}\sqrt{3}$	$\frac{1}{\sqrt{2}}$	$\frac{1}{2}$	0	$-\frac{1}{\sqrt{2}}$	-1	$-\frac{1}{\sqrt{2}}$	0
$\cos x$	1	$\frac{1}{2}\sqrt{3}$	$\frac{1}{\sqrt{2}}$	$\frac{1}{2}$	0	$-\frac{1}{2}$	$-\frac{1}{\sqrt{2}}$	$-\frac{1}{2}\sqrt{3}$	-1	$-\frac{1}{\sqrt{2}}$	0	$\frac{1}{\sqrt{2}}$	1

4 (a) $-\sin x$ (b) $\sin x$
   (c) $-\sin x$ (d) $-\sin x$

5 (a) $3.6 \sin x + 9.3 \cos x$
   (b) $9.4 \sin(x + 0.56)$

6 (a) Both sides give 0.955.
   (b) Both sides give -0.971.

7 $x + 0.4 = 1.12$ or $\pi - 1.12$ or $2\pi + 1.12$ or $3\pi - 1.12$ so $x = 0.72, 1.62, 7.00, 7.90$

8 (a)   (b)

(c)

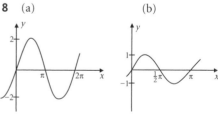

B   Differentiation (p. 37)

1D   (a) $BC = \sin\theta$, arc $AB = \theta$
For small θ, $BC \approx$ arc AB
The graph has gradient 1 at the origin.

(b) 0.0998

(c) $\cos x \approx 1 - \frac{1}{2}x^2$ for small x
When $x = 0.3$, error ≈ 0.0003

(d) $\dfrac{\sin(a+h) - \sin a}{h}$

$= \dfrac{\sin a \cos h + \cos a \sin h - \sin a}{h}$

$\approx \dfrac{\sin a\,(1 - \frac{1}{2}h^2 - 1) + \cos a \times h}{h}$
when h is small

$= \cos a - \frac{1}{2}h \sin a$

(e) This approaches $\cos a$ as h gets smaller and smaller. Hence
$y = \sin x \Rightarrow \dfrac{dy}{dx} = \cos x$

2   The cosine graph is the sine graph translated $\frac{1}{2}\pi$ to the left, i.e.
$\cos x = \sin(x + \frac{1}{2}\pi)$. Its gradient is therefore $\cos(x + \frac{1}{2}\pi) = -\sin x$

Exercise B (p. 38)

1

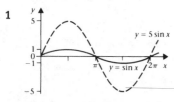

(a) $y = \sin x$ is mapped onto $y = 5 \sin x$ by a stretch of factor 5 in the y-direction.

(b) The gradient is multiplied by a factor of 5.

(c) $y = 5 \sin x \Rightarrow \dfrac{dy}{dx} = 5 \cos x$

2

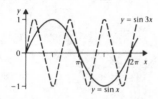

(a) $y = \sin x$ is mapped onto $y = \sin 3x$ by a stretch of factor $\frac{1}{3}$ in the x-direction.

(b) The gradient is multiplied by a factor of 3.

(c) $y = \sin 3x \Rightarrow \dfrac{dy}{dx} = 3 \cos 3x$

3 $y = 5 \sin 3x$ is obtained from $y = \sin x$ by applying both stretches from the previous questions.
$$y = 5 \sin 3x \Rightarrow \dfrac{dy}{dx} = 15 \cos 3x$$

4   (a) $-2 \sin 2x$ (b) $20 \cos 2x$
(c) $0.5 \cos 0.5x$

5

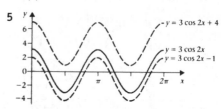

(b) These curves are mapped onto each other by translations in the y-direction. The derivatives are all the same:
$$\dfrac{dy}{dx} = -6 \sin 2x$$

6   (a) (i) $y = a \sin x \Rightarrow \dfrac{dy}{dx} = a \cos x$

(ii) $y = \sin bx \Rightarrow \dfrac{dy}{dx} = b \cos bx$

(iii) $y = a \sin bx \Rightarrow \dfrac{dy}{dx} = ab \cos bx$

(b) $y = a \cos bx \Rightarrow \dfrac{dy}{dx} = -ab \sin bx$

7   (a) $\frac{1}{2}\cos x$ (b) $-5 \sin x$
(c) $0.1 \cos x$ (d) $4 \cos 4x$
(e) $-2\pi \sin 2\pi x$ (f) $0.2 \cos 0.2x$
(g) $-6 \sin 2x$ (h) $3\pi \cos \frac{1}{2}\pi x$
(i) $\cos \frac{1}{3}x$

8

y	$\sin x$	$4 \sin 5x$	$2 \sin 3x$	$\cos x$	$10 \cos\frac{1}{2}x$	$-9 \cos\frac{1}{3}x$
$\dfrac{dy}{dx}$	$\cos x$	$20 \cos 5x$	$6 \cos 3x$	$-\sin x$	$-5 \sin\frac{1}{2}x$	$3 \sin\frac{1}{3}x$

9   (a) $8 \sin x + c$ (b) $-\frac{3}{7}\cos 7x + c$
(c) $40 \sin 0.1x - 30 \cos 0.1x + c$

10   (a) $\left[-\cos x\right]_0^\pi = 1 + 1 = 2$

(b) 3   (c) 4

C Applications (p. 39)

1D (a) 12 hours

(b) Since the period of $y = \sin \omega t$ is $\dfrac{2\pi}{\omega}$,

$$\frac{2\pi}{\omega} = 12 \implies \omega = \tfrac{1}{6}\pi$$

The amplitude is 2.5 and the mean height is 5 and so $h = 2.5 \sin \tfrac{1}{6}\pi t + 5$

2 $\dfrac{\mathrm{d}h}{\mathrm{d}t} = 2.5 \times \tfrac{1}{6}\pi \cos \tfrac{1}{6}\pi t = \tfrac{5}{12}\pi \cos \tfrac{1}{6}\pi t$

3 (a) $\dfrac{\mathrm{d}h}{\mathrm{d}t} = \tfrac{5}{12}\pi \cos \tfrac{4}{6}\pi = -0.65 \ (\mathrm{m\ h^{-1}})$

(b) The tide is falling at a rate of $0.65 \ \mathrm{m\ h^{-1}}$.

(c) When $t = 8$, $4 + 12 = 16$, $8 + 12 = 20$, $28, 32, \dots$

Exercise C (p. 41)

1 (a) $L = 12 + 2.5 \cos 2\pi t$

$$\implies \frac{\mathrm{d}L}{\mathrm{d}t} = -5\pi \sin 2\pi t$$

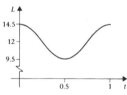

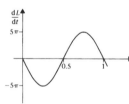

(b)

t	0	0.1	0.25	0.4	0.5
(i) Length (cm)	14.5	14.0	12	10.0	9.5
(ii) Velocity (cm s^{-1})	0	-9.2	-5π	-9.2	0

This represents the motion between the maximum and minimum positions. The velocity is momentarily zero at the extreme positions, and the speed is greatest at the midway position.

2 (a) $h = 0.8 \cos \tfrac{1}{6}\pi t + 6.5$

$$\implies \frac{\mathrm{d}h}{\mathrm{d}t} = -\tfrac{2}{15}\pi \sin \tfrac{1}{6}\pi t$$

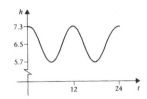

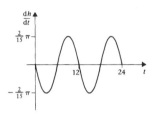

(b) $0.8 \cos \tfrac{1}{6}\pi t + 6.5 = 6$

$$\implies \cos \tfrac{1}{6}\pi t = -0.625$$
$$\implies t = 4.29, 7.71 \quad \text{(0417 hours and 0743 hours)}$$

When $t = 4.29$, $\dfrac{\mathrm{d}h}{\mathrm{d}t} = -0.33 \ (\mathrm{m\ h^{-1}})$

When $t = 7.71$, $\dfrac{\mathrm{d}h}{\mathrm{d}t} = 0.33 \ (\mathrm{m\ h^{-1}})$

The rates of change are numerically the same but opposite in sign because in one case the tide is falling and in the other it is rising.

(c) The tide is falling most rapidly at $t = 3$.

$$\frac{\mathrm{d}h}{\mathrm{d}t} = -0.42 \ (\mathrm{m\ h^{-1}})$$

(d) Tidal current is greatest when the tide is rising or falling most rapidly and is least near high and low tides.

Depth of water and strength of tidal current are the two important factors in deciding when it is safe to enter or leave harbour.

3 (a) $\dfrac{dh}{dt} = 0.16\pi \sin \frac{1}{30}\pi t$

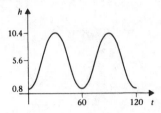

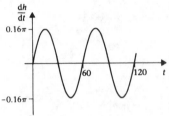

(b) $0.16\pi \sin \frac{1}{30}\pi t = -0.4$
$\Rightarrow t = 38.8, 51.2, 98.8, 111.2$

The speed is over 0.4 m s^{-1} between
$t = 38.8$ and $t = 51.2$ and again
between $t = 98.8$ and $t = 111.2$. The
chair descends most rapidly at $t = 45$;
speed = 0.5 m s^{-1}.

4 (a) (i)

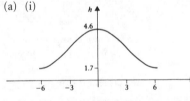

(ii) $h = 3.15 + 1.45 \cos \frac{1}{6}\pi t$

(b) (i)

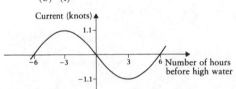

Since the period is 12 hours,
$\omega = \frac{2}{12}\pi = \frac{1}{6}\pi$

(ii) $c = -1.1 \sin \frac{1}{6}\pi t$

(iii) Since current represents the rate
at which water is entering or
leaving the harbour, this is
proportional to the rate of
change of the height of the tide.

(c) (i) $\dfrac{dh}{dt} = -0.76 \sin \frac{1}{6}\pi t$

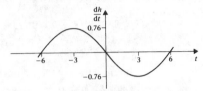

(ii) As indicated above, this is
directly proportional to the
current, demonstrating the direct
relationship between the speed of
the current and the rate of rise
and fall of the tide.

D More trigonometric functions (p. 42)

1

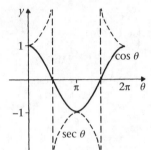

2 (a)

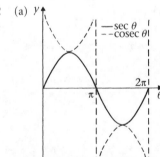

(b)

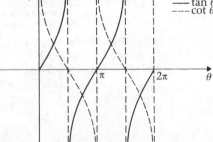

3 (a) $\dfrac{\sin^2\theta}{\cos^2\theta}+\dfrac{\cos^2\theta}{\cos^2\theta}=\dfrac{1}{\cos^2\theta}$

So, since

$\dfrac{\sin\theta}{\cos\theta}=\tan\theta$ and $\dfrac{1}{\cos\theta}=\sec\theta$,

$\tan^2\theta+1=\sec^2\theta$

(b) $\dfrac{\sin^2\theta}{\sin^2\theta}+\dfrac{\cos^2\theta}{\sin^2\theta}=\dfrac{1}{\sin^2\theta}$

So, since

$\dfrac{\cos\theta}{\sin\theta}=\cot\theta$ and $\dfrac{1}{\sin\theta}=\operatorname{cosec}\theta$,

$1+\cot^2\theta=\operatorname{cosec}^2\theta$

Exercise D (p. 43)

1 (a) $\sec^2\theta+\tan\theta=3$

$\Rightarrow\quad 1+\tan^2\theta+\tan\theta=3$

$\Rightarrow\quad \tan^2\theta+\tan\theta-2=0$

(b) Letting $t=\tan\theta$,

$t^2+t-2=(t+2)(t-1)$

(c) $\quad(\tan\theta+2)(\tan\theta-1)=0$

$\Rightarrow\quad \tan\theta=-2$ or $\tan\theta=1$

$\Rightarrow\quad \theta=-1.11,\ 2.03,\ 0.79,\ -2.36$

2 $2\cot^2\theta+\operatorname{cosec}\theta+1=0$

Using $\cot^2\theta=\operatorname{cosec}^2\theta-1$

$2(\operatorname{cosec}^2\theta-1)+\operatorname{cosec}\theta+1=0$

$\Rightarrow\ 2\operatorname{cosec}^2\theta+\operatorname{cosec}\theta-1=0$

$\Rightarrow\ (2\operatorname{cosec}\theta-1)(\operatorname{cosec}\theta+1)=0$

Since $\operatorname{cosec}\theta$ cannot equal $\frac{1}{2}$, we have

$\operatorname{cosec}\theta=-1$

$\Rightarrow\ \sin\theta=-1$

$\Rightarrow\ \theta=-\frac{1}{2}\pi$

3 (a) $\tan\theta=-\frac{1}{2}$ or 5,

$\theta=2.68,\ 5.82,\ 1.37,\ 4.51$

(b) $\cot\theta=4$ or -1, so $\tan\theta=\frac{1}{4}$ or -1

$\theta=0.24,\ 3.39,\ 2.36,\ 5.50$

4 (a) $\tan\theta+\cot\theta$

$=\dfrac{\sin\theta}{\cos\theta}+\dfrac{\cos\theta}{\sin\theta}$

$=\dfrac{\sin^2\theta+\cos^2\theta}{\sin\theta\cos\theta}$

$=\dfrac{1}{\sin\theta\cos\theta}$

$=\operatorname{cosec}\theta\sec\theta$

(b) $\sec^2x+\operatorname{cosec}^2x$

$=\dfrac{1}{\cos^2x}+\dfrac{1}{\sin^2x}$

$=\dfrac{\sin^2x+\cos^2x}{\sin^2x\cos^2x}$

$=\dfrac{1}{(\sin x\cos x)^2}$

$=\dfrac{4}{(2\sin x\cos x)^2}$

$=\dfrac{4}{\sin^2 2x}$

5 (a) $\sin^3x$ (b) 1

6 (a) $\tan\theta=\dfrac{\sin\theta}{\cos\theta}\Rightarrow\cot\theta=\dfrac{1}{\tan\theta}=\dfrac{\cos\theta}{\sin\theta}$

$\cot\theta\sec\theta=\dfrac{\cos\theta}{\sin\theta}\times\dfrac{1}{\cos\theta}$

$=\dfrac{1}{\sin\theta}=\operatorname{cosec}\theta$

(b) $\cot\theta=\frac{1}{3}$, $\sec\theta=\pm\frac{1}{3}\sqrt{10}$,

$\operatorname{cosec}\theta=\pm\frac{1}{3}\sqrt{10}$

7 $\tan(x+\frac{1}{4}\pi)=\dfrac{\tan x+\tan\frac{1}{4}\pi}{1-\tan x\tan\frac{1}{4}\pi}=\dfrac{1+\tan x}{1-\tan x}$

$\cot(x+\frac{1}{4}\pi)=\dfrac{1-\tan x}{1+\tan x}=\dfrac{\cot x-1}{\cot x+1}$

dividing each term by $\tan x$.

5 Proof

A Introduction (p. 45)

Exercise A (p. 45)

1 $x=-1$, $y=0$ disproves the statement.

2 False. The three-dimensional Cartesian axes are a counter-example.

3 False. 21 is the first counter-example.

4 $t_1=1$, $t_2=2$, $t_3=3$, $t_4=4$, $t_5=29$. The value of t_5 is *not* 5 as might be expected if you considered only the first four terms.

B Making a proof (p. 46)

1D Think about proofs you have already met, for example, deductive proofs in geometry such as *the angle subtended by a chord at the centre of a circle is twice the angle it*

subtends at the circumference, or the result
$\sin^2 x + \cos^2 x = 1$. Consider the difference
between a scientific law, which is
strengthened by the accumulation of
evidence but not normally proved (for
example, Newton's inverse square law of
gravitation: a mathematical model later
refined by Einstein), and a mathematical
'law', which must remain merely a
conjecture until proved.

2   The fourth L-shaped shell has dimensions
as shown.

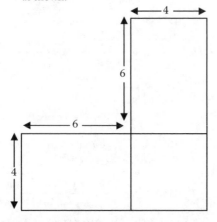

The area is $(4 \times 6) + (4 \times 4) + (6 \times 4) = 64$.
The areas of the other shells can similarly
be checked.

3   $A = k \times \frac{1}{2}k(k-1) = \frac{1}{2}k^2(k-1)$

$B = \frac{1}{2}k^2(k-1)$

$C = k^2$

$A + B + C = \frac{1}{2}k^2(k-1) + \frac{1}{2}k^2(k-1) + k^2$
$= k^2(k-1) + k^2 = k^3$

4   We know that mn has a factor of 7. Since 7
is a prime number, either m or n (or both)
must have a factor of 7. (Why would this
argument fail for, say, a factor of 6?)

Suppose n has a factor of 7, so $n = 7k$
(k being a positive integer). Since
$n + m = 7k + m$ also has a factor of 7, m
must be a multiple of 7 as well.

5   $7 \times 11 \times 13 = 1001$

Since n has factors of 7, 11 and 13, we
must have $n = 1001k$ for some positive
integer k.

So $n \geqslant 1001$.

Similarly, $m \geqslant 1001$.

Exercise B (p. 48)

1   (a) $2n$ is $2 \times n$ and is therefore even
         because it is divisible by 2.

    (b) $2n + 1$. This number is $2 \times n + 1$ and is
         therefore odd because it has a
         remainder of 1 when divided by 2.

    (c) $(2n+1) + (2n+3) + (2n+5) = 6n+9$
         $= 3 \times (2n+3)$ is divisible by 3.

2   (a) $10b + a$

    (b) $11a + 11b = 11 \times (a + b)$

    (c) The rule does *not* work for three-digit
         numbers, for example
         $102 + 201 = 303$.

         The rule *does* work for four-digit
         numbers.

         $(1000a + 100b + 10c + d)$
         $\quad + (1000d + 100c + 10b + a)$
         $\quad = 1001a + 110b + 110c + 1001d$
         $\quad = 11 \times (91a + 10b + 10c + 91d)$

3   (b) $(10a + b) \times 11 = 110a + 11b$
         $\qquad\qquad = 100a + 10a + 10b + b$
         $\qquad\qquad = 100a + 10(a + b) + b$

         So   'ab' $\times 11 = \boxed{a}\ \boxed{a+b}\ \boxed{b}$

    (c) For examples of this kind you have to
         'carry' digits in the addition.

         The method works, but you have to
         be more careful!

         $11 \times 392 = 3\ \boxed{12}\ 11\ \boxed{2}$
         $\qquad\qquad = 4\ 2\ \boxed{11}\ 2$
         $\qquad\qquad = 4\ 3\ 1\ 2$

4   In the 5×13 'rectangle' a very thin
    parallelogram of area 1 is missing.

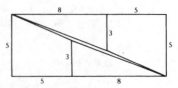

    A 'similar triangles' argument shows this:
    $\frac{3}{8} \neq \frac{5}{13}$

5   (a) The numbers may in general be
         written as $(2a - 1)$ and $(2a + 1)$, with
         sum $4a$.

(b) The sum of the numbers may be written as

$$(2a+1)+(2a+3)+(2a+5)$$
$$+\dots+(2a+2n-1)$$
$$=(2a+2a+2a+2a+\dots+2a)$$
$$+(1+3+5+\dots+2n-1)$$
$$=2na+n^2$$
$$=n(2a+n)$$

This expression is divisible by n. For n even, it is divisible by $2n$.

6E There are a number of ways in which this proof can be made. The following is based on the classic method attributed to Euclid, which employs contradiction.

Suppose $\sqrt{2}=\dfrac{a}{b}$, where a and b have no common factors.

$$\sqrt{2}=\frac{a}{b}\Rightarrow 2b^2=a^2$$
$$\Rightarrow a^2 \text{ is even (has a factor of 2)}$$
$$\Rightarrow a \text{ is even}$$

Let $\quad a=2m$
$$a^2=4m^2$$

Since $b^2=\dfrac{a^2}{2},\ b^2=\dfrac{4m^2}{2}=2m^2$
$$\Rightarrow b^2 \text{ is even}$$
$$\Rightarrow b \text{ is even}$$

If $\sqrt{2}=\dfrac{a}{b}$ then we have shown that *both* a and b are even and consequently have a common factor of 2.

This contradicts our original statement, so

$$\sqrt{2}\neq\frac{a}{b}$$

and so $\sqrt{2}$ is an irrational number.

C Fermat and proof (p. 49)

Exercise C (p. 51)

1

n	1	2	3	4
r_n	1	2	4	8

n is the number of points, and r_n is the corresponding number of regions.

Apparently the number of regions doubles every time a point is added, i.e.

$$r_{n+1}=2\times r_n, \text{ in which case}$$
$$r_n=2^{n-1}$$

2 $r_5=16$, which agrees with the conjecture. However, $r_6=31$, so the conjecture is false.

3

n	1	2	3	4	5	6	7
r_n	1	2	4	8	16	31	57

4 First differences   1   2   4   8   15   26
Second differences   1   2   4   7   11
Third differences   1   2   3   4
Fourth differences   1   1   1

5 The formula for r_n is probably a quartic polynomial.

A polynomial

$$r_n=an^4+bn^3+cn^2+dn+e$$

can be found by solving five equations (for the five unknown coefficients), obtained by substituting corresponding values of n and r_n. The first is

$$a+b+c+d+e=1$$

and the second is

$$16a+8b+4c+2d+e=2$$

6 1, 2, 4, 8, 16, 31, 57

Though these are the same numbers as those tabulated above, nothing has been *proved*.

D Prime number formulas (p. 51)

1 The first 10 numbers are 41, 43, 47, 53, 61, 71, 83, 97, 113, 131. These are all prime numbers.

2 Any number of the form $41k$ or $41k+1$, for example 82 or 83.

3 It is worth spending some time in exploring particular cases and establishing subsidiary results such as that if an^2+bn+c is always to be odd then c must be odd and a and b must have the same parity.

4 In the first attempt at a proof, the cases $c=\pm1$ and $ac+b+1=\pm1$ all invalidate the method. It is worth remembering that any one of these suffices as a counter-example.

5 When $n=1+2p$,

$$an^2+bn+c=a(1+2p)^2+b(1+2p)+c$$
$$=4ap^2+(4a+2b)p+a+b+c$$
$$=(4ap+4a+2b+1)p$$

The second attempt is sound and the method may be extended to show that no polynomial form P(n) of degree one or more generates only primes. If the degree of the polynomial is k it is sufficient to show that P(n) takes the same value for ($k+1$) different values of n.

E Differentiation from first principles (p. 52)

1 With 'normal' scales, the graph looks like that of $y = x$, with gradient 1 at all points. As you zoom in, the fact that a sine curve has been superimposed on the line $y = x$ becomes clear.

As you zoom in further, the curve starts to look like a straight line again. The gradient depends upon the point at which you zoom in and varies between 0 and 2.

2D (a) $(3+h)^2 = 9 + 6h + h^2$

(b) $6h + h^2$

(c) $\dfrac{6h + h^2}{h} = 6 + h$

(d) The gradient of PQ becomes closer and closer to 6.

(e) The main advantage of using h rather than a particular numerical value is that you have a general answer, $6 + h$, for the gradient PQ, for *any* point Q on the curve. A result like that of part (d) can be seen much more easily from the algebraic expression than it would be from several numerical results. Furthermore, you can see that for *any* small h, the gradient is close to 6. You therefore know that zooming in further (by taking smaller values of h) cannot cause any change in this result: *the graph is locally straight at $x = 3$ and has gradient 6 at that point.*

3 (a) -2 (b) 3

4 (a) $\lim\limits_{h \to 0} (h + 2) = 2$

(b) $\lim\limits_{h \to 0} (5h - 2) = -2$

(c) $\lim\limits_{h \to 0} (4h - h^2) = 0$

(d) $\lim\limits_{h \to 2} (h + 2) = 4$

(e) $\lim\limits_{h \to -3} \dfrac{2(h-3)(h+3)}{h+3} = \lim\limits_{h \to -3} 2(h-3)$
$\phantom{(e) \lim\limits_{h \to -3} \dfrac{2(h-3)(h+3)}{h+3}} = -12$

5 (a) 1   (b) 0   (c) 1

Exercise E (p. 57)

1 (a) $\lim\limits_{h \to 0} \dfrac{3(1+h)^2 - 3}{h} = \lim\limits_{h \to 0} \dfrac{\cancel{3} + 6h + 3h^2 - \cancel{3}}{h}$
$\phantom{(a) \lim\limits_{h \to 0} \dfrac{3(1+h)^2 - 3}{h}} = \lim\limits_{h \to 0} (6 + 3h) = 6$

(b) $\dfrac{dy}{dx} = \lim\limits_{h \to 0} \dfrac{3(x+h)^2 - 3x^2}{h}$
$\phantom{(b) \dfrac{dy}{dx}} = \lim\limits_{h \to 0} (6x + 3h) = 6x$

2 $\lim\limits_{h \to 0} \dfrac{[5(x+h)^2 + 3(x+h)] - [5x^2 + 3x]}{h}$
$= 10x + 3$

3 $\lim\limits_{h \to 0} \dfrac{[4(x+h)^2 - 2(x+h) + 7] - [4x^2 - 2x + 7]}{h}$
$= 8x - 2$

4 $\dfrac{dy}{dx} = \lim\limits_{h \to 0} \dfrac{(x+h)^3 - x^3}{h}$
$= \lim\limits_{h \to 0} \dfrac{x^3 + 3hx^2 + 3h^2x + h^3 - x^3}{h}$
$= \lim\limits_{h \to 0} \dfrac{3hx^2 + 3h^2x + h^3}{h}$
$= \lim\limits_{h \to 0} [3x^2 + 3hx + h^2] = 3x^2$

So $y = x^3 \implies \dfrac{dy}{dx} = 3x^2$

5E $\dfrac{dy}{dt} = \lim\limits_{h \to 0} \dfrac{\dfrac{1}{2(t+h)+5} - \dfrac{1}{2t+5}}{h}$
$= \lim\limits_{h \to 0} \dfrac{-2\cancel{h}}{\cancel{h}(2t+5)(2t+2h+5)}$
$= \dfrac{-2}{(2t+5)^2}$

6 (a) $x^5 + 5x^4h$ (b) $x^9 + 9x^8h$

(c) $x^n + nx^{n-1}h$

$$\lim_{h\to 0} \frac{(x+h)^n - x^n}{h}$$

$$= \lim_{h\to 0} \frac{nx^{n-1}h + h^2(\ldots)}{h}$$

$$= \lim_{h\to 0} \left[nx^{n-1} + h(\ldots) \right]$$

$$= nx^{n-1}$$

7E $\displaystyle\lim_{h\to 0} \frac{\sin(x+h) - \sin x}{h}$

$$= \lim_{h\to 0} \frac{\sin x \cos h + \cos x \sin h - \sin x}{h}$$

$$= \lim_{h\to 0} \left[\frac{\cos h - 1}{h} \sin x + \frac{\sin h}{h} \cos x \right]$$

$$= 0 \times \sin x + 1 \times \cos x$$

$$= \cos x$$

6 The chain rule

A Functions of functions (p. 58)

1D (a) $C = 50 + 2t$

(b) $F = 32 + 1.8C$

$$\Rightarrow F = 32 + 1.8(50 + 2t)$$

$$F = 122 + 3.6t$$

(c) $\dfrac{dF}{dt} = 3.6, \quad \dfrac{dF}{dC} = 1.8, \quad \dfrac{dC}{dt} = 2$

$$\frac{dF}{dt} = \frac{dF}{dC} \times \frac{dC}{dt}$$

For all your examples you should find that the rate of change of the composite function is the product of the other two rates of change.

2 If you zoom in at any chosen point on a locally straight function, then it will look increasingly like a linear function. You might, therefore, expect the chain rule to be true for any *locally straight* functions.

3 (a) $\dfrac{dy}{du} = 3u^2$ and $\dfrac{du}{dx} = \cos x$

$$\Rightarrow \frac{dy}{dx} = \frac{dy}{du} \times \frac{du}{dx}$$

$$= 3u^2 \times \cos x$$

$$= 3(\sin x)^2 \times \cos x$$

$$= 3 \sin^2 x \cos x$$

(b) $y = e^{x^2}$

$$\frac{dy}{dx} = \frac{dy}{du} \times \frac{du}{dx}$$

$$= e^u \times 2x$$

$$= e^{x^2} \times 2x$$

$$= 2xe^{x^2}$$

(c) $y = (e^x)^2 = e^{2x}$

$$\frac{dy}{dx} = \frac{dy}{du} \times \frac{du}{dx}$$

$$= 2u \times e^x$$

$$= 2e^x \times e^x$$

$$= 2e^{2x}$$

4 The chain rule does in fact apply to any locally straight functions and you should have found that your results were confirmed by whatever numerical methods you tried.

Exercise A (p. 60)

1 (a) $\dfrac{dR}{dt} = 2t, \dfrac{dS}{dR} = 2R$

$$\frac{dS}{dt} = 4Rt = 4t(3 + t^2)$$

(b) $S = 9 + 6t^2 + t^4$

$$\frac{dS}{dt} = 12t + 4t^3$$

$$= 4t(3 + t^2)$$

2 (a) (i) $2(x+1)$ (ii) $4(2x-1)$

(iii) $4x(x^2 - 2)$

(b) (i) $2x + 2$ (ii) $8x - 4$

(iii) $4x^3 - 8x$

3 By the chain rule: let $R = 5 + 4t \Longrightarrow S = R^3$

$$\frac{dR}{dt} = 4, \frac{dS}{dR} = 3R^2$$

$$\frac{dS}{dt} = 12R^2 = 12(5 + 4t)^2$$

By expanding: $S = 125 + 300t + 240t^2 + 64t^3$

$$\Rightarrow \frac{dS}{dt} = 300 + 480t + 192t^2$$

$$= 12(25 + 40t + 16t^2)$$

$$= 12(5 + 4t)^2$$

The chain rule is preferable!

4 Let $R = 4 + 3t^2 \implies \dfrac{dR}{dt} = 6t$

$S = R^3 \qquad \implies \dfrac{dS}{dR} = 3R^2$

$\dfrac{dS}{dt} = 18t(4 + 3t^2)^2$

5 $\dfrac{dy}{du} = \cos u, \quad \dfrac{du}{dx} = 2$

$\dfrac{dy}{dx} = 2 \cos u = 2 \cos 2x$

6 Let $u = 3x, \quad y = \cos u$

$\dfrac{dy}{dx} = 3 \times -\sin u = -3 \sin 3x$

7 Let $u = ax, \quad y = \sin u$

$\dfrac{dy}{dx} = a \cos u = a \cos ax$

B Differentiating by inspection (p. 61)

Exercise B (p. 62)

1 (a) $8x(x^2 + 3)^3$ (b) $10(5 + 2x)^4$
  (c) $3(4x - 3)(2x^2 - 3x)^2$
  (d) $12x^7(x - 2)(x - 3)^3$

2 (a) $-2x \sin x^2; \quad 0$ (b) $2 \cos 2x; \quad 2$
  (c) $3e^{3x}; \quad 3$

3 (a) $-3x^2 \sin x^3$ (b) $3 \sin^2 x \cos x$
  (c) $-8 \cos^3 x \sin x$
  (d) $2 \sin x \cos x$ (e) $2xe^{x^2}$
  (f) $-6 \sin 2x$ (g) $12x(x^2 + 1)^2$

4 (a) $\dfrac{dV}{dt} = 200, \quad \dfrac{dV}{dr} = 4\pi r^2$

  (b) $200 = 4\pi r^2 \dfrac{dr}{dt}$

  $\dfrac{dr}{dt} = \dfrac{50}{\pi r^2}$

  When $t = 1, V = 200$

  $\implies \quad 200 = \tfrac{4}{3}\pi r^3$

  $\implies \quad r = 3.63$

  $\implies \quad \dfrac{dr}{dt} = \dfrac{50}{\pi \times 3.63^2}$

  $\quad = 1.21 \text{ cm s}^{-1} \text{ (to 2 d.p.)}$

5 (a) $r = 3 + 0.04t^2 \implies \dfrac{dr}{dt} = 0.08t$

  Assuming the balloon is spherical,

  $V = \dfrac{4}{3}\pi r^3 \implies \dfrac{dV}{dr} = 4\pi r^2$

  (b) $\dfrac{dV}{dt} = \dfrac{dV}{dr} \times \dfrac{dr}{dt}$

  $\dfrac{dV}{dt} = 4\pi r^2 \times 0.08t$

  (c) When $t = 2, r = 3.16$

  $\implies \dfrac{dV}{dt} = 0.32\pi \times (3.16)^2 \times 2$

  $\dfrac{dV}{dt} = 20.1 \text{ m}^3 \text{ per minute (to 3 s.f.)}$

6 (a) $V = x^3 \implies \dfrac{dV}{dx} = 3x^2$

  (b) $\dfrac{dx}{dt} = -0.5, \quad \dfrac{dV}{dt} = -1.5x^2$

  $\dfrac{dV}{dt} = -1.5(4 - 0.5t)^2$

  (c) When $t = 2, \dfrac{dV}{dt} = -13.5 \text{ cm}^3 \text{ per hour}$

7 (a) $2 \times \sin 2x \times 2 \cos 2x = 4 \sin 2x \cos 2x$
  $\qquad = 2 \sin 4x$
  (b) $-24 \cos 4x \sin 4x = -12 \sin 8x$
  (c) $-\sin x \, e^{\cos x}$
  (d) $4e^{4x}$ (e) $-3e^{-3x}$
  (f) $4(e^{x^2} - 3x)^3(2x \, e^{x^2} - 3)$

8 (a) 0 (b) $-4 \sin x \cos x$
  (c) $-4 \sin x \cos x$

  For (a), $\dfrac{d}{dx}(\cos^2 x + \sin^2 x) = \dfrac{d}{dx}(1) = 0$
  For (b) and (c), $\cos^2 x - \sin^2 x =$
  $1 - 2 \sin^2 x = \cos 2x$ and
  $\dfrac{d}{dx}(\cos 2x) = -2 \sin 2x = -4 \sin x \cos x$

C Applications to integration (p. 63)

1D $y = (5x - 3)^4 \implies \dfrac{dy}{dx} = 4(5x - 3)^3 \times 5$
  $\qquad = 20(5x - 3)^3$

  $\implies \displaystyle\int_1^2 (5x - 3)^3 \, dx = \left[\tfrac{1}{20}(5x - 3)^4 \right]_1^2$

  $\qquad = 119.25$

Exercise C (p. 64)

1 (a) $\frac{1}{3}\sin 3x + c$

This is an indefinite integral and so the constant of integration must be included.

(b) $-2\cos\frac{1}{2}x + c$　(c) $-\frac{2}{5}\cos 5x + c$

(d) $\frac{1}{2}e^{2x} + c$　　(e) $\frac{1}{28}(4x+2)^7 + c$

2 (a) $\left[2e^{0.5x}\right]_1^2 = (2e) - (2e^{0.5})$

$$= 2.14 \text{ (to 2 d.p.)}$$

(b) $\left[-\frac{1}{2}\cos 2x\right]_{-1}^0 = (-\frac{1}{2}) - (-\frac{1}{2}\cos(-2))$

$$= -0.71 \text{ (to 2 d.p.)}$$

Note: the angle is in radians.

(c) $\left[6\sin\frac{1}{2}x\right]_0^2 = (6\sin 1) - (0) = 5.05$

(to 2 d.p.)

(d) $\left[\frac{1}{6}(2x+3)^3\right]_0^1 = (\frac{1}{6} \times 125) - (\frac{1}{6} \times 27)$

$$= \frac{98}{6} = 16\frac{1}{3}$$

3 (a) A is $\left(\frac{\pi}{2}, 0\right)$,

$$\int_0^{\pi/2} \sin 2x \, dx = \left[-0.5\cos 2x\right]_0^{\pi/2} = 1$$

(b) B is $(\pi, 0)$,

$$\int_0^\pi \frac{1}{2}\cos\frac{1}{2}x \, dx = \left[\sin\frac{1}{2}x\right]_0^\pi = 1$$

(c) C is $\left(\frac{\pi}{4}, 0\right)$,

$$\int_0^{\pi/4} 3\sin 2x \, dx = \left[-1.5\cos 2x\right]_0^{\pi/4} = 1.5$$

4E The leading term in $\frac{1}{8x}(x^2+7)^4$ is

$\frac{1}{8x} \times x^8 = \frac{1}{8}x^7$. On differentiation, this

gives $\frac{7}{8}x^6$ which is *not* in the expansion of $(x^2+7)^3$. You can adjust with numbers as in example 4 but not with functions of x.

5E (a) $2\sin\frac{1}{2}x + c$　(b) $\frac{2}{5}e^{2.5x} + c$

(c) Not possible by the methods of this chapter. The expression would have to be multiplied out before it could be integrated.

(d) $\frac{1}{25}(5x+3)^5 + c$　(e) $-\frac{1}{5}\cos 5x + c$

(f) Not possible

6E (a) $-\frac{1}{2}\cos x^2 + c$　(b) $\frac{1}{3}e^{x^3} + c$

(c) $\frac{1}{10}(2x^2+1)^5 + c$

7E $\int_0^1 \sin^2 x \, dx = \int_0^1 \frac{1}{2}(1 - \cos 2x) \, dx$

$$= \left[\frac{1}{2}x - \frac{1}{4}\sin 2x\right]_0^1$$

$$= 0.27 \text{ (to 2 d.p.)}$$

D　Inverse functions and x^n (p. 65)

1D (a) For a locally straight curve:

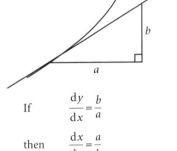

If　　$\dfrac{dy}{dx} = \dfrac{b}{a}$

then　$\dfrac{dx}{dy} = \dfrac{a}{b}$

Hence,　$\dfrac{dx}{dy} \times \dfrac{dy}{dx} = \dfrac{a}{b} \times \dfrac{b}{a} = 1$

(b) From the chain rule,

$$\frac{dy}{dy} = \frac{dy}{dx} \times \frac{dx}{dy}$$

However, $\dfrac{dy}{dy}$ is 1 and so

$$\frac{dy}{dx} \times \frac{dx}{dy} = 1 \Rightarrow \frac{dx}{dy} = 1 \div \frac{dy}{dx}$$

Exercise D (p. 66)

1 $\dfrac{dy}{dx} = 4u^3 \times -\dfrac{1}{x^2}$

$= 4x^{-3} \times -x^{-2}$

$= -4x^{-5}$

2 $\dfrac{dx}{dy} = 4y^3 \implies \dfrac{dy}{dx} = \dfrac{1}{4}y^{-3} = \dfrac{1}{4}x^{-\frac{3}{4}}$

3 $\dfrac{dx}{dy} = e^y = x$

Then $\dfrac{dy}{dx} = \dfrac{1}{dx/dy} = \dfrac{1}{x}$

4 Let $u = 2x \implies \dfrac{du}{dx} = 2$

$y = \ln u \implies \dfrac{dy}{du} = \dfrac{1}{u}$

$\dfrac{dy}{dx} = \dfrac{2}{2x} = \dfrac{1}{x}$

5 (a) $y = \ln 3x \implies \dfrac{dy}{dx} = \dfrac{1}{x}$

$y = \ln 5x \implies \dfrac{dy}{dx} = \dfrac{1}{x}$

(b) $y = \ln ax \implies \dfrac{dy}{dx} = \dfrac{1}{x}$

(c) $\qquad y = \ln ax$

$\implies y = \ln a + \ln x$

(because $\ln(A \times B) = \ln A + \ln B$)

$\implies \dfrac{dy}{dx} = 0 + \dfrac{1}{x}$

(ln a is a constant value and so has a zero derivative.)

6 (a) $\dfrac{2}{x}$ (b) $\cot x$ (c) $\dfrac{3}{x+2}$

7 (a) $\qquad y = x^{1/q} \implies x = y^q$

$\implies \dfrac{dx}{dy} = qy^{q-1} \implies \dfrac{dy}{dx} = \dfrac{1}{q}y^{-q+1}$

$\implies \dfrac{dy}{dx} = \dfrac{1}{q}x^{(-q+1)/q} = \dfrac{1}{q}x^{\frac{1}{q}-1}$

(b) $\qquad y = x^{p/q} \implies y = u^p$ where $u = x^{1/q}$

$\implies \dfrac{dy}{dx} = pu^{p-1} \times \dfrac{1}{q}x^{1/q-1}$

$= \dfrac{p}{q}x^{(p-1)/q} \times x^{1/q-1}$

$= \dfrac{p}{q}x^{p/q-1}$

8 (a) $-\dfrac{1}{16}$ (b) $-\dfrac{1}{256}$

(c) $\dfrac{3}{4}$ (d) $\dfrac{1}{4}e$

(e) 1 (f) π

9 (a) $-\dfrac{\cos x}{\sin^2 x}$ (b) $\dfrac{\sin x}{\cos^2 x}$

10 (a) $(1, -2)$, minimum

(b) $(2, 3)$, minimum

(c) $(2, 1)$, maximum

(d) $(\frac{1}{3}, 1 + \ln 3)$, minimum

11 (a) $y = \sin^{-1} x$ and $-1 < x < 1$

$\implies -\frac{1}{2}\pi < y < \frac{1}{2}\pi$

$\implies \cos y > 0$

(b) $\dfrac{dx}{dy} = \cos y = \sqrt{1 - \sin^2 y} = \sqrt{1 - x^2}$

(positive square root because of (a))

So $\dfrac{dy}{dx} = \dfrac{1}{\sqrt{1 - x^2}}$

12 (a) $-\dfrac{1}{\sqrt{1 - x^2}}$ (b) $\dfrac{1}{\sqrt{64 - x^2}}$

7 Algebra and functions

A Remainders (p. 68)

1 (a) $Q(x) = x^2 + 5x + 4$, $R = 13$

(b) $P(2) = 13$

2 (a) $Q(x) = x^3 - 3x^2 + 9x - 27$, $R = 81$

(b) $P(-3) = 81$

3D See the summary after question 4.

4 (a) If $x = 4$, then $x - 4 = 0$ and

$P(4) = 0 + 6 = 6$

(b) Similarly $P(a) = 0 + R = R$

5 If $P(a) = 0$, then $R = 0$ and

$P(x) = (x - a)Q(x)$, so $(x - a)$ is a factor.

Exercise A (p. 69)

1 $Q(x) = 2x^2 + 3x + 5$, $R = 10$

$P(3) = 10$ gives a check.

2 (a) -2 (b) -79

3 6

4 $a = 2\frac{1}{2}$, $b = -4\frac{1}{2}$

5 $3x - 5 + \dfrac{6}{x+1}$

6   The student's long division and calculation of the remainder to check.

B   Rational fractions (p. 70)

1   (a)   When $x = 2.01$, $y \approx 500$
    (b)   When $x = 1.99$, $y \approx -500$

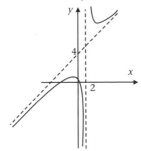

2   When $x = 100$, $y \approx 104.05$ and the graph is just above $y = x + 4$. When $x = -100$, $y \approx -96.05$ and the graph is just below $y = x + 4$.

3 $(1, 0)$, $(-3, 0)$, $(0, 1\frac{1}{2})$

Exercise B (p. 71)

1

(a)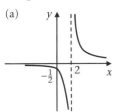

(b)

(c)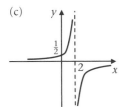

(d)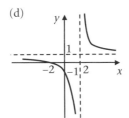

(e)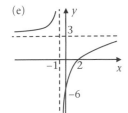

(f)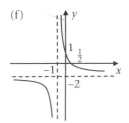

2

(a)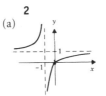

(b)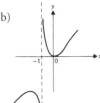

(c)

(d)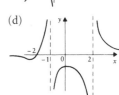

(e)

(f)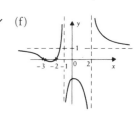

(g)

(h)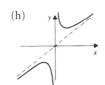

(i)

3 (a)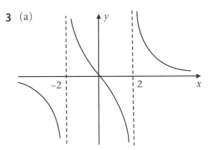

(b)

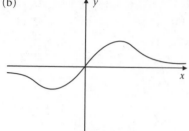

(c)

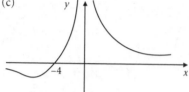

4

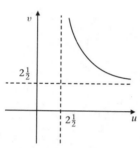

Negative values are excluded by the context. $u > 2\frac{1}{2}, v > 2\frac{1}{2}$

5

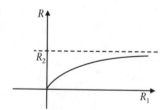

For small R_1, $R \approx R_1$
For large R_1, $R \approx R_2$

C Inequalities (p. 72)

1   $x = -1\frac{1}{2}$

2   $x < -2$ or $x > -1\frac{1}{2}$
    $x + 2$ takes negative values for $x < -2$

Exercise C (p. 73)

1   (a) $x = 8$
    (b) $4 < x < 8$
    (c)

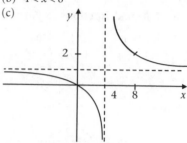

2   (a) $2 < x < 5$
    (b) $x < -2$ or $x > 5$
    (c) $2\frac{3}{4} < x < 3$
    (d) $x < -2\frac{1}{3}$ or $x > -1$

3   (a)

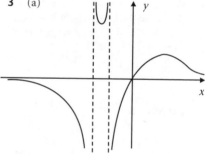

    Asymptotes are $x = -2$, $x = -3$, $y = 0$
    (b) $x = -1\frac{1}{2}, -4$
    (c) $x < -4$ or $-3 < x < -2$ or $x > -\frac{3}{2}$

4   (a) $-3 < x < -2$ or $x > -1$
    (b) $x = 0, 1$
    (c) $-1 < x < 0$ or $x > 1$

5E $-5 < x < 1$ or $x > 2$

D Quadratic equations (p. 74)

1   $(x - \alpha)(x - \beta) = 0$
    $x^2 - (\alpha + \beta)x + \alpha\beta = 0$

2   $\alpha\beta = 3$
    $\alpha + \beta = -5$

3   $2\alpha + 2\beta = -10$
    $2\alpha \times 2\beta = 12$

4   Sum of roots $= -10$
        $= -(\text{coefficient of } x)$
    Product of roots $= 12$
        $= \text{constant term}$

Exercise D (p. 75)

1 $\alpha + \beta = -4 \quad \alpha\beta = -7$

(a) $\alpha^2 + \beta^2 = (\alpha + \beta)^2 - 2\alpha\beta$
$$= 16 + 14$$
$$= 30$$

$\alpha^2\beta^2 = 49$

Equation is $x^2 - 30x + 49 = 0$

(b) $(\alpha - 1) + (\beta - 1) = \alpha + \beta - 2 = -6$
$(\alpha - 1)(\beta - 1) = \alpha\beta - (\alpha + \beta) + 1 = -2$

Equation is $x^2 + 6x - 2 = 0$

2 $\alpha + \beta = 5 \quad \alpha\beta = 8$

(a) $2\alpha + 2\beta = 10$
$2\alpha \times 2\beta = 32$

Equation is $x^2 - 10x + 32 = 0$

(b) $\dfrac{\alpha}{b} + \dfrac{\beta}{\alpha} = \dfrac{\alpha^2 + \beta^2}{\alpha\beta} = \dfrac{(\alpha + \beta)^2 - 2\alpha\beta}{\alpha\beta}$
$$= \dfrac{25 - 16}{8} = \dfrac{9}{8}$$

$\dfrac{\alpha}{\beta} \times \dfrac{\beta}{\alpha} = 1$

Equation is $x^2 - \frac{9}{8}x + 1 = 0$
or $\quad 8x^2 - 9x + 8 = 0$

(c) $(-\alpha) + (-\beta) = -5$
$(-\alpha) \times (-\beta) = 8$

Equation is $x^5 + 5x + 8 = 0$

3 $\alpha\beta = 3 \qquad ①$
$\alpha + \beta = k \qquad ②$
$\alpha - \beta = 3 \qquad ③$

$② + ③ \Rightarrow \quad 2\alpha = k + 3$
$② - ③ \Rightarrow \quad 2\beta = k - 3$

So $\quad 4\alpha\beta = (k + 3)(k - 3) = 12$
$\Rightarrow k^2 = 21$
$\Rightarrow k = \pm\sqrt{21}$

8 Differentiation

A The product rule (p. 76)

1D $e^x - 2 \sin x$ is the difference of two functions, both of which you know how to differentiate. The derivative is $e^x - 2 \cos x$.
$e^{\sin x}$ is a 'function of a function'. Its derivative is $\cos x \times e^{\sin x}$.
A numerical method will be needed to find the gradient of $y = x \sin x$. As yet, you do not have an algebraic method for differentiating products.

2 (a) $\dfrac{dy}{dx} = 2x \sin x + x^2 \cos x$
$$= 2.22 \text{ at } x = 1$$

(b) $\dfrac{1.01^2 \sin 1.01 - 1^2 \sin 1}{0.01}$
$$= 2.24$$

3 (a) $\dfrac{dy}{dx} = -\frac{1}{2} \sin(\frac{1}{2}x) \times (4x - \frac{1}{2}x^2)$
$$+ \cos(\tfrac{1}{2}x) \times (4 - x)$$
$$= (\tfrac{1}{4}x^2 - 2x)\sin(\tfrac{1}{2}x) + (4 - x)\cos(\tfrac{1}{2}x)$$

4 Whatever functions you choose you should find that the product rule gives correct gradient functions.

5 (a) $\dfrac{d}{dx}(x^3 \times x^2) = 3x^2 \times x^2 + x^3 \times 2x$
$$= 3x^4 + 2x^4$$
$$= 5x^4 \text{ as expected}$$

(c) $\dfrac{d}{dx}(x^a \times x^b) = ax^{a-1} \times x^b + x^a \times bx^{b-1}$
$$= ax^{a+b-1} + bx^{a+b-1}$$
$$= (a + b)x^{a+b-1}$$
$$\text{as expected}$$

6E A well-behaved function is continuous and locally straight.

Exercise A (p. 78)

1 (a) $x \times 2x + (x^2 + 1) \times 1 = 3x^2 + 1$
$\dfrac{d}{dx}(x^3 + x) = 3x^2 + 1$

(b) $3x^2 - 20x + 25$ (c) $12x^2 - 16x - 3$
(d) $6x^5 - 2x$

2 (a) $e^x(\sin x + \cos x)$
(b) $xe^x(2 + x)$
(c) $x^2(3 \cos x - x \sin x)$
(d) $\sqrt{2x + 3} + \dfrac{x}{\sqrt{2x + 3}}$
(e) $\frac{5}{2}x\sqrt{x}$
(f) $-e^{-x}x^2$

3 (a) 147.8   (b) 16.3

4 The gradient is 1.1.
The equation of the tangent is
$y = 1.1x - 0.16$.

5 (a) (i) $\dfrac{dA}{dt} = 2t \sin t + t^2 \cos t$

At $t = 1$, the rate of change of area is 2.22 .

(ii) When $t = 2.5$, $\dfrac{dA}{dt} = -2.01$, so the area is decreasing.

(b) (i) $A = \sin t \cos t$

$\dfrac{dA}{dt} = \cos^2 t - \sin^2 t$

When $t = 0.5$ the rate of increase of area is 0.540 .

(ii) The area stops increasing when

$\dfrac{dA}{dt} = 0$.

So $\cos^2 t = \sin^2 t$

$\tan^2 t = 1$

This first occurs when $\tan t = 1$.

$t = \frac{1}{4}\pi = 0.785$

6 The gradient at $x = 1$ is 1.36 .
The equation of the tangent is
$y = 1.36x - 0.68$.

7 At the turning point $e^x(1 + x) = 0$,
so $x = -1$.
So the coordinates of the turning point are $(-1, -0.37)$.

8 (a) At the stationary point,
$e^x(2x + x^2) = 0$, so $x = 0$ or -2.
When $x = 0$, $y = 0$, so $(0, 0)$ is a stationary point.

(b) e^x cannot equal 0, so the only stationary points are at $x = 0$ and $x = -2$.
The coordinates of the other stationary point are $(-2, 0.54)$.

9 (a) $0 = \dfrac{1}{x} + x\dfrac{dv}{dx}$

So $\dfrac{1}{x} = -x\dfrac{dv}{dx}$

or $\dfrac{dv}{dx} = -\dfrac{1}{x^2}$

10E $\dfrac{dy}{dx} = \sin x + x \cos x$, so at the stationary

point, $\sin x + x \cos x = 0$.
Dividing by $\cos x$ gives $\tan x + x = 0$.
One stationary point is $(0, 0)$.
The others are $(-2.03, 1.82)$ and $(2.03, 1.82)$, to 3 s.f.

B Product rule and chain rule (p. 80)

Exercise B (p. 80)

1 (a) $\dfrac{du}{dx} = 4(2x - 3)$

(b) $\dfrac{dv}{dx} = 15(3x + 7)^4$

(c) $\dfrac{dy}{dx} = v\dfrac{du}{dx} + u\dfrac{dv}{dx}$

$= 4(3x + 7)^5(2x - 3)$

$+ 15(2x - 3)^2(3x + 7)^4$

$= (2x - 3)(3x + 7)^4(42x - 17)$

2 (a) $\dfrac{du}{dx} = -2 \cos x \sin x$

(b) $\dfrac{dv}{dx} = 5 \cos 5x$

(c) $\dfrac{dy}{dx} = v\dfrac{du}{dx} + u\dfrac{dv}{dx}$

$= 5 \cos^2 x \cos 5x$

$- 2 \sin 5x \cos x \sin x$

3 (a) $e^{3x}(6 \sin 2x + 4 \cos 2x)$

(b) $e^{2x}(2 \cos 3x - 3 \sin 3x)$

(c) $e^{x^2}(2x \sin 4x + 4 \cos 4x)$

4 (a) $\dfrac{2x}{x^2 + 1}$ (b) $\ln x + 1$

(c) $\sin^2 x + 2x \sin x \cos x$

(d) $2x^2 \cos x^2 + \sin x^2$

(e) $2(x + \sin x)(1 + \cos x)$

(f) $e^x(\cos x - \sin x) + \sin x + x \cos x$

(g) $-2(2x + 3)^{-2}$

(h) $2xe^{3x} + 3x^2 e^{3x} = xe^{3x}(2 + 3x)$

5 (a) $x = \frac{5}{3}, 5$ (b) $x = \frac{1}{5}$

(c) $x = 1$ (d) $x = 0, 2$

(e) $x = -\frac{5}{3}$ (f) No turning points
(for $x < \frac{5}{2}$, y is not defined)

6 (a) $\dfrac{dy}{dx} = e^{0.5x}(0.5 \sin x + \cos x)$

The gradient at $x = 2$ is 0.105 .

(b) The gradient at $x = 2$ is -0.343 .

7 (a) Displacement $= 0$;

velocity $= \dfrac{ds}{dt}$

$= 0.4 \times 512\pi \cos(512\pi t)$

$= 643.4$ cm s^{-1} (when $t = 1$)

(b) $\dfrac{512\pi}{2\pi} = 256$

8 $(x+1)^{-1} - (x+2)(x+1)^{-2}$

$$= \frac{1}{(x+1)} - \frac{(x+2)}{(x+1)^2}$$

This is equal to $\dfrac{(x+1) - (x+2)}{(x+1)^2}$

or $\dfrac{-1}{(x+1)^2}$.

$\left(\text{Note that } \dfrac{x+2}{x+1} = 1 + \dfrac{1}{x+1}.\right)$

C Differentiating quotients (p. 82)

1 $\dfrac{dy}{dx} = (\sin x)^{-1} - x \cos x (\sin x)^{-2}$

$$= \frac{1}{\sin x} - \frac{x \cos x}{\sin^2 x}$$

$$= \frac{\sin x - x \cos x}{\sin^2 x}$$

2 (a) The derivative is

$$e^x(\sin x)^{-1} - e^x \cos x (\sin x)^{-2}$$

or $\dfrac{e^x}{\sin x} - \dfrac{e^x \cos x}{\sin^2 x}$

This is equal to

$$\frac{e^x \sin x - e^x \cos x}{\sin^2 x}$$

which is the expression obtained by using formula (1) on p. 82.

3 By the chain rule,

$$\frac{d(v^{-1})}{dx} = -1v^{-2} \frac{dv}{dx}$$

So $\dfrac{dy}{dx} = v^{-1} \dfrac{du}{dx} - uv^{-2} \dfrac{dv}{dx}$

$$= \frac{1}{v} \frac{du}{dx} - \frac{u}{v^2} \frac{dv}{dx}$$

$$= \frac{v \dfrac{du}{dx} - u \dfrac{dv}{dx}}{v^2}$$

Exercise C (p. 83)

1 (a) $\dfrac{x \cos x - \sin x}{x^2}$

(b) $\dfrac{e^x(1-x)}{e^{2x}}$ or $\dfrac{1-x}{e^x}$

(c) $\dfrac{e^x(\sin x - \cos x)}{\sin^2 x}$

(d) $\dfrac{e^{3x}(3 \sin 2x - 2 \cos 2x)}{\sin^2 2x}$

2 (a) $\dfrac{dy}{dx} = \dfrac{e^x \cos x - e^x \sin x}{e^{2x}}$

$$= \frac{\cos x - \sin x}{e^x}$$

At $x = -1$, the gradient is 3.76.

(b) $\dfrac{dy}{dx} = \dfrac{2x^2 e^{2x} - 2x e^{2x}}{x^4} = \dfrac{2e^{2x}(x-1)}{x^3}$

At $x = 0.8$, the gradient is -3.87.

3 The derivative obtained by using the quotient rule is $\dfrac{-2}{(2x+3)^2}$ and by using the chain rule it is $-2(2x+3)^{-2}$.

The two answers are equivalent.

4 (a) $\dfrac{dy}{dx} = \dfrac{(1+x^2) - 2x^2}{(1+x^2)^2} = \dfrac{1-x^2}{(1+x^2)^2}$

At the stationary points, $1 - x^2 = 0$ so $x = \pm 1$.

When $x = -1$, $y = -0.5$; when $x = 1$, $y = 0.5$

$x = -1.1 \Rightarrow \dfrac{dy}{dx} = -0.043$ and

$x = -0.9 \Rightarrow \dfrac{dy}{dx} = 0.058$,

so there is a local minimum at the point $(-1, -0.5)$.

$x = 0.9 \Rightarrow \dfrac{dy}{dx} = 0.058$ and

$x = 1.1 \Rightarrow \dfrac{dy}{dx} = -0.043$,

so there is a local maximum at the point $(1, 0.5)$.

(b) There is a local minimum at the point $(0, 0)$.

There is a local maximum at the point $(-8, -16)$.

5 (a) $(-2, -\frac{1}{8})$

(b) No turning points

(c) $(2, \frac{1}{4}), (-2, -\frac{1}{4})$

(d) $(6, 14), (-2, -2)$

(e) $(-2, -1), (-5, -\frac{1}{4})$

6 (a) $\dfrac{1}{\cos^2 x} = \sec^2 x$

(b) $\dfrac{dx}{dy} = \sec^2 y$

$\Rightarrow \dfrac{dy}{dx} = \dfrac{1}{\sec^2 y} = \dfrac{1}{1 + \tan^2 y} = \dfrac{1}{1 + x^2}$

7 (a) $\dfrac{-\sin^2 x - \cos^2 x}{\sin^2 x}$ (b) $\dfrac{0 - \sec^2 x}{\tan^2 x}$

(c) Both simplify to $\dfrac{-1}{\sin^2 x}$ or $-\csc^2 x$.

8 (a) $\dfrac{d}{dx}(\sec x) = -(\cos x)^{-2} \times (-\sin x)$

$= \dfrac{1}{\cos x} \times \dfrac{\sin x}{\cos x}$

$= \sec x \tan x$

(b) $\dfrac{d}{dx}(\sec x) = \dfrac{\cos x \times 0 - 1 \times (-\sin x)}{\cos^2 x}$

$= \sec x \tan x$

$\dfrac{d}{dx}(\csc x) = -\csc x \cot x$

9E $\dfrac{du}{dx} = y\dfrac{dv}{dx} + v\dfrac{dy}{dx}$

$v\dfrac{dy}{dx} = \dfrac{du}{dx} - y\dfrac{dv}{dx}$

$= \dfrac{du}{dx} - \dfrac{u}{v}\dfrac{dv}{dx}$

$= \dfrac{v\dfrac{du}{dx} - u\dfrac{dv}{dx}}{v}$

So $\dfrac{dy}{dx} = \dfrac{v\dfrac{du}{dx} - u\dfrac{dv}{dx}}{v^2}$

D Differentiation practice (p. 85)

Exercise D (p. 85)

1 (a) $-3\sin(3x+2)$
(b) $-4\sin(4x-1)$
(c) $5\cos(5x-11)$

2 (a) $2\sin x \cos x = \sin 2x$
(b) $2x\cos x^2$
(c) $-3\cos^2 x \sin x$
(d) $-6\cos 3x \sin 3x = -3\sin 6x$

3 (a) $6(3x+5)$ (b) $4\cos 4x$
(c) $3x^{-\frac{1}{2}}$ (d) $(2x-7)^{-\frac{1}{2}}$
(e) $-8\sin(2x-7)$ (f) $-3x(x^2-5)^{-\frac{3}{2}}$
(g) $-2\sin x \cos x$ (h) $-10\sin 5x \cos 5x$
(i) $\frac{1}{2}(2x-3)(x^2-3x)^{-\frac{1}{2}}$
(j) $1 + x(x^2+1)^{-\frac{1}{2}}$ (k) $-9(3x+4)^{-4}$

4 (a) $6x(3x-1)$ (b) $2\cos x - 2x\sin x$
(c) $(x+5)^2(4x+5)$ (d) $\dfrac{-11}{(4x-1)^2}$
(e) $\dfrac{-3x\sin 3x - \cos 3x}{x^2}$
(f) $2\sin 3x + 3(2x+1)\cos 3x$
(g) $2x\tan 2x + 2x^2\sec^2 2x$
(h) $3\cos 4x \cos 3x - 4\sin 3x \sin 4x$
(i) $2\cos^2 x \sin x - \sin^3 x$

5 (a) $\frac{1}{2}\sec^2 \frac{1}{2}x$ (b) $-3\csc^2 3x$
(c) $2\tan x \sec^2 x$ (d) $2\tan x \sec^2 x$
(e) $\dfrac{3}{9+x^2}$

6 $\dfrac{dy}{dx} = \dfrac{1}{1+\cos x} = \dfrac{1}{2\cos^2 \frac{1}{2}x} = \frac{1}{2}\sec^2 \frac{1}{2}x$

$y = \dfrac{2\sin \frac{1}{2}x \cos \frac{1}{2}x}{2\cos^2 \frac{1}{2}x} = \tan \frac{1}{2}x$

7 (a) $-2x^{-3}$ (b) $-2(2x+5)^{-2}$
(c) $\frac{5}{2}(5x)^{-\frac{1}{2}}$ (d) $12x(2x^2-3)^2$
(e) $(2x-3)^4 + 8x(2x-3)^3$
(f) $10x^4 - 12x^3$ (g) $-2x^{-\frac{3}{2}} + \frac{1}{2}x^{-\frac{1}{2}}$
(h) $\dfrac{\frac{1}{2}(4+x)x^{-\frac{1}{2}} - x^{\frac{1}{2}}}{(4+x)^2}$
(i) $-12\sin 4x$ (j) $12\sin 6x \cos 6x$
(k) $\dfrac{1}{x}$ (l) $\frac{1}{2}e^{2x}\cos \frac{1}{2}x + 2e^{2x}\sin \frac{1}{2}x$
(m) $\dfrac{\cos 2x \cos x + 2\sin 2x \sin x}{\cos^2 2x}$
(n) $\frac{2}{3}x(x^2-12)^{-\frac{2}{3}}$ (o) $2xe^{-3x} - 3x^2e^{-3x}$

8

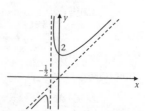

Maximum at $(-1\frac{1}{2}, -2\frac{1}{2})$
Minimum at $(\frac{1}{2}, 1\frac{1}{2})$

9E (a) $\dfrac{dy}{dx} = \dfrac{1}{1 - \sin x}$

(b) $\dfrac{\cos x}{1 - \sin x} = \dfrac{\cos x \, (1 + \sin x)}{1 - \sin^2 x}$

$= \dfrac{\cos x \, (1 + \sin x)}{\cos^2 x}$

$= \dfrac{1 + \sin x}{\cos x}$

$= \sec x + \tan x$

$\dfrac{1}{1 - \sin x} = \dfrac{1 + \sin x}{\cos^2 x}$

$= \sec^2 x + \sec x \tan x$

$= \dfrac{d}{dx}(\sec x + \tan x)$

This question requires $\cos x \neq 0$.

10E (a) $\cot x$ (b) $-\tan x$

(c) $\tan x$

$\displaystyle\int_0^{\frac{1}{4}\pi} \tan x \, dx = \Big[-\ln \cos x \Big]_0^{\frac{1}{4}\pi}.$

$= \ln \sqrt{2} = \tfrac{1}{2} \ln 2$

≈ 0.347

11E $\dfrac{d}{dx}(\ln \tan x) = \dfrac{\sec^2 x}{\tan x}$

$= \dfrac{1}{\cos^2 x} \times \dfrac{\cos x}{\sin x}$

$= \dfrac{2}{2 \sin x \cos x}$

$= 2 \operatorname{cosec} 2x$

9   Numerical methods

A   Numerical integration (p. 88)

1 (a)

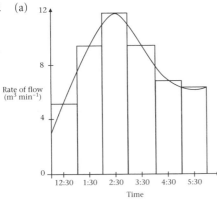

Rate of flow
(m³ min⁻¹)

Time

(b) $5 \times 60 + 9.5 \times 60 + 12 \times 60 + 9.5 \times 60$
$\qquad + 7 \times 60 + 6.5 \times 60$
$\qquad = 2970$

(d) Over-estimate

2 & 3

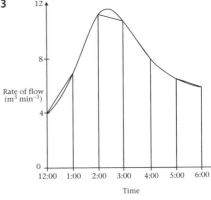

Rate of flow
(m³ min⁻¹)

Time

4 $30 \times (4 + 7) + 30 \times (7 + 11.5)$
$\qquad + 30 \times (11.5 + 11) + 30 \times (11 + 8)$
$\qquad + 30 \times (8 + 6.5) + 30 \times (6.5 + 6)$
$\qquad = 2940$

5   Under-estimate

Exercise A (p. 90)

1 (a) Assuming that the cross-section is always circular, you can first calculate the cross-sectional area, A, from the circumference, C, by the formula

$$A = \dfrac{C^2}{4\pi}$$

Height, h (cm)	10	30	50	70	90
Area, A (cm²)	198.9	127.3	71.6	31.8	8.0

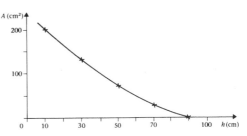

(b) Area under graph

$\approx 20[198.9 + 127.3 + 71.6 + 31.8 + 8.0]$

≈ 8750

This area represents the volume of the stalagmite in cm³.

2   The train comes to rest when $t = 10$.

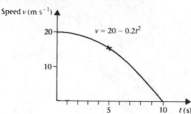

By the trapezium rule, the area under the graph from $t = 0$ to $t = 10$ is approximately

$$\tfrac{1}{2} \times 2 \times (20 + 19.2) + \tfrac{1}{2} \times 2 \times (19.2 + 16.8)$$
$$+ \tfrac{1}{2} \times 2 \times (16.8 + 12.8)$$
$$+ \tfrac{1}{2} \times 2 \times (12.8 + 7.2)$$
$$+ \tfrac{1}{2} \times 2 \times (7.2 + 0) = 132$$

The distance travelled is about 132 m.

3   (a)

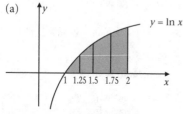

$$\int_1^2 \ln x \, dx \approx 0.125(\ln 1 + \ln 1.25)$$
$$+ 0.125(\ln 1.25 + \ln 1.5)$$
$$+ 0.125(\ln 1.5 + \ln 1.75)$$
$$+ 0.125(\ln 1.75 + \ln 2)$$
$$= 0.384$$

B   Increasing the accuracy (p. 90)

1D   (a)   (i)   0.2
         (ii) $x_1 = 0.1$, $y_1 = 1.997\,50$
                $x_2 = 0.3$, $y_2 = 1.977\,37$
         (iii) Strip 1 = 0.3995
                Strip 2 = 0.3955

         (b)   Strip 7 = 0.3040
                Strip 10 = 0.1249

         (c)   Total area = 3.1525
                Percentage error = 0.35%

2   (a) $h = \dfrac{b - a}{n}$

         (b) $x_1 = a + \tfrac{1}{2}h$

         (c) x is increased by h each time.

3   (a)   (i)   3.152 41   (ii)   3.145 43
               (iii) 3.142 95   (iv)   3.142 07

               $\pi \approx 3.141\,59$. The error is approximately divided by 3 each time the number of strips is doubled.

         (b)   About 400

4   Area $= \tfrac{1}{2}h\,(y_0 + y_1) + \tfrac{1}{2}h\,(y_1 + y_2) + \dots$
         $\qquad + \tfrac{1}{2}h\,(y_{n-1} + y_n)$
         $= \tfrac{1}{2}h\,(y_0 + 2y_1 + 2y_2 + \dots + 2y_{n-1} + y_n)$

So

$$\int_a^b f(x)\,dx \approx \tfrac{1}{2}h\,(y_0 + 2y_1 + \dots + 2y_{n-1} + y_n)$$

5   (i)   3.104 52   (ii)   3.128 47
         (iii) 3.136 95   (iv)   3.139 95

         The trapezium rule under-estimates π (by more than the corresponding mid-ordinate rule over-estimates π). Again, the errors are approximately divided by 3 each time the number of strips is doubled.

Exercise B (p. 94)

1   (a)   Too small
         (b)   Neither – exactly the same
         (c)   Neither clearly too large nor too small
         (d)   Too large

2   (a)   Too large   (b)   Exact
         (c)   Not clear   (d)   Too small

3   (a)   0.6919, error $\approx -0.001\,24$
         (b)   0.6956, error ≈ 0.0025

4   (a)   1.57   (b)   1.26   (c)   1.71

C   The Newton–Raphson method (p. 95)

1D

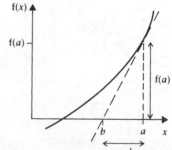

Since $f'(a)$ is the gradient of the graph at $x = a$,

$$\frac{f(a)}{a-b} = f'(a)$$

$$\Rightarrow \frac{f(a)}{f'(a)} = a - b$$

$$\Rightarrow b = a - \frac{f(a)}{f'(a)}$$

2   (a) $f'(x) = 2x - 3\cos x$

    (b) $b = a - \dfrac{a^2 - 3\sin a}{2a - 3\cos a}$

        If $a = 2$, $b = 2 - \dfrac{2^2 - 3\sin 2}{2 \times 2 - 3\cos 2} = 1.7576$

        (Remember to work in radians.)

    (c)   If $a = 1.7576$, $b = 1.7230$

3   $f(x)$

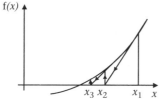

Exercise C (p. 98)

1   (a) $f'(x) = 3x^2 - 3$

        $x_{n+1} = x_n - \dfrac{x_n^3 - 3x_n + 1}{3x_n^2 - 3}$

    (b) -1.9, 0.3, 1.5

    (c) 1.53, -1.88

2   0.739

3   3.032

4   $2 \rightarrow 2.48 \rightarrow 2.424\ 79 \rightarrow 2.423\ 99$
    $3 \rightarrow 2.49 \rightarrow 2.425\ 10 \rightarrow 2.423\ 99$

5   $x = 0.487\ 404$

6   The area of sector OACB is $\frac{1}{2}\theta r^2$.
    Triangle OAB is isosceles and has area
    $r^2 \sin\frac{1}{2}\theta \cos\frac{1}{2}\theta = \frac{1}{2}r^2 \sin\theta$.

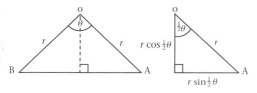

Hence the area of the segment is
$$\tfrac{1}{2}\theta r^2 - \tfrac{1}{2}r^2 \sin\theta = \tfrac{1}{10}\pi r^2$$
$$\Rightarrow \theta - \tfrac{1}{5}\pi = \sin\theta$$
$$\theta = 1.627 \text{ to 3 decimal places}$$

7   (a) $2\theta r^2 - r^2 \sin 2\theta$

    (b) $\theta = 0.8832$

8   (a)   (i)   Model B

          (ii)   Model A – exponential growth
              will always out perform
              quadratic growth eventually.

    (b) $t = 19.03$ hours

9   (a) 0.2486 (b) 0.5988

    (c) 0.2486

    The equations in (a) and (c) are
    equivalent.

10   0.4569, 5.998

11

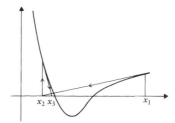

The Newton–Raphson method will not
converge to the nearest root.

12   (a) $x = 3.8730$ to 4 decimal places

    (b)   All values greater than 2.87 will give
        the root 3.8730.

    (c)   Any start position between $-0\ 67$ and
        2.87 will give the root $x = 2$.

    (d)   (i) $x_1 = -0.68$ gives the root 3.87.

          (ii) $x_1 = -0.69$ gives the root -3.87.

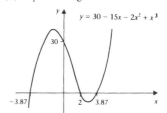

You cannot always predict to which
root an iteration will converge. If the
starting position is reasonably close to
the root, you will usually home in on
the root very quickly. However, if the
iteration takes you near a turning
point, then the method becomes very
unpredictable. In this case, the
method takes you near the turning
point at $x = 3$.

(e)

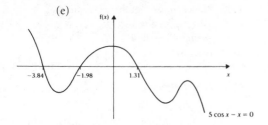

$5 \cos x - x = 0$

From an initial value of -1, the iteration quickly converges to the root -1.977. However, a starting value of -0.5 is near a turning point and the iteration converges to the root -3.837 and not -1.98, the nearest root. Starting values of -7 and -6.5 are some way from any of the roots, as well as being near turning points. In each case, the root which is eventually reached is difficult to predict and depends upon the accuracy of your calculator.

(f)

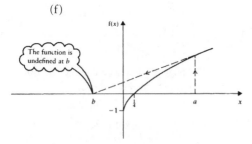

The function is undefined at b

This is an equation which is easily solved by simple algebraic manipulation and you would not normally use the Newton–Raphson method to solve it. It does, however, illustrate how the method can fail to work even if the starting value is not near a turning point. In this case, a starting value must be chosen below $x = 1$.

10 Applications of integration

A Volumes of revolution (p. 101)

1 (a) $h \approx 40$ cm (b) $h \approx 83$ cm

2 The width w of the slab increases uniformly from 0 to 2 as the height h increases from 0 to 2. So $w = h$.

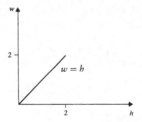

The length l of the slab increases uniformly from 2 to 3 as the height h increases from 0 to 2. So $l = 2 + \frac{1}{2} h$.

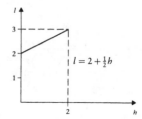

3 The volume of a slab at height h is $h\left(2 + \frac{1}{2} h\right) \delta h$. Hence, the volume of the container is

$$V = \int_0^2 h\left(2 + \tfrac{1}{2} h\right) \mathrm{d}h$$

$$= \int_0^2 \left(2h + \tfrac{1}{2} h^2\right) \mathrm{d}h$$

$$= \left[h^2 + \tfrac{1}{6} h^3\right]_0^2$$

$$= 5\tfrac{1}{3} \, \mathrm{m}^3$$

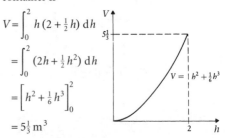

4 The container is half full when $V = 2\frac{2}{3}$.
$$h^2 + \tfrac{1}{6} h^3 = 2\tfrac{2}{3} \Rightarrow h \approx 1.46 \, \mathrm{m}$$
The equation can be solved by using the Newton–Raphson method from the previous chapter.

5 The increase in volume is
$$\left[h^2 + \tfrac{1}{6} h^3\right]_{1.1}^{1.4} = 0.9855 \, \mathrm{m}^3.$$

6 $\sqrt{2}\left[\tfrac{2}{3} h^{1.5} + \tfrac{2}{5} h^{2.5}\right]_0^2 = 5.87 \, \mathrm{m}^3$

7 (a) If the rectangle of height y and width δx is rotated completely about the x-axis, it describes a cylinder of radius y and width δx and hence will have volume $\pi y^2 \delta x$.

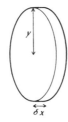

  (b) If $y = x^2$, $y^2 = (x^2)^2 = x^4$

  (c) Volume $= \displaystyle\int_0^2 \pi y^2 \, dx = \int_0^2 \pi x^4 \, dx$

$$= \left[\tfrac{1}{5}\pi x^5 \right]_0^2 = \tfrac{1}{5}\pi 2^5 - \tfrac{1}{5}\pi 0^5 = \tfrac{32}{5}\pi$$

8 (a) Volume $= \displaystyle\int_0^2 \pi y^2 \, dx = \int_0^2 \pi(x^2 + 1)^2 \, dx$

$$= \int_0^2 \pi(x^4 + 2x^2 + 1) \, dx$$

$$= \left[\pi(\tfrac{1}{5}x^5 + \tfrac{2}{3}x^3 + x) \right]_0^2 = 13\tfrac{11}{15}\pi$$

  (b) The graph $y = x^2 - 2x$ cuts the x-axis where $x^2 - 2x = 0$

$$\Rightarrow x(x - 2) = 0 \quad \Rightarrow x = 0 \quad \text{or} \quad x = 2$$

Volume $= \displaystyle\int_0^2 \pi(x^4 - 4x^3 + 4x^2) \, dx$

$$= \left[\pi(\tfrac{1}{5}x^5 - x^4 + \tfrac{4}{3}x^3) \right]_0^2$$

$$= \tfrac{16}{15}\pi$$

9 When a rectangle of length x and height δy is rotated about the y-axis, it describes a cylinder of volume $\pi x^2 \delta y$. It follows that the volume of the solid obtained by rotating the area about the y-axis is equal to

$$\int_0^4 \pi x^2 \, dy = \int_0^4 \pi y \, dy = \left[\pi \tfrac{1}{2} y^2 \right]_0^4 = 8\pi$$

10 $y = \dfrac{1}{x} \Rightarrow x = \dfrac{1}{y}$

Volume

$$= \int_1^2 \pi x^2 \, dy$$

$$= \int_1^2 \pi \dfrac{1}{y^2} \, dy$$

$$= \tfrac{1}{2}\pi$$

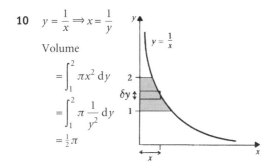

11D Many people would expect the two volumes to be equal. It is easy to prove otherwise. Both volumes formed will be cones.

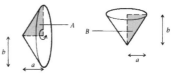

The volume of a cone is given by the formula $V = \tfrac{1}{3}\pi r^2 h$.

The two cones formed will have volumes $\tfrac{1}{3}\pi b^2 a$ for area A and $\tfrac{1}{3}\pi a^2 b$ for area B. These volumes will only be equal if $a = b$.

You could have calculated the volumes formed using integration. The volume formed by rotating area A about the x-axis is

$$\int_0^a \pi y^2 \, dx = \int_0^a \pi m^2 x^2 \, dx$$

$$= \left[\tfrac{1}{3}\pi m^2 x^3 \right]_0^a$$

$$= \tfrac{1}{3}\pi m^2 a^3$$

$$= \tfrac{1}{3}\pi b^2 a \qquad \text{because } m^2 a^2 = b^2$$

This confirms the formula for the volume of a cone.

Exercise A (p. 106)

1 $\tfrac{31}{5}\pi$

2 (a)

$$V = \pi \int_0^2 x^2 \, dy$$

$$= \pi \int_0^2 (2 - y) \, dy$$

$$= \pi \left[2y - \tfrac{1}{2}y^2 \right]_0^2$$

$$= 2\pi$$

  (b) $\tfrac{32}{15}\pi\sqrt{2}$

3 (a) $\frac{7}{3}\pi$

(b)

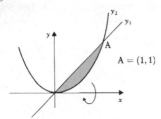

$A = (1, 1)$

$$V = \pi \int_0^1 y_1^2 \, dx - \pi \int_0^1 y_2^2 \, dx$$

$$= \pi \int_0^1 x^2 \, dx - \pi \int_0^1 x^4 \, dx$$

$$= \pi \left[\frac{1}{3} x^3 \right]_0^1 - \pi \left[\frac{1}{5} x^5 \right]_0^1 = \frac{2}{15} \pi$$

(c) $\frac{1}{30}\pi$

4 $(0, 0)$ and $(2, 4)$

$V = \frac{32}{5}\pi$

5 1.75

B   Integration by inspection (p. 106)

1D (a) Differentiating the function $\sin x^2$ seems to be a sensible starting point.

$$\frac{d}{dx}(\sin x^2) = 2x \cos x^2$$

using the chain rule,

so $\int x \cos x^2 \, dx = \frac{1}{2} \sin x^2 + c$

(b) Differentiating the function $x \sin 2x$ by the product rule,

$$\frac{d}{dx}(x \sin 2x) = 2x \cos 2x + \sin 2x$$

$\Rightarrow$

$$x \sin 2x = 2 \int x \cos 2x \, dx + \int \sin 2x \, dx$$

$\Rightarrow$

$$2 \int x \cos 2x \, dx = x \sin 2x - \int \sin 2x \, dx$$

$\Rightarrow$

$$2 \int x \cos 2x \, dx = x \sin 2x + \frac{1}{2} \cos 2x + c$$

$\Rightarrow$

$$\int x \cos 2x \, dx = \frac{1}{2} x \sin 2x + \frac{1}{4} \cos 2x + c$$

(c) Differentiating the function $\sin 2x$ by inspection,

$$\Rightarrow \frac{d}{dx}(\sin 2x) = 2 \cos 2x$$

so $\int \cos 2x \, dx = \frac{1}{2} \sin 2x + c$

(d) It is not possible to find an algebraic solution to $\int \cos x^2 \, dx$.

Exercise B (p. 108)

1 (a) $\frac{1}{3} \sin 3x + c$

(b) $\int (x^2 - 4) \, dx = \frac{1}{3} x^3 - 4x + c$

(c) $\frac{1}{5} e^{5x} + c$ (d) $\ln |x| + c$

2 (a) $3x^2 \cos x^3$ (b) $-4x \sin 2x^2$

(c) $6x (x^2 - 3)^2$

3 (a) $\frac{1}{3} \sin x^3 + c$ (b) $-\frac{1}{4} \cos 2x^2 + c$

(c) $\frac{1}{6}(x^2 - 3)^3 + c$

4 (a)

$y = 3(1 - x^2)$

(b) $V = \pi \int_0^3 x^2 \, dy$

$$= \pi \int_0^3 (1 - \frac{1}{3} y) \, dy$$

$$= \pi \left[y - \frac{1}{6} y^2 \right]_0^3 = \frac{3}{2} \pi$$

5 (a)

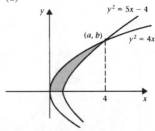

$y^2 = 5x - 4$

(a, b)

$y^2 = 4x$

At the point of intersection,

$b^2 = 5a - 4, \; b^2 = 4a$

$\Rightarrow 4a = 5a - 4$

$\Rightarrow a = 4$ and $b = 4$

(b) $V_1 = \pi \int_0^4 y^2 \, dx$

$= \pi \int_0^4 4x \, dx = 32\pi$

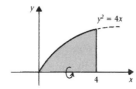

$V_2 = \pi \int_{0.8}^4 y^2 \, dx$

$= \pi \int_{0.8}^4 (5x - 4) \, dx = 25.6\pi$

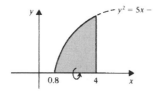

The volume of material is
$32\pi - 25.6\pi = 6.4\pi$ cubic units.

6 (a) (i) $2\pi(e^2 - e^{-2}) \approx 45.6$

(ii) $4\pi \ln 4 \approx 17.4$

(iii) $7\frac{1}{8}\pi \approx 22.4$

(b) (i) $\frac{1}{2}(e^4 - 4e^2 + 7)\pi \approx 50.3$

(ii) $(2 \ln 2 - 1)\pi \approx 1.21$

(iii) $17\frac{1}{3}\pi \approx 54.5$

C Integrating trigonometric functions
(p. 109)

1D (a)
$$\cos(A + B) = \cos A \cos B - \sin A \sin B$$
$$\cos(A - B) = \cos A \cos B + \sin A \sin B$$
$$\cos(A + B) + \cos(A - B) = 2 \cos A \cos B$$
(b)
$$-\cos(A + B) = -\cos A \cos B + \sin A \sin B$$
$$\cos(A - B) = \cos A \cos B + \sin A \sin B$$
$$-\cos(A + B) + \cos(A - B) = 2 \sin A \sin B$$
(c)
$$\sin(A + B) = \sin A \cos B + \cos A \sin B$$
$$\sin(A - B) = \sin A \cos B - \cos A \sin B$$
$$\sin(A + B) + \sin(A - B) = 2 \sin A \cos B$$

2 (a) $2 \cos A \cos B = \cos(A + B) + \cos(A - B)$

$$A = B = x$$
$$\Rightarrow 2 \cos^2 x = \cos 2x + \cos 0$$
$$= \cos 2x + 1$$

(b) $2 \sin A \sin B = -\cos(A + B) + \cos(A - B)$

$$A = B = x$$
$$\Rightarrow 2 \sin^2 x = -\cos 2x + \cos 0$$
$$= -\cos 2x + 1$$

(c) $2 \sin A \cos B = \sin(A + B) + \sin(A - B)$

$$A = B = x$$
$$\Rightarrow 2 \sin x \cos x = \sin 2x + \sin 0$$
$$= \sin 2x$$

Exercise C (p. 110)

1 (a) $\int \frac{1}{2} \sin 2x \, dx = -\frac{1}{4} \cos 2x + c$

(b) $\int (\frac{1}{2} \sin 5x + \frac{1}{2} \sin x) \, dx$

$$= -\frac{1}{10} \cos 5x - \frac{1}{2} \cos x + c$$

(c) $\int (\frac{1}{2} \sin 4x + \frac{1}{2} \sin(-2x)) \, dx$

$$= \int (\frac{1}{2} \sin 4x - \frac{1}{2} \sin 2x) \, dx$$

$$= -\frac{1}{8} \cos 4x + \frac{1}{4} \cos 2x + c$$

2 (a) $\int (\frac{1}{2} \cos 6x + \frac{1}{2} \cos 4x) \, dx$

$$= \frac{1}{12} \sin 6x + \frac{1}{8} \sin 4x + c$$

(b) $\int (-\frac{1}{2} \cos 5x + \frac{1}{2} \cos x) \, dx$

$$= -\frac{1}{10} \sin 5x + \frac{1}{2} \sin x + c$$

(c) $\int (-\frac{1}{2} \cos 5x + \frac{1}{2} \cos(-3x)) \, dx$

$$= \int (-\frac{1}{2} \cos 5x + \frac{1}{2} \cos 3x) \, dx$$

$$= -\frac{1}{10} \sin 5x + \frac{1}{6} \sin 3x + c$$

3 $\left[\frac{1}{2}x + \frac{1}{4} \sin 2x \right]_0^{\frac{1}{4}\pi} = \frac{1}{8}\pi + \frac{1}{4}$

4 $\pi \int_0^{\frac{1}{2}\pi} \sin^2 x \, dx = \frac{1}{4}\pi^2$

5E $\int_0^{\frac{1}{6}\pi} (\frac{1}{2} - \frac{1}{2} \cos 2x)^2 \, dx$

$$= \int_0^{\frac{1}{6}\pi} (\frac{1}{4} - \frac{1}{2} \cos 2x + \frac{1}{8} + \frac{1}{8} \cos 4x) \, dx$$

$$= \frac{1}{16}\pi - \frac{7}{64} \sqrt{3} \approx 0.0069$$

D Two further integrals (p. 110)

Exercise D (p. 111)

1 (a) 0.308 (b) $\frac{1}{3}\tan^{-1}\frac{4}{3} \approx 0.309$

2 (a) 0.525 (b) $\frac{1}{6}\pi \approx 0.524$

3 (a) 2.50, 2.94

(b) π

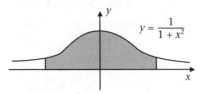

$$y = \frac{1}{1+x^2}$$

11 More integration techniques

A Integration by parts (p. 112)

1D (a) $u = \cos 2x \Longrightarrow \dfrac{du}{dx} = -2\sin 2x$

and $\dfrac{dv}{dx} = x \Longrightarrow v = \frac{1}{2}x^2$

$\Longrightarrow \displaystyle\int x\cos 2x\,dx$

$= \frac{1}{2}x^2\cos 2x + \displaystyle\int x^2\sin 2x\,dx$

This rearrangement of the integral does not make it simpler to evaluate. If you make the wrong choice as to which part of the product should be u and which should be $\dfrac{dv}{dx}$, then you will generally find that the integral has become more, rather than less, complicated. Experience will enable you to spot which part of the product to integrate and which to differentiate.

(b) If you let $u = x$ and $\dfrac{dv}{dx} = \cos x^2$, then

$\dfrac{du}{dx} = 1$ looks promising. However,

$\dfrac{dv}{dx} = \cos x^2$ has no algebraic solution and so the integral cannot be rearranged using the technique of integration by parts.

If you let $u = \cos x^2$ and $\dfrac{dv}{dx} = x$, then

$\dfrac{du}{dx} = -2x\sin x^2$ and $v = \frac{1}{2}x^2$. The resulting rearrangement becomes

$\int x\cos x^2\,dx = \frac{1}{2}x^2\cos x^2$
$\qquad\qquad + \int x^3\sin x^2\,dx$

which does not help you.

In fact, this integral can be evaluated by inspection.

$$\int x\cos x^2\,dx = \frac{1}{2}\sin x^2\,dx + c$$

which makes the point that integration by parts will not necessarily be a sensible method to choose just because an integral can be written as the product of two functions.

Exercise A (p. 113)

1 (a) $xe^x - e^x + c$

(b) $\frac{1}{3}xe^{3x} - \frac{1}{9}e^{3x} + c$

(c) $\dfrac{1}{a}xe^{ax} - \dfrac{1}{a^2}e^{ax} + c$

2 (a) $x\sin x + \cos x + c$

(b) $\dfrac{x}{3}\sin 3x + \dfrac{1}{9}\cos 3x + c$

(c) $\dfrac{x}{a}\sin ax + \dfrac{1}{a^2}\cos ax + c$

3 (a) $\displaystyle\int x^2 e^x\,dx = x^2 e^x - \int 2xe^x\,dx$

$\qquad\qquad = x^2 e^x - 2xe^x + 2e^x + c$

(b) $\displaystyle\int x^2\sin x\,dx = -x^2\cos x$

$\qquad = -x^2\cos x + \displaystyle\int 2x\cos x\,dx$

$\qquad = -x^2\cos x + 2x\sin x + 2\cos x + c$

4 (a) $-\frac{1}{2}\cos(-2) - \frac{1}{4}\sin(-2) \approx 0.44$

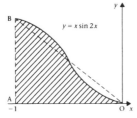

The area found is shaded in the diagram. When $x = -1$, $x\sin 2x \approx 0.91$.

The shaded area is close to that of triangle AOB $\approx \frac{1}{2} \times 0.91 \times 1 = 0.455$, which indicates that the answer is reasonable.

(b) $12e^{-1.5} - 8 + 8e^{-1.5} \approx -3.54$

The area found is shaded in the diagram. The minimum value, -1.47, of $2xe^{0.5x}$ is between $x = -3$ and $x = 0$.

An estimate of the integral is approximately -3×1.2 (negative because it is below the x-axis), which indicates that the answer is reasonable.

5E (a) $\frac{1}{3}x^3 \ln x - \int \frac{1}{3}x^2 \, dx$

$= \frac{1}{3}x^3 \ln x - \frac{1}{9}x^3 + c$

(b) $\ln x + 1 - 1 = \ln x$

(c) $I = \int x^2 \ln x \, dx$

$= x^2(x \ln x - x) - \int 2x(x\ln x - x) \, dx$

$= x^3 \ln x - x^3 - 2I + \frac{2}{3}x^3 + c'$

$3I = x^3 \ln x - \frac{1}{3}x^3 + c'$

$I = \frac{1}{3}x^3 \ln x - \frac{1}{9}x^3 + c$

B Change of variable in integration (p. 114)

1D (a) $\dfrac{1}{2\sqrt{x^2+1}}$ (b) $\dfrac{1}{2\sqrt{u}}$

Exercise B (p. 114)

1 $\dfrac{dy}{du} = 2x(2x+1)^3 = u^4 - u^3$

2 $\dfrac{dy}{du} = 2x\sqrt{\frac{1}{2}x+1} = 4u^{\frac{3}{2}} - 4u^{\frac{1}{2}}$

3 $\dfrac{dy}{du} = 4x(\frac{1}{2}x+1)$

4 $\dfrac{dy}{du} = \sin^3 x = u^3$

5 $\dfrac{dy}{du} = \dfrac{1}{2(1+x^2)^2} = \dfrac{1}{2}u^{-2}$

6 $\dfrac{dy}{du} = \dfrac{\sqrt{1-x^2}}{-2x} = \dfrac{\sqrt{u}}{-2\sqrt{1-u}}$

C Integration by substitution (p. 115)

Exercise C (p. 116)

1 (a) $u = x+3 \Rightarrow \dfrac{du}{dx} = 1$

$\int u^5 \, du = \frac{1}{6}u^6 + c$

$= \frac{1}{6}(x+3)^6 + c$

(b) $u = 2x - 5 \Rightarrow \dfrac{du}{dx} = 2$

$\int \frac{1}{2}(u+5)u^6 \frac{1}{2} \, du = \frac{1}{4}\int (u^7 + 5u^6) \, du$

$= \frac{1}{32}u^8 + \frac{5}{28}u^7 + c$

$= \frac{1}{32}(2x-5)^8 + \frac{5}{28}(2x-5)^7 + c$

(c) $\int (u+2)^2 u^7 \, du$

$= \int (u^9 + 4u^8 + 4u^7) \, du$

$= \frac{1}{10}(x-2)^{10} + \frac{4}{9}(x-2)^9 + \frac{1}{2}(x-2)^8 + c$

(d) $\frac{1}{18}(x^2-4)^9 + c$ (e) $\frac{2}{9}(x^3-2)^{\frac{3}{2}} + c$

2 (a) $\frac{1}{3}\sin^3 x + c$ (b) $-\frac{1}{3}\cos^3 x + c$

3 (a) $u = x^3 + 3 \Longrightarrow \dfrac{du}{dx} = 3x^2$

$$\int x^2\sqrt{x^3 + 3}\,dx = \int x^2\sqrt{x^3 + 3}\,\frac{1}{3x^2}\,du$$

$$= \int \frac{1}{3}u^{\frac{1}{2}}\,du = \frac{2}{9}(x^3 + 3)^{\frac{3}{2}} + c$$

(b) $\frac{1}{7}(x-3)^7 + \frac{1}{2}(x-3)^6 + c$

(c) $\frac{2}{5}(x-2)^{\frac{5}{2}} + \frac{4}{3}(x-2)^{\frac{3}{2}} + c$

(d) $\frac{1}{4}\sin^4 x + c$

(e) $-\frac{1}{6}\cos^6 x + c$

(f) $\dfrac{1}{(x+2)^2} - \dfrac{1}{(x+2)} + c$

4 $u = x - 1 \Longrightarrow \dfrac{du}{dx} = 1$

$$\int_0^2 x^2(x-1)^6\,dx = \int_0^2 (u+1)^2 u^6\,dx$$

$$= \int_0^2 (u^8 + 2u^7 + u^6)\,du$$

$$= \left[\tfrac{1}{9}u^9 + \tfrac{1}{4}u^8 + \tfrac{1}{7}u^7\right]_{x=0}^{x=2}$$

$$= \left[\tfrac{1}{9}(x-1)^9 + \tfrac{1}{4}(x-1)^8 + \tfrac{1}{7}(x-1)^7\right]_{x=0}^{x=2}$$

$$= \tfrac{1}{9} + \tfrac{1}{4} + \tfrac{1}{7} + \tfrac{1}{9} - \tfrac{1}{4} + \tfrac{1}{7}$$

$$= \tfrac{32}{63}$$

5 (a) $\frac{1}{8}x(2x+1)^4 - \frac{1}{80}(2x+1)^5 + c$

$$= \tfrac{1}{80}(2x+1)^4[10x - (2x+1)] + c$$

(b) $\frac{1}{20}(2x+1)^5 - \frac{1}{16}(2x+1)^4 + c$

$$= \tfrac{1}{80}(2x+1)^4[4(2x+1) - 5] + c$$

$$= \tfrac{1}{80}(2x+1)^4(8x - 1) + c$$

D   Definite integrals (p. 117)

1 When $x = 0$, $u = -1$ and when $x = 2$, $u = 1$. Working as before, but making the above substitutions for the limits, we have

$$\int_{u=-1}^{u=1} (u+1)^2 u^6\,dx$$

$$= \int_{u=-1}^{u=1} (u^8 + 2u^7 + u^6)\,du$$

$$= \left[\tfrac{1}{9}u^9 + \tfrac{1}{4}u^8 + \tfrac{1}{7}u^7\right]_{u=-1}^{u=1}$$

$$= \tfrac{1}{9} + \tfrac{1}{4} + \tfrac{1}{7} + \tfrac{1}{9} - \tfrac{1}{4} + \tfrac{1}{7}$$

$$= \tfrac{32}{63}$$

Exercise D (p. 118)

1 (a) $\displaystyle\int_0^2 (u+1)u^4\,du = 17\frac{1}{15}$

(b) $\displaystyle\int_1^3 (2u^{\frac{3}{2}} - 2u^{\frac{1}{2}})\,du = 6.08$

(c) $\displaystyle\int_1^{13} (\tfrac{1}{3}u^{\frac{3}{2}} + \tfrac{2}{3}u^{\frac{1}{2}})\,du = 33.8$

(d) $\displaystyle\int_1^3 (2u^{-4} - u^{-3})\,du = \frac{16}{81}$

E   Integrating $\dfrac{1}{x}$ (p. 118)

1 $\ln|3x^2 + 1| + c$

Exercise E (p. 120)

1 (a) $3\ln|x-2| + c$ (b) $3\ln|2x+7| + c$

(c) $\frac{1}{3}\ln|3x-1| + c$

2 (a) $\frac{2}{3}\ln|4| - \frac{2}{3}\ln|1| = 0.924$ (to 3 d.p.)

(b) $\frac{2}{3}\ln|-5| - \frac{2}{3}\ln|-8| = -0.313$
(to 3 d.p.)

3 The function is not defined for $x = 2$.

4 (a) $\displaystyle\int \frac{\sin x}{\cos x}\,dx = -\ln|\cos x| + c$

$$= \ln|\sec x| + c$$

(b) $\displaystyle\int \frac{\cos x}{\sin x}\,dx = \ln|\sin x| + c$

5 (a) $-\frac{1}{3}\ln|4 - x^3| + c$

(b) $\ln|3 + x^2| + c$

(c) $\ln|\ln x| + c$

(d) $-\ln|1 + \cos x| + c$

6 $\dfrac{1}{x-1} - \dfrac{1}{x+1} = \dfrac{2}{x^2 - 1}$

$$\Longrightarrow \int \frac{1}{x^2 - 1}\,dx$$

$$= \tfrac{1}{2}[\ln|x-1| - \ln|x+1|] + c$$

$$= \tfrac{1}{2}\ln\left|\frac{x-1}{x+1}\right| + c$$

7 (a) $\dfrac{d}{dx}\{\ln|\ln x - a| - \ln|x + a|\} = \dfrac{2a}{x^2 - a^2}$

$\Rightarrow \displaystyle\int \dfrac{1}{x^2 - a^2}\,dx = \dfrac{1}{2a}\ln\left|\dfrac{x-a}{x+a}\right| + c$

(b) $\left[\dfrac{1}{8}\ln\left|\dfrac{x-4}{x+4}\right|\right]_2^3 = \dfrac{1}{8}(\ln\frac{1}{7} - \ln\frac{1}{3})$

$\qquad\qquad = -\dfrac{1}{8}\ln\frac{7}{3} \approx -0.1059$

(c) The mid-ordinate rule gives -0.1058.

8 (a) $\left[\sin^{-1} x\right]_{-\frac{1}{2}}^{\frac{1}{2}} = \dfrac{1}{3}\pi \approx 1.047$

(b) $\pi \ln 3 \approx 3.451$

(c) Average y-value is just greater than 1
$\Rightarrow$ area just greater than 1 and
volume $\approx \pi r^2 h$ with $r \approx 1$, $h = 1$

$\qquad V \approx \pi$

F Integration practice (p. 121)

Exercise F (p. 121)

The constant of integration is omitted.

1 $\dfrac{2}{3}\ln|3x + 1|$

2 $-\dfrac{1}{20}(1 - 5x)^4$

3 $-\dfrac{1}{4}(1 - x^2)^4$

4 $-\dfrac{1}{500}(1 - 5x)^4(1 + 20x)$

5 $\dfrac{1}{4}e^{4x} - 3e^{2x} + 9x$

6 $\dfrac{1}{2}\tan^{-1}\left(\dfrac{x}{2}\right)$

7 $\dfrac{1}{2}\ln|4 + x^2|$

8 $(4 + x^2)^{\frac{1}{2}}$

9 $-\dfrac{1}{2}(4 + x^2)^{-1}$

10 $-x^2\cos x + 2x\sin x + 2\cos x$

11 $-\dfrac{1}{3}xe^{-3x} - \dfrac{1}{9}e^{-3x}$

12 $\dfrac{2}{3}(3 - x)^{\frac{3}{2}} - 6(3 - x)^{\frac{1}{2}}$

13 $\dfrac{1}{5}\ln|\sec 5x|$

14 $\dfrac{1}{2}x + \dfrac{1}{2}\sin x$

15 $x - \dfrac{1}{2}\cos 2x$

16 $\ln|x - 9| - 9(x - 9)^{-1}$

17 $\dfrac{1}{2}\ln|x^2 - 9|$

18 $\dfrac{3}{2}\ln\left|\dfrac{x-3}{x+3}\right|$

19 $\ln|x^2 - 9| + \dfrac{1}{2}\ln\left|\dfrac{x-3}{x+3}\right|$

$\qquad = \dfrac{3}{2}\ln|x - 3| + \dfrac{1}{2}\ln|x + 3|$

20 $3\sin^{-1}\left(\dfrac{x}{3}\right)$

21 $-3(9 - x^2)^{\frac{1}{2}}$

Index